Mollie Gross

CONFESSIONS

of a
Military Wife

SB

Savas Beatie

California

Cataloging-in-Publication Data is available from the Library of Congress.

ISBN 978-1-61121-250-1

05 04 03 02 01 5 4 3 2 1
First paperback edition, first printing

SB
Published by
Savas Beatie LLC
989 Governor Drive, Suite 102
El Dorado Hills, CA 95762

Phone: 916-941-6896
E-mail: sales@savasbeatie.com

Our titles are available at special discounts for bulk purchases by corporations, institutions, and other organizations. For details, contact Special Sales, P.O. Box 4527, El Dorado Hills, CA 95762, or you may e-mail us at sales@savasbeatie.com, or visit our website at www.savasbeatie.com for additional information.

All photos courtesy of the author unless otherwise stated.

Opinions expressed by the author are not necessarily held by others who appear in this book, the United States Marine Corps, or the United States Department of Defense. Some names and identifying characteristics have been changed to protect the privacy of individuals.

Printed in the United States of America.

This book is lovingly dedicated to my amazing Grandma Ruby . . .

for all she taught me, for all the support she gave me,
and for all the things we share.

Contents

Contents *(continued)*

A gallery of photos appears after page 130

INTRODUCTION

This book is based on my life in the military as well as jokes from my stand up comedy act, "Mollie Gross, Military Wife."

It covers my experiences as a Marine Corps wife, specifically talking about life on base and enduring wartime deployments. To protect their privacy, I have changed the names of some of the women mentioned in the book.

My husband and I lived on base from 2002 to 2006. During that time, Jon went through two war-time deployments as part of 2nd Battalion 1st Marines. He was an Infantry Platoon Commander and was attached to the 15th Marine Expeditionary Unit aboard the USS *Tarawa*.

During his first deployment Jon was part of the initial invasion of Iraq.

His second deployment was to Camp Baharia, just outside the city of Fallujah. At that point, he was a Company Executive Officer and participated in various combat operations within the city of Fallujah.

This book can be read from beginning to end. But, if you're like me, you may want to skip around—reading a topic that appeals to you.

I suffer with Attention Deficit Disorder, so I tend to flip through books stopping to read what interests me.

This is not meant to be a "How to Guide" to provide wives with resources on base or those offered by the military. There are plenty of those books already. In fact, I have at least five.

This book is meant to make you laugh and help you understand your situation. Since I believe in the healing power of laughter, I have tried to provide you with a resource for the times when you need a pick me up.

I have reached so many military wives through my stand up shows, on line videos, and on my social media or my website. And they all tell me, over and over, "I really needed that. I needed to laugh!"

Since this book is an extension of my comedy routine, I expanded on many of the stories I don't have time to spell out on stage.

I want military wives to know they are not alone and that wacky things happen. Let's laugh at ourselves. Or at least laugh at me and know I can laugh at myself.

All deployments are different; each marriage is unique. I also acknowledge there are differences within and between the branches of the military. This book is written from my perspective, but we share a common thread—the love of country and honor for our spouses who serve.

My goal in writing this book is to lift the spirits of any wife—no matter the branch of service or her spouse's rank. I want the Silent Ranks to understand there is no right way to be a "dependent." It all boils down to support and love.

To any women considering marrying a military man, I hope this book helps you understand what you're facing. The role of military wife is a tough one. It demands a commitment not only to your spouse, but also to the service.

You need to be aware that your needs will be second to the military, that you may be alone for months at a time and will find yourself moving to a new home every four years.

It takes a special type of person to commit to that. It is not for everyone. Be honest with your needs.

For civilians reading this book, I offer an honest picture of what it's like being married to the military. We have our own culture and priorities, but we also have a lot of pride in what we are doing.

Military wives are described as members of the Silent Ranks. We wear no rank nor do we receive medals or ribbons of achievement for our years of service. We serve silently beside our servicemen.

At times you will see these women are "not so silently ranked." They are not women sitting at home crying and tying yellow ribbons around trees.

We also laugh, thrive, and live.

I hope this book inspires the military wives to laugh and live. It has been an honor representing you. Although the military clubs dub us as our husbands' "dependents," I encourage you to continue your journey to become your husband's "independent."

Since I had trouble understanding the language of the military, I felt it was important to include a glossary explaining the acronyms used throughout the book.

Thanks for picking up my book. Here's to many laughs together.

Semper Fiesty!

Mollie Gross

ACKNOWLEDGMENTS

Years ago during a deployment I told Natalie and Kat, "I'm going to write a book about all this." Six years later my comedy coach, Bill Word, told me over lunch, "Just write it all ready. You have to just do it."

He was right and so was the timing. I had had enough time to recover from the deployments and could rationally process my thoughts again. I had piles of notes and stories scratched down on notepads. Many of the comedy events were already being played out on stage. So, I began to write.

At the same time I also started touring military bases using an hour of material I had written. I launched a social media platform, which resulted in a fan base across the world and in every branch of the military. Six months later, I had a finished manuscript. Thanks Bill!

There are so many people to thank. One of the first is my comedy writing partner Andy Salamone, who helped me decide what is funny, or showed me how to make certain material even funnier. Just hearing Andy's voice makes the creative wheel in my brain start cranking at full speed! We are a great team.

Many thanks go out to the military wives in all different branches who read my manuscript and encouraged me to approach topics no other military wives have ever discussed. They kept me focused on what was important and what needed to be confessed—as brutally honest as it may be. Their feedback was priceless.

Writing a book is one thing. Getting it published is an entirely different experience. Meeting Melody Abshear at Camp Pendelton was my first gift from God. She is my muse and as Type-A as I am! Melody always fills in the blanks and heads me in the right direction. I can't really get by without her. She put me on the right track to getting this book published and helped me put together my proposal.

I cannot thank my husband enough for his hours of commitment to my book. From spell checking to proof reading (which was not easy to do when it's his wife's story about the deployments he put her through), from his cutting and pasting, dealing with my frequent outburst and tantrums, researching online to find proposal copies and templates, finding resources, and then the right publishing house, he helped with it all. It was a team effort. He is a good man.

Finding Savas Beatie (or did they find me?) was a perfect fit. Managing Director Theodore P. Savas and I hit it off instantly on the phone. I was so impressed by what Ted and his company had done with their other books, especially Nick "Gunny Pop" Popaditch's *Once a Marine: An Iraq War Tank Commander's Inspirational Memoir of Combat, Courage, and Recovery* (2008). Nick's story is incredible and inspirational! What was even more incredible was when my Marine husband told me he was pretty sure he knew "Gunny Pop." When my husband was in Fallujah, he heard about an "eccentric Gunny tank commander." When Gunny Pop was hit in the head with a rocket and largely blinded in April of 2004 during the First Battle of Fallujah, my husband helped medivac Gunny to Camp Fallujah. The world is indeed a small place. The pieces for my book were falling into place.

Meeting Gunny Pop and his wife April at one of my shows was amazing. I felt like we had known them forever! I know that moving forward with Savas Beatie is the best fit for *Confessions of a Military Wife.*

Ted understands and supports all I am trying to do for military wives and their families. I deeply appreciate it. Not many people shed light on the "Silent Ranks," and Ted is helping to bring them right out front and center. Thank you, Ted, for not only giving me this opportunity but also for allowing me to reach these women.

Ted assigned Gloria Beverage as my editor (AKA: "genius extraordinaire"). "G", as I nicknamed her early on, is a wordsmith with the ability to cut through 100 words of ADHD gibberish and make it into two sentences that make sense. When I was way too in my head, she explained my thoughts fluidly. Thank you for your patience, especially when I would not let go of a topic that I just had to include. Thank you for assuring me that, "Yes, Mollie, it's still funny."

Sarah Keeney, Savas Beatie's Marketing Director, kept me focused and directed. Her patience has been greatly appreciated during this process. Thanks for answering all my questions! Thanks also to marketing assistants Tammy Hall and Veronica Kane, who are doing wonderful work to help make this book successful.

Indrek Mändmets of Indrek Mändmets Photography brought my idea of combat boots, dog tags, and heels to life. His attention to detail is superb! James Zach of ZGrafix, assigned to the project by Savas Beatie—and the same great designer who did the stunning jacket cover for *Once a Marine*—took this idea and created a book cover that had me screaming with excitement! The hot pink sent me over the top! I could not have imagined anything more perfect. Thanks, Jim!

Henry Ho is the genius behind my marketing, press kit, and web site. His skills and creativity synced everything together and the outcome was streamlined. Henry brought me to the level of professionalism I had been striving for. If I have the idea, he can make it happen. He gets me focused and tolerates my midnight emails.

To my attorneys Michael and Scott at Loeb & Loeb (who I drive nuts): thank you for letting me have my way.

Special thanks to Christi Smith, who designed and created "**Semper Flesty**" for my tour! I love your positive energy! "**Semper Flesty**" encapsulates the energy and pride all military wives should feel. There are so many military wives, military small business owners, veterans, and friends who have done so much for me as far as getting the word out there about what I do—from taking pictures of me on location to writing something up on me for the newspaper or an online blog.

Special thanks to "KK" and my biggest fan Hank Salmans at Devil Dog Brew. Your encouragement kept me going.

To our parents and family, thank you for all your love and support, especially during those tough years. We love you.

I know there are others out there, and if I forgot to mention you, please know I know how much you meant to me and this project. Each relationship I have made along the way means so much to me. I keep you all in my prayers every night. Thank you again for your support while I am on tour, writing, or just trying to lift your spirits on line!

Chapter One

BEFORE

A noise startles me awake. I look over at the clock on my nightstand and see it's 2:00 a.m. My heart starts racing. I reach out for my husband—seeking comfort and safety—but realize he's not there. My Marine is in the field, which means I'm on my own.

I hear more noises and now I'm sure an intruder is in my house. While I'm scared, I'm also pissed. As the wife of an infantryman who is always gone, I have had to learn to fend for myself.

I slowly reach for the Taser under the bed, but can't find it. Now I'm in complete panic mode and begin to move quickly.

"Where is the damn mace?" I wonder as I crawl along the floor headed for the bathroom. That's when I realize the mace is by the front door.

Adding to my rising anxiety, I am now on the opposite side of the room. I'm too far away from the phone to be able to quickly call for help.

I hear someone rummaging through our cabinets! I take comfort in the fact that we survive on a meager $400 a week, which means there is nothing worth stealing in this house.

Still, I am chilled to the bone with fear. I try to take comfort in the fact that I live in base housing, which is guarded by men carrying guns. I'm one of the few who continues to lock my doors. I know anyone who really wanted to could get on base.

I grab a can of generic strawberry body spray and hold it in front of me in a defiant gesture of self-defense as I slowly move down the hall.

I find myself thinking, "Why did I leave South Carolina to be here by myself all the time? My husband is never around to protect me; he's too busy fighting for other people! Why didn't I marry a banker? Do banker's wives have to fight off intruders by themselves in the middle of the night?"

By now my breathing is so shallow that I have become dizzy with fear and a lack of oxygen.

I creep into the laundry room, where I hear the intruder. I hold up the can, ready to fight him off with body spray. There is someone in the room with me.

I flip on the light and come face-to-face with a nude man! As he spins toward me I see his camouflage-painted face and we both scream. I spray him directly in the face with a generous amount of my special strawberry and cream repellent before taking off running down the hall.

Within seconds, a pair of muscled arms grab me around the waist and I begin yelling "RAPE!" I turn to face my attacker. His black, brown, and green face is staring at me just inches from my own.

That's when it registers. The face with the strange colors belongs to my husband. By now his eyes are swollen and he's coughing.

In unison, we ask, "What is wrong with you? What are you doing?"

He's the first to answer.

"We got done in the field early, so I thought I'd surprise you."

"Some surprise," I respond angrily. "You're lucky I keep the mace by the front door."

Relieved, I escort my nude and very dirty Marine to the bathroom, where I spray him down to get all the dirt and camo face paint off.

As his smile emerges, my fear and anger begin to melt away. I haven't seen him for days, and realize how good it is to have my love home.

My anxiety melts away as he takes me in his arms. I feel safe and whole again.

We laugh and then I kiss lips that still smell of strawberries.

As we head for the bedroom, I think, "Let those other women marry bankers. I've got myself a Marine."

FINDING LOVE AT A FISH FRY

Jon and I met at a fish fry. My roommate was dating a graduate from the Citadel, a military college in South Carolina. His mother decided to host a company party at the end of the summer to reunite the boys of Hotel (H) Company.

I wasn't interested in going to the party. I already had a date with another Citadel graduate I had picked up while driving my car down Rosewood Avenue.

Plus, I was, well, boy crazy. As my mother put it, "blink and you might miss one" of my boyfriends.

So I had other plans for that night and they didn't involve a fish fry in the country. However, my girlfriend begged me to come with her so she wouldn't be the only girl there. She cinched the deal by assuring me there would be plenty of cute boys to flirt with throughout the day.

As we were getting ready for the party, she pulled out the Citadel yearbook so I could check out some of the guys who would be at the party.

That's when my eyes settled on 2nd Lieutenant Jon Gross. He was the most gorgeous man I had ever seen—a great tan, dark hair, and gorgeous hazel eyes.

I couldn't contain myself. "Who's that," I screamed.

"Jon? He joined the Marines right after college, but no one's heard from him since. He won't be attending the party," she assured me. I was bummed.

"He's too quiet for you anyway, Mollie," she explained. "He never had a girlfriend in college—spent all his time studying instead."

At the fish fry I did my best to flirt with all the guys, but my heart wasn't really into it. (I had been raised in the South, so flirting comes naturally.)

While I was eating, I looked up and caught my breath! Walking up the driveway was the guy from the yearbook—Jon Gross.

As the other guests cheered his arrival, I knew my mystery cutie from the yearbook had walked into my life.

His friends exclaimed, "Gross, where have you been?"

They were all surprised to see him, particularly since no one knew where he was. He replied that he driven to South Carolina on a whim after completing his training at TBS (The Basic School) with the USMC in Virginia. "I was hoping to visit with some of my old buddies."

When I finally got to meet him, I found myself tongue-tied. I just couldn't get any words out. This struck me as odd, as I never run out of things to say.

Later I was able to talk to him as we stood outside by the fry pits. I had been flirting hard with Ging Gaddy, the host's 80-year-old grandfather, when I caught Jon's eye.

As we talked about his training in Quantico I told him my grandparents always shopped at the PX there, but that my grandfather had just died.

He looked in my eyes and replied, "I'm so sorry to hear that."

The more we talked, the more I was drawn to this powerfully intense and yet quiet man. I could sense his humility. He had such an air of calmness and quiet confidence. I was falling in love, but didn't realize it yet.

Then it was time for me to leave since I had a date with another Citadel graduate. The boys at the party knew what a party girl I was and tried to keep me from leaving. I told them I had a hot date and was more interested in making out with my date than I was in hanging out with them.

As I headed home to get prepared for my evening, something told me to change my plans. I called my roommate and asked her to invite the boys over for an after-party. Then I drove home and called my date to invite him to the Citadel party at my house.

My date and I sat on the couch and chatted until my roommate showed up with the rest of the party. I looked up to see my yearbook mystery man walking over to sit beside me on the couch. It felt odd, but also completely comfortable.

We began talking about everything—movies we liked, what was on the TV—and then my cat climbed up on his lap and started purring. I had never seen him do this with any of my dates. That was it for me. I knew I wanted to spend more time with this man.

As we talked through the evening, I decided he was the most sincere, humble, and honorable man I had ever met. In fact, he reminded me so much of my grandfather.

There are many men who could be your boyfriend, but there is only one type of man you want to marry and spend the rest of your life with. He was just that man.

We agreed to become pen pals since he was training about forty-five minutes away from my parent's home in Virginia.

While I was writing my address in his daily planner, I asked him a serious question: "If you aren't married in ten years, will you marry me?"

He didn't miss a beat: "Yes. You're the most exciting person I've ever met. I wanted to be with you from the first moment I saw you."

Well, that just took my breath away.

My poor date, in the meantime, was sitting on the porch talking to a group of people. I arranged to have one of Jon's buddies get rid of him.

I knew I wanted to be with Jon for the rest of that night. We continued to talk and later shared our first kiss.

We still argue about who kissed whom, but I think it was pretty mutual.

OPPOSITES DO ATTRACT

After that first kiss we wrote every week and talked on the phone whenever we could. We savored every conversation and poured our hearts into every letter. It was painful being separated from Jon.

Meeting Jon was like a completion of me. He had every quality I lacked and yet always admired. He was patient, calm, stable, and content.

In me, he found all the attributes he didn't possess. I was the center of attention, loud, hyper, enthusiastic, and outgoing.

For the first time we each had found a partner we could trust completely without judgment. Although our temperaments were complete opposites, we realized we had much in common. It was easy to fall in love.

I would drive seven hours to my parents' house on Fridays so we could see each other. On our first dinner date, Jon tried to explain what I was getting myself into. He stressed that he was attached to the Navy and could be deployed at any time. And he wanted me to know that the Marine Corps had an eighty-five percent divorce rate.

I suggested we slow down a little and try talking about hobbies or books we had read. My girlfriend had been right about this guy; he really didn't date much. Why, I didn't know: he was so cute and charming.

And he attempted to seduce me by rattling off random statistics about the Marine Corps. We all know Marines are natural romantics.

The attack of September 11 unfolded right after we started dating. I became frightened when I couldn't get through on the phone to Quantico. I had no idea where he was or what he was doing. American lives were forever changed, and so did my relationship with this incredible man.

I think we both realized then that life in the military would mean more than being stationed around the world. We both recognized that war was a very real part of our future together.

Jon had started IOC (Infantry Officers Course) after he finished TBS (The Basic School) at Quantico. Now he drove seven hours every weekend to visit me in South Carolina. I was so honored by the sacrifices he was making just to spend time together.

Jon got orders to ship out to Camp Pendleton. I knew that his Military Occupational Service (MOS) in the infantry would mean he would be deployed for six of every eighteen months. This also meant that he would soon be sent into the war zone.

I was living in South Carolina and could not imagine how difficult it would be to maintain a long-distance relationship. When I initially began to date Jon I hadn't thought much about it when he was stationed three states away. We treasured our time, but I knew that I couldn't nurture or add to the relationship when I was so far away. I had made up my mind.

I had known from the beginning that I would marry Jon. The only question was when. Of course, I also realized that the military dictates the "whens" in your life.

Jon, meanwhile, was worried he was asking so much of me. He wasn't sure I would like life as a military wife, or that I would like being alone. By marrying him, I would be leaving my friends, family, and career. It was a lot to ask of a woman. After all, you have to be strong to give up so much for someone else.

But marrying Jon was a no-brainer for me. I was in love and knew I wanted to be with him. I wanted to support him in what he was about to endure.

The reasons Jon gave to convince me to marry him:

1. "I'll never get on your nerves, 'cuz I'll always be gone."

2. "You can have all the closet space, 'cuz I wear the same thing every day."

3. "You can have as many babies as you want, 'cuz it's free."

Jon went to Idaho to spend Christmas with his family and made arrangements to fly me to his hometown on Christmas Day. I know my parents were disappointed. We had always spent Christmas together. But they didn't complain because they thought the world of Jon. They had grown fond of him during those weekends in Virginia.

Not only had I not flown by myself in a really long time, but I was also nervous about meeting Jon's family. I knew this visit was significant.

On the flight I was seated next to a guy who was more freaked about his holiday trip than I was. Before the plane took off, he confided that he was afraid of flying. He said the doctor had given him some pills, but he was concerned they hadn't taken effect. That's when he popped open a lunch box that looked like a miniature pharmacy and swallowed half of another pill.

We continued chatting about our destinations. I, of course, kept going on and on about Jon.

By the time the plane hit some turbulence, this guy's nervous energy had gotten to me. Now I was in full panic mode.

He cracked open the lunch box again. This time he offered me half a pill. Being young and naïve, I accepted it. What was I thinking taking pills from a stranger seated next to me on an airplane? Can you say Roofie?

No matter. I was no longer worried about the flight. When the flight attendant offered each of us a free drink because it was Christmas, I thought, "How nice of the airline!" We each indulged in a Bloody Mary and continued bonding over our free drinks and the free spirit we had ingested.

When I woke up an hour later, my new best friend and I were cuddled up drooling all over each other. As the plane was landing, I also realized I was completely wasted.

It had been three weeks since I had seen Jon and there he was, standing in the baggage area holding a bouquet of flowers! And there I was, stumbling along with my arm around my new best friend, who was carrying my luggage.

Can you imagine what Jon must have been thinking? Thank God my barbiturate peddling friend had the presence of mind to shake Jon's hand and tell him how he had saved the day on the flight by providing calming narcotics while I provided the wonderful, calming conversation throughout the flight.

Even though Jon proposed that weekend, he didn't have a ring to give me, nor had he asked my father for his blessing. The next weekend he went to see my dad armed with a jumbo bag of pistachio nuts and a case of Miller Lite. It was probably the toughest mission my Marine had faced up to that point.

My poor quiet Jon. He sat through two hours of basketball before he got the courage to ask for my hand in marriage. How many of my dad's farts did he have to endure over those hours? He should have brought his gas mask for this mission!

When he showed my parents the ring, my daddy cried. They were so pleased to have Jon as their "newest" son. With their blessing we decided to elope the following weekend.

THE DILLON COUNTY WEDDING CHAPEL

Six months after our first meeting, Jon and I said, "I do" in a cheesy place called South of the Border, which is known for its cheap cigarettes and fireworks. It was the only place we could find in three states that would process the paperwork while Jon was in the field.

Part of the urgency stemmed from Jon's need to make sure that I would be PCSing (permanent change of station: moving) with him to Camp Pendelton. Bottom line: time was of the essence. I needed to become his "dependent" and get that amazing military ID card that opens all the doors.

I was thrilled. I'd always wanted to elope. My parents were very supportive since they had eloped themselves. Because mother's parents were stationed in the Philippines, they knew they couldn't wait three years for their return to the states. My mother had grown up as an Air Force brat, so she understood the military doesn't give you time to plan a big wedding.

Some people were freaked about our plans, however. After all, I had only known this guy for six months and now we were moving across country where I would have no family, no friends, and no job. Worst of all, he would constantly leave me. People were less than supportive, and they let me know about it.

Regardless, I continued making plans. I found a wedding dress for $20 and waited to hear from Jon, who was in the field.

Finally, it was time. My girlfriend and Jon's college buddy, who would be our witnesses, joined us for the drive to the wedding chapel.

On the front door was a sign announcing, "Shoes and shirts required." Apparently some of the couples getting married were not complying with these simple rules.

The couple in front of us informed the clerk that their divorces had been finalized the day before and they wanted to wear matching sweatsuits as they walked down the aisle.

She completed her lovely ensemble with a rented veil from the quaint boutique adjacent to the chapel. In fact, they had a number of items for rent to enhance your wedding day. Imagine: red cummerbunds, an all-white tuxedo, and a complete selection of plastic flower bouquets. Thank God my roommate had thought to buy me an elegant bouquet of white roses with a single red one in the center.

Our Justice of the Peace called us in to discuss the arrangements. He looked like a cross between Gomez Adams and Rhett Butler. I couldn't stop looking at his pencil-thin black mustache. I swear he drew it on.

He was about 5' 4" and greasy-looking. And then there was this four-carat diamond ring on his pinky finger!

Worst of all, this guy talked a hundred miles an hour. For a second I thought I was at a used car auction. Seriously, I think he was on crack.

He had an array of options for a perfect wedding. He said we could—for just $50.00 more—have our marriage license printed on paper with a unicorn leaping over an airbrushed rainbow.

For an additional $100.00, we could be married in the second chapel, which featured an airbrushed landscape of a Greek temple. He offered a host of other options, but that was all I could catch because he was talking so fast.

We finally settled on the marriage license on plain paper, which I now regret. How cool would it be to have an air brushed marriage license?

And we agreed to say our vows in the plain chapel. When we explained we were in the military and didn't have much money, he threw in two T-shirts that said, "I got married at the Dillon County Wedding Chapel." He even offered to have his wife and brother take pictures of the ceremony.

By the time the ceremony started, I could no longer contain myself. I couldn't even make eye contact with Gomez or I would start laughing. His spiel was so over-the-top. He began yelling to a room of six people, "Dearly Beloved!" in the thickest Southern accent he could muster.

When he began to roar a prayer beginning with "Jesus Christ, Lamb of God!" I was laughing so hard that tears were rolling down my face. I may have even peed a little in my pants.

Finally I heard, "I now pronounce you man and wife. You may kiss your bride." I turned to Jon and French-kissed him! I was thrilled to be married!

Although the ceremony was a bit cheesy, I was confident Jon and I had made the right decision. I chose to marry Jon because I would not move across country without making a commitment. I refused to shack up. Jon said that said something about my character.

After being in the military community for a while, I discovered that many couples eloped. Military life has its own culture and different practices from those found in civilian life. We have a higher calling. What is most important is being there for our men.

I knew I didn't want Jon to go through this duty station or other deployments alone.

Our wedding day was one of the most beautiful days of my life. I'm glad that Jon and I did it alone because so many of the challenges we had ahead of us would also have to be done alone.

THE HONEYMOON

Nancy and Carol, two wonderful women I had worked for in South Carolina, gave Jon and me an overnight stay at a B & B in Camden.

They knew we couldn't afford it. The sales job I had just quit had paid more than Jon's salary. Now we were going to have to live on $400 a week.

These ladies decided to give us a special wedding night. What they did was beyond thoughtful. By the time we checked into the room, we were feeling romantic and filled with marital bliss. But what happened next just was not fair.

THE ICEMAN COMETH

We were trying to consummate our marriage when someone knocked on the door. We tried to ignore it, but the knocking wouldn't stop. I could hear the person at the door saying, "Ice. I have your ice."

We continued to ignore the knocks as our clothes came off.

The knocks became more persistent. Now the voice was saying, "Hello, I have your ice." Then I saw the knob on the door begin to turn and I realized the ice man was coming in. The door was unlocked!

"He's coming in!" I screamed.

My chivalrous husband, my knight in shining armor, my Marine, who four hours earlier had pledged to protect me and honor me all the days of my life, jumped out of bed and ran into the bathroom.

There I was, sitting up bare-chested in bed, when a 13-year-old boy walked into the room carrying a bucket of ice. I screamed again. He made eye contact with my milk white breasts and screamed. From somewhere in the bathroom, Jon screamed. The boy, who we dubbed "Sheldon," dropped the ice and ran. He had gotten an eyeful of my D-cup boobs, while Jon stood in the bathroom trying to cover himself up with a washcloth.

All our happiness washed out the embarrassment of the "mid-coitus walk in." That is, until we sat down for breakfast the next morning and realized "Sheldon" was our waiter. Humiliation washed over me as I saw the young boy's eyes light up before slowly settling on my breasts.

He walked right up to us and asked, "Were you two in room 101? Was that your honeymoon last night?" We avoided making eye contact. "Yes," we mumbled.

He didn't stop there. He kept apologizing, making the excuse that he thought we simply had to have the ice. We ate as fast as we could, but we could see him hiding behind plants gazing at us, eyes glazed over and frozen in a flashback of breasts and ice cubes flying through the air.

After our brief honeymoon, my new husband drove back to Virginia and I returned to South Carolina. We started writing detailed love letters and making phone calls.

While I missed him so much that it hurt, I took comfort in knowing we were starting a wonderful life together. Jon and I spent the first three months of marriage living in different states. It was surreal, but over the next few months I began to settle into married life.

GRANDMA: THE GREATEST GENERATION

The next time I was able to see Jon was during a weekend stay at my Grandma's house in Virginia. She invited us over because she wanted to give me some advice on being a military wife.

This woman had been married to the U.S. Air Force for more than thirty years. She and my grandfather went through World War II and Korea, seven children, and assignments all over the world. I knew she could teach me a thing or two about being a good military wife as well as how to embrace the lifestyle.

Grandma is what we call "Old South," which means she still holds a grudge against the British. In fact, she got really mad at my cousin, Dean Charles, calling him a traitor because he went to college "in one of them Union states."

Grandma is extremely charming and outspoken. In fact, I learned manipulation techniques from her. I think a lot of what she says is done in an effort to get a reaction out of others.

A few years back, she had more than four feet of her colon removed. That's hard to imagine since she's not too much taller than five feet. Her grandchildren like to tell her that since her surgery she does everything half ass. To get back at us, she hides all her secret family recipes in her medical files next to the color photos of her colonoscopies.

Anyway, during our visit, we noticed she was mixing up words. She started referring to Muslims as Mormons. After 9/11, she told Jon and me how it was important for America to stop the radical Mormons because they had perpetrated the attacks on the Twin Towers.

There was no way we could convince her of the difference. We'd just smile and nod. "That's right, Grandma, all the Mormons got together on September 11th and ran their bicycles into the Twin Towers!"

Then she started using "Dildo" instead of "Dickey," the word for the mock turtleneck worn under a sweater. We weren't quite sure where she heard that "new" word, but we assumed it came from one of the "stories" (soap operas) she watched every day.

It seemed harmless enough until she misplaced her "Dildo" and started calling her neighbors to ask if she could borrow one of theirs!

Needless to say, Jon was concerned about what advice this woman would give me.

Here's what she offered:

1. It is imperative you have a baby before he deploys. He won't want to give you one. So take care of that yourself.

2. Never have "relations" with your husband right before he leaves. He will need something to look forward to, so take care of that yourself as well.

3. Always remember, when he comes back from deployment you will be in stiff competition with Asian hookers. So I got prepared. I bought a kimono and a bag of Ping-Pong balls.

Grandma was also eager to go with me when I picked up my military ID card. Mostly, I think it was because she wanted to get out of the house. She had stopped driving after the "Dollar General Shopping Bonanza Incident."

One day she called my Aunt Martha to report, "I went through the Dollar General today."

"That's great mom, what did you buy?" Aunt Martha asked.

"No, dear, I WENT THROUGH the Dollar General today," Grandma explained.

She went on to explain that the Herman Munster-style shoe she wore (scoliosis had left one leg shorter) had created a "lead foot." Instead of hitting the brakes, the "lead foot" had hit the gas pedal and she had gone "through the Dollar General." I believe she put the car in park in aisle five.

On the drive to Quantico, Grandma warned me about keeping my ID card with me at all times. She went on to tell me about the time she had gone to the commissary (grocery store on a military base) to buy a week's worth of groceries for seven children. When she got to the checkout stand, she realized she didn't have the military ID.

The militant clerk refused to ring her up, so she had to leave without the groceries.

She also gave me a complete rundown on military health care. Grandma had had seven children—six girls and one boy.

She told me that when my Uncle George was born after a slew of girls, my granddad suggested naming him "Caboose." He is actually not the baby; he is the fourth of seven!

Since Grandma was pregnant throughout her years as a military wife, she knew the health care system well. She explained that calling military medicine TRICARE is a joke. Obviously they don't try and they really don't care!

One time when they were stationed in England (and she wasn't pregnant) she developed a terrible ear infection. She decided she needed to go to the hospital, so she asked a neighbor to watch her five children.

When she checked in, she told the receptionist that she needed to see the doctor.

"I am sorry, ma'am, but the doctor only sees pregnant women on Wednesdays."

Grandma calmly replied, "If that's the case, I will call my husband and take care of that at lunch, but I would prefer to skip it and just get my ear checked out."

The doctor happened to overhear her reply and agreed to see her.

I know my marriage to Jon brought back so many memories for her. My grandfather had passed away less than eight months before our wedding. The similarities between my grandfather and Jon were more than temperament and military career. My grandfather was a man who also walked softly, but carried a big stick.

We treasured our talks with Grandma, who became my rock when Jon was deployed. During World War II, she had gone for two years without seeing my grandfather, surviving only on limited letters. I knew she understood what I was going through and I was thankful to be able to talk to her.

MADE FOR EACH OTHER

Jon and I are complete opposites, physically and emotionally.

He's six feet tall, has dark hair, a great tan, and dark hazel eyes. He's quiet, calm, patient, content, intelligent, and polite, but absent-minded when it comes to anything that is not Marine-related. He's a great researcher with the ability to retain vast amounts of information. I also admire that he never says a bad thing about anyone or anything.

In contrast, I'm short—at just five feet—have blonde hair and hazel eyes. I am loud, hyper, energetic, extremely organized, controlling, bossy, opinionated, and tend to whine. I often pop off—saying outrageous things no matter where I am or who I am around.

Jon is more comfortable communicating one on one, while I do better in a group. I'm street smart, while Jon is book smart. He's under control, while I'm out of control.

We make a great team!

We balance each other out.

Chapter Two

THE DITY MOVE FROM HELL

I was now married to the military, and they were calling the shots. We had fifteen days to get to my husband's new duty station in California. I was ready for my first PCS. I had a yard sale, threw out half my belongings, packed, and got ready to go.

My husband said we'd do a DITY (Do It Yourself) move to save money, which meant we would pack and move ourselves across the U.S.

What my new husband didn't tell me was the military could pack every single piece of my belongings and ship them across country in a TMO move. We could even have had our cars shipped. I could have traveled across the country on a plane, but I was never told about this option.

Instead, my husband insisted on using a U-haul truck to move. The first truck he brought home on moving day was the tiniest thing I had ever seen.

I calmly told him our belongings would not fit. He brushed me off and walked inside to begin loading.

We carried the couch out and put it inside the truck, but the end hung out over tailgate.

I was baffled. We still had to get two more couches, a bed, multiple dressers, a kitchen table, and all the books and clothes into a U-haul. It was clear to me this truck wasn't large enough. He stared at the truck for a while, and then said, "Well, I guess I may need to get one size bigger."

What I didn't realize was my husband could not admit I was right. Seriously, this would continue until we were in our 30s. With time and maturity, my husband would finally break this nasty habit.

For the first six years of our marriage I would tell my husband something, but he would go to at least one other source to hear exactly what I said. It really hurt my feelings.

Now, I understand my husband went from his parents' home to a military college to the Marine Corps. Someone else had always called the shots. Obviously, he was uncomfortable. It was the first time in his life he had to be in charge. And now he had to learn how to be a partner.

I, on the other hand, had lived on my own since I was eighteen. I had paid my bills and taken care of myself for six years.

I think it was a tough pill for Jon to swallow. He's a warrior and a big, bad ass Marine. And here I was expecting him to take care of me. He was out of his element.

It quickly became apparent that I would be taking care of him. So I had to tread lightly to avoid bruising his ego. I very delicately pointed out that we needed a much larger U-haul. Still, my husband was sure he knew what he was doing and went off to get the next size up.

He showed up an hour later with a trailer only a few feet longer than the last one. I was at a loss for words. Instead of getting mad, I reminded myself that my husband is the smartest person I ever met, but that he had never moved a house full of furniture.

I decided it was time to speak up. I did so kindly, gently, pointing out that before we broke our backs trying to haul more furniture that wouldn't fit, I needed to go with him to get another trailer.

I was not sassy or rude, but I stood my ground. He was not receptive at first, insisting he had the right size. I gently pointed out that when I had moved the previous summer, it had taken many trips in a large truck.

He agreed and we went together to get one of the biggest trailers they had. After two days of loading, we had managed to fit all our stuff in a truck. It was a tight squeeze.

During the process Jon realized we made a good team and that I would be able to handle life as a military wife. Taking charge on this first move would not be the first time I would have to step up to the plate when it came to the home front.

Finally we had the truck packed and his SUV on a tow bar behind it. I followed in my tiny SUV with TWO cats—at thirty-five miles per hour.

It took ten days and was one of the most miserable experiences of my life. In fact, we had our first fight on this DITY move.

Believe it or not, I had not cursed him out because I was picking my battles carefully. However, after driving at that speed for eight hours a day with one cat sitting on the dashboard and meowing every three seconds and the other cat between my neck and the head rest, I was ready to fight.

TO PEE OR NOT TO PEE

We had been driving for days. My butt was permanently numb. One day we drove a long stretch and I had to go to the restroom. I called to Jon on the walkie talkie. "We need to stop. I need to go to the bathroom."

"Ok, we'll stop soon," he promised.

Ten exits went past. I was following behind him so I had to wait for him to exit.

I called him back. "Sweetheart, I need to use the restroom."

"Ok, we'll stop in a few exits."

Ten more exits go by and I began to get angry. Didn't this man get it? I had to go pee!

Finally, I called back and patiently, sweetly, and gently said, "Sweetheart, I really need to stop and use the restroom."

He apologized and assured me we would stop at exit 64. I thanked him. I was wrong to be upset. My husband was a sweet, caring man. He had his reasons for not stopping. He truly was thinking of my needs.

I started checking to see how close exit 64 was. That's when I saw we were passing exit 30.

Let's just say there was no confrontation. There were no more requests to stop. I simply called him and said that if he wanted to continue this trip with me, he could meet me at the next exit. I would be stopping at exit 31 to use the bathroom. I hit the gas, sped up, and passed his ass.

DON'T TALK TO ME LIKE I AM
ONE OF YOUR MARINES!

He was waiting for me when I emerged from the restroom. He hung his head down avoiding eye contact. That's when I cursed him out—a Southern expression for letting someone know what's up.

Anyway, I let him know I was his wife, not one of his Marines. I told him he could not talk to me like I am one of his men, or even treat me like one of them.

Unlike his Marines, I continued, I could not pee in an empty Mountain Dew bottle kept under the car seat!

He admitted that when I passed him on the highway he envisioned me getting back on the opposite highway and heading back home. He thought I was leaving him.

We still had some challenges ahead of us, but after that we communicated better. And my husband was getting better at stopping frequently to let me go to the bathroom or get a snack.

We even stopped in Graceland to look for the King. I fell asleep at the wheel in Arkansas and nearly ran off the road. One cat escaped in Arizona while we were trying to take its picture next to a cactus. OK, not a bright idea.

We both went the wrong way on a one-way street in Texas. (Why are there so many Dairy Queens in Texas?) This is all I ate for three days straight. Yes, it took three days to get through the Lone Star State.

The highlight of the trip was when we stayed at a "by-the-hour" hotel in New Mexico.

Jon had this goal of driving exactly 500 miles a day. I agree that it is good to have daily goals. However, I think if you're driving and there is a huge city with plenty of hotels and restaurants just 475 miles out, maybe you should stop there instead of making your daily goal.

My husband didn't agree. So there we were at ten at night in God knows where New Mexico with no hotels or restaurants in sight. He refused to turn around and go back to the big city. We had to push on to the 500-mile mark.

Forty miles and an hour later we found a lonely hotel that looked like it belonged in a ghost town.

The clerk was surprised we wanted the room for the entire night. He continued to look at us suspiciously like he thought Jon had kidnapped me and was stashing me there before making a dash for the border. His face said, "Amber Alert."

Our room was equally frightening. I was afraid I'd catch some rare disease (like scurvy) just by sitting on the bed. There was a lipstick kiss and a "Thanks for everything" message on the mirror. There were even used condoms under the bed. I was afraid to take a shower.

Since we thought there were hidden cameras in the room, we slept with our clothes on.

Let's just say, we didn't christen New Mexico.

CALIFORNIA DREAMING

When we finally crossed into California, I was becoming nervous about my new life. Since I had always lived in the South, it was quite a shock to see the scenery change from rolling hills and trees to tumbleweeds and cactus.

When I saw my first cactus, I was awestruck by its size. Now I was gazing at my first palm tree!

I have joked about how different Southerners can be from state to state. My personal mantra is "I am from Virginia. We are not slow enough to be Southern or rude enough to be Yankee. We are like the porridge that Goldilocks chose 'cuz we're just right!" Virginians are just country snobs.

We wait till you leave the room to talk trash about you because it would be rude to do so in front of your face. This is not two-faced behavior; it is being polite.

All good Southern girls are taught to flirt with everyone no matter their sex or age. Southerners are critical of Yankees—even if we're friends.

History and character are a common link that all East Coasters share. It's our common thread. Both Yankees and Southerners agree that something odd happens to a person's personality if they are raised west of the Mississippi River. These people came from pioneers who were completely happy living on their own with nobody around for miles.

As my husband, who is from the Northwest puts it, "my people were too weak to go West."

Why would we have moved, I counter. We were happy with the way it was. We didn't need to live alone.

We both agree that people's personalities are influenced by where they live. This perspective, I found, was not going to help me adapt to being a military wife and living next to people from around the world. Over the years I was exposed to other cultures and lifestyles. I learned that we all have differences, but we are all individuals first. As I was exposed to more people, I stopped being so close-minded.

I didn't know what to think about Californians. I had heard too many rumors about their wacky ways and their strange hobbies—surfing and roller-blading throughout the year. I thought they would be Yankees with tans.

And then there were their food hang-ups like the South Dog Beach diet or whatever the latest craze was. I knew little about their personalities except they were liberal and extremely body conscious.

In fact, the only Californian I had ever met was a vegan, who was quite militant about her decision not to eat animal products.

At the South Carolina State fair, she encountered a dairy farmer who was demonstrating the contraptions he used to get milk from the cows. There were suction cups that he hooked up to the teats and giant pumps that gyrated when he flipped a switch.

I was digging the whole thing until the vegan started screaming, "Oh, my God, this is an atrocity! Animal abuse at its worst! This would never happen in California! That's why I am vegan! I don't want any of that in my body."

All I could think was, "Gee, lady, I can't really speak for the cow, but I will say this. I would love it if my job was to sit around all day and have someone play with my teats!"

Before we headed for Camp Pendleton, we spent a few days exploring Southern California. I began to think the people of California were obsessed with Hollywood. Every night the news reported what this star had done or what the industry was doing.

It looked to me like Hollywood had a massive influence on everything everyone did, thought, or wore.

I started feeling the pressure instantly. All the women were getting their hair and teeth bleached. And yes, I dare to say it, bleaching their anuses.

I was freaked out. I had no idea how I would make friends if I couldn't conform to the masses. So I called my grandma and sought her advice.

"Grandma, everyone out here is bleaching their anuses. What do I do?"

Her advice? "Baby, go outside in the sun and squirt a little lemon juice on it."

Ten days and too many miles to count, we finally arrived at Camp Pendleton.

I couldn't understand why the Marines would "Oooh-Rah," grunt, or bark at each other whenever they passed. It happened so frequently I tried to give my husband a suppository!

Everywhere I looked there were guards carrying huge guns, helicopters flying overhead, and tanks rolling down the road!

Was I really going to have to live in this surreal place?

We hadn't been assigned housing yet so we went to the BOQ where we would stay until we could get a house on base.

I thought we were at a hotel. When Jon opened the door, I was horrified to see a room with cement block walls, a crusty old recliner, and a lumpy bed that smelled of mildew.

When I looked in the bathroom, I found a leaky shower. There was mold and water everywhere.

A panic attack gripped me, but my husband didn't react. It didn't matter to him where we stayed. He had been sleeping outside for the past four months!

But reality had hit me. "Is this how we will be living?" I screamed.

He looked at me in complete fear; he had no words with which to reply. Once again he was sure I regretted my decision to marry him.

I collapsed on the bed and started bawling. I had left my friends, my family, my acting and stand up comedy career as well as my pets and sweet tea—just to live with this man who was now a mute.

Worst of all, he had brought me across the country to live in this hell hole cement room for the rest of my life!

I cried myself to sleep. Jon was too scared to touch me or say a word.

Needless to say, we did not christen the BOQ either.

The next day Jon approached a friend on base and asked if we could stay with them until we found housing.

I was about to experience my first dose of military hospitality. John and Jenn opened their doors to us and even welcomed our cats! They cooked us dinner and made us feel incredibly comfortable in their home.

Best of all, they told us we could stay as long as we needed. I was blown away by their kindness.

Once I saw how charming base housing could be I calmed down. Jon was no longer afraid of me.

My husband's friend also gave us pointers on dealing with the base housing people.

Basically, we were told we had to play "nice nice." You may go in and they'll tell you there is a three-month wait. While this may be true on some bases, it was not so on Camp Pendleton at that time.

Following our friend's advice, we went down to the housing office and kissed butt.

We were given keys to check out two houses on Camp Del Mar in Oceanside—right by the beach.

Jon and I had been earnestly praying to the Lord that we would get base housing and, if God could be so kind, please let it be a house near the beach. Our prayers had been answered.

The first key was to a cute and cozy townhouse. But the second key was for a home that technically was above our rank. It was a one level with two yards, a driveway, and a garage! God had showed His favor on us!

The gentleman with the reputation of being difficult had allowed us to check out a home that was above our rank. Without hesitation, we decided on that one.

Still, I wondered why this man had been so kind to us. Later on, it dawned on me what happened that changed his attitude.

I have suffered from Irritable Bowel Syndrome my whole life. This condition keeps me from digesting pretty much everything. My belly often fills with gas and swells. Seriously, I look like I'm about six months pregnant.

As a result, I avoid wearing tight fitting clothes. I often get lots of gas and sometimes have "emergencies" when eating out.

Let's put it this way. My husband doesn't get upset when I come home without my panties on. He knows I'm not cheating on him. I've simply had another accident.

Sometimes when there's a line at a public bathroom, the women will let me cut in front. After this happened several different times, it occurred to me that these women thought I was pregnant!

Flash back to the base housing office. Before we went in, we had had lunch at a Mexican restaurant. This type of food doesn't suit my condition.

While we were sitting in the base housing office I became very uncomfortable and bloated. I began rubbing my stomach and shifting around in my seat. I even had to excuse myself at least twice to use the bathroom.

Jon and I are so used to my stomach problems that we didn't think about the impression I was making.

Once we were in the house with the extra bedrooms, we figured out that the man at the housing office was under the impression I was pregnant.

We had a good laugh, but we also accepted the blessing of our first home.

Chapter Three

SETTLING IN: MY FIRST WEEKS

I quickly realized base housing is not like living in a typical subdivision. Men run in formation every morning down the street. This is nice to watch, especially if they are wearing their green silkies (green shorts similar to the ones worn by exercise guru Richard Simmons).

At any given time there may be a Marine in full camouflage and face paint hiding under a tree during a stake-out exercise. The first time I saw this it scared me so bad I almost peed in my pants!

In addition to cars driving slowly down the street, there are helicopters constantly overhead and tanks or light armored vehicles rolling down the street.

There's also a lot of saluting. I wondered if I was supposed to salute back. But, what is a proper "dependent's salute?" Boy Scouts have a two-finger salute. I figured I wasn't as skilled as they were, so I gave one finger salutes. I used the pointer finger on my right hand for my salute whenever I drove onto base.

I found this one finger salute convenient. You could switch fingers depending on who you were "saluting" or how you felt about them.

I didn't have much time to bask in being a military wife newlywed. Within days of arriving at Camp Pendleton, we had been assigned a house in Del Mar, but had a limited amount of time to unload the boxes and return the U-haul before we had to get on a plane for a visit with Jon's family.

Jon and I learned the hard way that I can't lift heavy objects.

While we were unpacking, I lifted this long Tupperware box and started to carry it to the edge of the truck. When I started to walk, the weight and length of the box pulled me forward. I couldn't stop myself and was trying to regain my balance when I ran toward the open tailgate.

Jon appeared in the front door of our new home just in time to watch me fly through the air. I looked like a child at a water park with my long mat in my hands diving into the waves.

I flew ten feet through the air riding my Tupperware boogie board. I felt nothing when I landed because the box broke my fall.

Jon stood in the door watching in horror.

I stood up and started yelling, "Did you see that? That was awesome!"

Jon was all serious, telling me that if that box had not been there to break my fall, I would have crushed my face on the driveway.

I angrily responded that if I hadn't had the box, I wouldn't have fallen.

Jon wasn't yet used to my clumsiness and tendency for disasters. To this day he insists I wear a helmet when I'm going up and down the stairs. He has since realized that it's much safer if I don't help with any strenuous tasks. I just make them more difficult.

Anyway, after the "tripping incident," I was no longer allowed to carry any boxes, which really slowed down the unpacking process.

I was worried because we had a plane to catch! We were going to Jon's hometown for a wedding reception in our honor. Most of Jon's family had not met me and his parents were eager to introduce us. It was a thoughtful gesture, but the timing only added to our stress.

Four days later, we returned to Camp Pendleton and Jon put on his Alphas (I just love that little hat that looks like a hotdog!) and reported for duty.

I look back at that move—unpacking and settling into a new home followed by the hometown visit—and realize we had not planned well.

First, we had not realized it would take so long to get across country or to get base housing. We learned the hard way that PCS leave is time to get settled—not take vacations or visit family.

We had let family pressure be our top priority when our new life should have been.

Thank God, Jon's Company Commander took pity on him and allowed him a few more days to get settled. We unpacked all my disgusting college furniture and random wedding gifts in an attempt to make the house livable.

Somewhere in the midst of settling in, a debilitating panic seized me. I was facing culture shock—both of California and military life—adjusting to Jon's family while missing my own, and then facing long days alone with no one to talk to.

Bizarre, unrealistic fears about military life and the base took hold of me.

My husband had no idea what was going on. He was in full Marine mode, heading back to work.

It didn't help that I was afraid to speak up. I thought he should be able to read my thoughts and know I was upset. It took me a while to realize men do not communicate like women do.

I look back at those first few months on base and realize many of my thoughts were completely irrational. If only I had had someone to explain things to me, maybe then I would not have blown everything out of proportion.

FAILURE TO COMMUNICATE

The military lifestyle has its own language. Everything is called something different from what I knew. Not only that, everything is described in acronyms.

I don't even know where they came up with some of these terms.

Why would you call the potty a "head?" What about "ink stick" to "moonbeam" and "go fasters."

And for all this, "Don't ask, don't tell" business, whose bright idea was it to describe a bunch of men hiking in the woods as a "HUMP."

I couldn't understand what my husband was talking about—SOP, BAH, or PCS? Why didn't he just tell me what they meant. When he didn't, I decided to make up my own meanings.

Here are my translations:

BAH: Broke Ass House payment/Husband

SOP: Same Old Problem

PCS: Pretty Crappy Situation

MRE: Most Rejected Entree

TAD: Tight Assed Decision

I think this style of talk is OOC: Out of Control!

I remember thinking those first few months on base: "What are you talking about? Could someone please tell me what time 1300 is?"

SHAKE, RATTLE, AND ROLL

All the noises and weapons on base started making me jumpy. Everyone was armed with a weapon. The LAVs and the "FROGS" (CH-46 helicopter) were really loud. There was always a random assault vehicle on the road.

I couldn't get used to it. I had been hearing about California earthquakes, and now had to put up with bomb tests and on-base explosions.

We were in bed one night when I heard the loudest boom and the house started to shake.

I jumped up screaming: "EARTHQUAKE! Grab the valuables and get into the basement. Get the cats, and put them in the tub!"

My husband grabbed me and tried to calm me down.

"Mollie, that's not a bomb. There's no earthquake. That's our neighbors. You see, he's leaving on deployment tomorrow and his wife is just saying goodbye."

How embarrassing! Thank you, base housing, for giving us neighbors who share a driveway AND a bedroom wall.

THE COMMISSARY: AN INTRODUCTION

I refused to drive anywhere on base. The strange vehicles, the Marines in formations, and the many rules on base frightened me. As a result, Jon was forced to drive me everywhere.

I had been in a PX, but not the commissary. I was afraid to go inside. My grandmother had scared me with her tales of militant clerks.

In fact, the entire base atmosphere had me in a fit of anxiety. I was afraid I would forget my ID and get tackled and cuffed by some hourly government worker.

My husband had to beg me to get out of the car. Once inside, I wouldn't push the shopping cart.

What woman doesn't want to push the cart? Pushing the cart is something women instinctively do. Just watch two women shopping together. They are constantly fighting over who gets to push. Even if it's a mother and her six-year-old daughter shopping for two items, they will fight over the handlebars. The woman wants control of the cart.

I worried about what the food would be like in the commissary. Was it "military issue?" Was everything in boxes? Was it government labeled? Was it given military names like "Don't ask? Don't tell Fruit Loops"?

I didn't know what to expect. I was in full panic mode.

Then I had to start making decisions about what to buy.

I had never shopped for us. While we were dating, we had either gone out to eat or my mom had cooked for us.

The pressure to buy the right food became too much for me. Jon kept watching me like he expected me to know what I was doing.

At that time I only knew how to cook two things: chicken enchiladas and tuna fish casserole.

But I couldn't even remember what ingredients I needed. I gave up. We bought a box of rice, beef bouillon, and ketchup.

By this time I was becoming claustrophobic and wanted out of there.

I found myself surrounded by really old veterans wearing hats that said, "Retired Marine—SEMPER FI." These hats didn't appear to fit on their heads, but instead seemed to hover over them.

At one point, I mistakenly tried to take the last box of crackers that a veteran also wanted. He started yelling, "I ran away from home at seventeen, lied about my age, and joined the Corps! I fought in World War II, Korea, and NAM! I have no cartilage in my right knee! It's bone-on-bone, but every morning I run six miles! I did not sacrifice my knee for this country to come here today and have you disrespect me at the commissary. Oooh-RAH!"

I dropped the crackers and walked away.

More bizarreness followed.

Why did everyone have two carts? There were so many children—all under three years old and all screaming. Was there a special? Buy two three-year-olds and get a toddler free.

Then there were all those uniforms. I was going cross-eyed. Why weren't any of these Marines and Navy service people working?

Really. I was losing it. By the time the checker asked for my ID, I was shaking.

I was sure she was going to want a full body search to make sure I was legit.

I looked around for Jon and spotted him standing at the magazine rack reading *Marine Corps Times*.

I handed the clerk my ID, but she barely looked at it before she started scanning my items.

THAT WAS IT? I was still suspicious.

My Grandma's stories were still playing over in my head. Somehow I had made it through my first trip to the commissary.

MY DAYS

Life for the first few weeks went like this. I stayed home all day unpacking, and my husband brought supplies home each night.

He would then help me move around the big stuff. The house was finally coming together.

During the day I would watch "Lifetime" movies or "Unsolved Mysteries" as I unpacked and cried.

I told Jon I had no one to talk to all day. He was at work and so were all my friends on the East Coast. By the time I called anyone on the East Coast they were already in bed. I was feeling isolated and alone.

My husband was afraid that I thought I had made a mistake.

He encouraged me to explore the base. I refused. I was sure I'd be shot by one of the Marines, get lost, or get run over by a tank.

Jon was patient at first, but became stern when he realized he would be in the field the following week.

He told me I would have to go out by myself because he would not be around to help me.

I became paralyzed by fear. At one point I was so panic-stricken that I wouldn't even let Jon take an evening jog. I was sure he would fall into a ditch and no one would discover his body. Then I'd be stuck in the house for the rest of my life.

My anxiety was at an all time high.

My first trip past the driveway became a nightmare. I was headed for the commissary again, but all the roads began to look the same.

I panicked and went down the wrong street finding myself on a dirt road, screaming as Hummers and LAVs surrounded my vehicle.

I fully expected to be blown up because I was trespassing. This was it! Any minute now, I was a goner.

Instead, the Marines took pity on me and got me turned around and off in the right direction.

Maybe no one was going to kill me after all. Slowly my anxiety started to subside.

After three weeks on base, I was finally able to drive myself out of the driveway.

GRUNT WORK

Was it just me or were all of you wives really confused when your husband called from work and said he would be home late because he and the guys were going on a five-mile HUMP?

I now knew I had married a Grunt and that he was staying true to the promises he had made. He couldn't get on my nerves because he was always gone.

When he came home from the field he was totally disgusting and had to be hosed off. I would make him undress in the laundry room, leaving his boots and utilities (camouflage uniform) on the floor.

After a shower he would fall asleep—only to wake up at 4:45 a.m. to go out and do it again the next day. There would be times he'd be gone for an entire week.

I didn't have kids, but was constantly doing laundry.

"Do bankers' wives have to hose their husbands off when they get home from work?" I wondered. "Do other wives have to guess when or if their husbands are coming home?"

I learned I couldn't plan to have a warm dinner ready for Jon because I never knew when he would walk through the door. I started adding two hours to when I thought he'd be home. I just figured since he was used to eating all those MREs that my reheated dinners would be just fine.

TAP OUT!

Bombs and explosions aren't the only strange noises you'll hear on a base. Revelry woke me up every morning. Retreat was played when they lowered the flag at sundown. Taps was played at night.

The bugle music is blasted on loud speakers throughout the base letting everyone know the American flag is being lowered or raised.

If you are outside during these times, you are required to stop what you are doing and face the flag in respect.

I learned the hard way not to be driving while they are lowering or raising the flag, because you're not allowed to drive.

My husband and I were coming home around five one evening. Jon had treated me to ice cream at the Cold Stone Creamery—a delicious treat on a hot day.

However, it's not as special when you're lactose intolerant. If I look at dairy products, I crap my pants unless I take medicine. On this occasion, I had forgotten to bring my pills.

We were only five minutes from base, so I didn't think that my IBS would be an issue. I thought we could get home before the emergency struck. Then the chills started, followed by a hot flash and the anus spasms.

I urgently needed to get to the bathroom!

I was still a newlywed and certainly wasn't to the point where I felt comfortable yelling, "I'm going to shit my pants any second!"

But the sweating had started, which was followed by the tears. "I'm not feeling well, and need to get home," I told him.

"Ok, but I have to obey the speed limit because of all the kids in the neighborhood," he replied.

I was pleading with him to hurry up when he came to a complete stop.

I screamed at him, "Why are we stopping?"

He rolled down the window. "Retreat."

I could see the flag lowering in the distance, the beautiful orange sun setting behind it.

In the opposite direction I could see the roof line of our home—so close, yet so far away.

As Retreat played, I surrendered. I pooped my pants. I took one for the flag.

Now that's patriotism.

YES, SIR!!!

Rank was something else that really blew my mind. There are two categories of Marines: officers and enlisted.

Officers go to college first and then get their training.

Enlisted men usually do the exact opposite.

But there are also Warrant Officers, Staff NCOs, and Gunnies. The base where we lived also had Navy personnel.

Not only that, housing and clubs are divided by rank.

My husband told me certain people received salutes and were addressed as "Sir," while others were not entitled to that courtesy.

In the South, everyone is addressed as "Sir" or "Ma'am" even if they are your age or younger.

I found myself wondering why a 37-year-old man was calling my husband "sir"?

I also wondered why the guards would salute me when I drove onto base. Jon explained they were saluting the sticker on my car. Saluting a sticker? Now I was thoroughly confused.

Thank God the wife of my husband's CO, Trina, called me once a week to invite me to a LINKS class.

I'm glad I finally let her talk me into attending.

That LINKS (Lifestyle Insights Networking Knowledge Skills) class helped me understand the military lifestyle. I seriously think it should be a prerequisite for anyone marrying into the military.

These ladies taught me the differences in rank and the reasons for separating the ranks.

They explained what the various acronyms meant and why as well as the history of some of the silly words.

They even helped me figure out what time it was.

MEETING NEW FRIENDS

I was finally getting the hang of base housing–military lifestyle. But, I still hadn't made any friends yet.

I had met a few random women at the "Hail and Farewell" gatherings that my husband had to attend, but that was about it.

And I was suspicious of these women because they would come up to me and ask strange things like, "Who is your husband with?"

I was ready to fight! What were they insinuating? My husband was with me!

I kept clear of most of the women at these formal functions.

At one function I was approached by an older wife who handed me a book and said "Here, read this."

It was "Roses and Thorns," a guide to proper behavior for military wives. I flipped it open and looked at the copyright page: 1940.

"This will teach you to be a proper dependent," she continued.

I stared at her open-mouthed and wondered, "Are you nuts?"

Proper dependent!? With my husband gone all the time and me having to do everything by myself, I am anything but "dependent!" I am my husband's "Independent!" I knew right then that it was urgent that I make real friends.

MY MARINE MOM

I had been living on base for about a month when I saw my first familiar face outside the commissary. It belonged to Mary, the Colonel's wife I had met on a trip to Charleston a few months earlier.

Mary had a permanent smile on her face the entire four years we lived at Camp Pendleton. She was petite, had the cutest little dark brown bobbed haircut, and was covered with gold jewelry. She was a classy lady and always made me feel welcome.

Mary also liked everything to be perfect—even if it was not. She believed that if something was not OK, you should just pretend it was. Eventually you would get over it.

Over the next four years, she would become my military mom.

That day as we chatted she asked me how I was getting along. We realized this would not be a quick conversation, so she asked me to come over later.

She had not yet been assigned her base housing, so she invited me to meet her at the BOQ where they were staying.

Much to my horror, I discovered she was staying in the exact room that Jon and I had when I had my breakdown!

Unlike me, this woman, who had made a lifelong career as a military wife, settled into her temporary digs with no complaints, embracing her environment and adapting to all changes.

As a matter of fact, she flourished! She acted as if we were not surrounded by cement walls that smelled of stale mildew.

Watching her, I became ashamed of the way I had acted within these four walls just a month earlier. I knew then that I would learn quite a bit from this seasoned wife. Perhaps the biggest lesson was simply to make the best of every situation.

Mary asked if I had met any friends, joined any of the various clubs, or signed up with any volunteer organizations. I had to admit I had not.

She assured me that in time I would make lifelong friends. In fact, she said, "all it will take is one Bunco party."

I had no idea what she was talking about. According to Mary, Marine wives went crazy over the game. I figured if this lady had survived twenty years as a military spouse, then I could make it to the next Bunco game.

AUTUMN

As luck would have it, I met Autumn a couple weeks later.

Autumn is also Virginia-born and bred. We soon discovered we could talk and hang out for hours and never get on each other's nerves. We joked that it was because we were both Aries.

Autumn is petite like me, with shoulder-length, highlighted auburn hair and braces.

Her husband is a First Lieutenant with a "Horseshoe haircut" who had been deployed practically from their wedding day.

She speculated she had spent a grand total of three months with him during their first year of marriage. That thought freaked me out, but her attitude reassured and inspired me.

Her home was beautifully decorated and she began to give me suggestions on what to cook. Autumn was like a gorgeous 24-year-old Betty Crocker.

She also encouraged me to become a volunteer or to find a hobby. In fact, she was working on her Masters' Degree so she could become a teacher.

She had also just started running marathons.

And here I was, unable to get my fat ass off the couch or stop crying, in the presence of a woman on fire!

She had completely embraced the lifestyle, which helped me change my perspective.

Autumn showed me that as a military wife you can have hobbies and aspirations even when the military is calling all the shots for your family.

I decided I wanted to be like her—happy, thriving, and accepting.

The week after we met, Autumn invited me to a neighborhood Bunco game being hosted by one of the Captains' wives in Del Mar Housing.

A few days before the party, I received a call from the hostess, who told me I was in charge of table snacks.

In the Bunco etiquette book, each woman must bring an appetizer, table snack, or dessert, while the host provides prizes for the winners and losers.

I worried about bringing the right snack. After all, this would be my first social get together without my husband.

I needed to make a good impression. I didn't want to blow it by bringing something too "low brow" like a 6-pack of Mountain Dew and ranch-flavored combos.

I thought about my Mother's Bridge games when she would bring out her fine china and serve classy snacks. I decided to call her for advice. She suggested Goldfish, a casual, yet classy snack. Suitable for a lunch box as well as a dining room table.

"Goldfish," she assured me, "don't have the 'low brow' reputation of a potato chip."

THE BUNCO PARTY

That first evening was stiff and pretentious.

I recognized a few of the women I had met around the neighborhood. Many of the new wives, however, were nervous and unsure how to act. At first we stood around the kitchen snacking on Brie and sipping red wine.

Still, I wondered about the children hanging around. Wasn't this a wives' function? Why were kids here?

The only conversations going on were between the Captains' wives. They were talking about their husbands—what they did and who they knew.

It didn't seem right. After all, this was supposed to be a "welcome to the neighborhood" evening where we could get to know everyone in the area.

What did our husbands have to do with our likes, hobbies, and jobs? Didn't anyone care where we were from?

These "veteran" wives laughed loudly and spoke haughtily of their husband's faults and inadequacies in and around the home, and then bragged about their achievements at work.

None of the them made any effort to engage us in conversation.

Worst of all, they seemed to gather around one particular woman: Maggie. She seemed to be instigating their aggressive, bullying behavior. It felt like they were trying to intimidate the new wives.

I sat back and observed. The only person I knew was Autumn, who was busy in the kitchen.

I began to believe they didn't care about us. It seemed they had forgotten where they had come from. They had taken on the identities of their husbands. They wore their husband's rank, and not in a loyal, loving, proud way that the Silent Ranks do, but as a way of entitlement.

I found it quite sad. They were all trying so hard to fit a certain mold, to keep to a standard that only they were holding themselves to.

So, here I was trying to contain myself, (which means not saying the "F" word or talking about gas or bowel issues), as all these higher ranking wives spoke of military life in a manner meant to intimidate.

They basked in the glow of offering the truths of base housing life. "You know they can listen in to all our phone conversations," explained one. "Be careful what you talk about."

I wondered what General wanted to hear about my period or any other dumb ass chatty topic women gabbed on and on about over the phone?

Besides, I reasoned, I had no one to call on the phone. Seriously, I may have been green, but I hadn't been born yesterday.

And then Maggie got our attention. "They will kick you off base if you don't mow your yard. There are strict rules about yard care—no dead plants. We have standards in officers' housing!"

She went on and on about strict rules of base housing, proper dress code for officers' wives, yard care standards, hardships of deployments, babies being born while husbands were gone. Then there were the frightening stories about the naval hospital.

The Captains' wives seemed to relish each cringe on our faces, each furrowed brow. I really think they enjoyed scaring us.

Some of the wives began breaking into a sweat, double-checking their outfits in the mirror and running through lists in their minds, asking themselves, "Did I make it? Am I up to par?"

I thought it was ridiculous, but I managed to keep my mouth shut.

That's when Maggie's three-year-old daughter took a fork and started scrapping it down the side of the hostess' heirloom china cabinet.

Where was this type of behavior listed in the military wives' code of do's and don'ts?

No one said a thing.

Maggie had now started on her husband's USMC accomplishments—oblivious to her child's behavior.

Her daughter continued to carve and scratch away at the hutch.

The host came out of the kitchen and watched in horror as this child scraped away. I swear I saw a tear trickle down her cheek. And yet she didn't say a word.

None of the other wives said a word to Maggie or the child. Finally, one of the 2nd Lieutenants' wives, Natalie, calmly and assertively told the child to give her the fork and go back to the table.

Maggie didn't flinch!

The host, however, breathed a sigh of relief.

I could tell that her mother's preoccupation had not gone unnoticed. This child was used to doing outrageous things to get her mother's attention.

I invited the little girl to sit on my lap. She climbed up, grateful for the attention. I began to braid her hair while Natalie asked her to draw a picture.

The new wives began to make eye contact—silently confirming this select group of higher-ranking wives must be nuts.

I decided this group could not be representative of the whole.

Finally, the game started. We began to have fun once we were all playing and not talking.

Maggie was at my table and attempted small talk. Most of the girls were shy, so she directed her attention to me. She started by asking me where we lived.

"On Dolphin Drive," I replied.

She assumed I meant one of the townhouses, and said as much.

"No," I continued, "We were given one of the one-level homes farther down the street."

The entire room went silent. A gasp was heard from another table.

When we were given the larger one-level home, Jon knew the other women would have a problem with it. Housing is divided by rank, which in turn reflects status.

We had been placed in a home that belonged to someone with a higher ranking. We weren't supposed to be there.

In the handful of one-level homes in our neighborhood were Navy Captains, Marine Captains, Majors, many Warrant Officers, and one Marine Colonel.

Maggie's eyes narrowed and her lips pursed. "How did you possibly manage getting one of those homes!" she demanded.

I searched the faces of the other new wives. They just stared back open-mouthed. They had no idea what was going on.

"Your husband is only a Second Lieutenant," she continued. "How did you get a house with a garage, an extra bathroom, and backyard! You don't even have any children! Did you lie to get that house?"

I could feel my face burning. I wasn't about to tell them about the "gas baby" I was carrying when we were at the housing office. Somehow I didn't think they would find any humor in that.

I had no idea how to respond. I looked around the crowd. All of the higher ranking wives were glaring at me, their eyes filled with indignation and jealousy over the extra half-bathroom.

The new wives remained silent. They knew we were outnumbered.

I was cornered. I had been called a liar!

Autumn saved the day. She jumped up and screamed, "BUNCO." It broke the tension. She won the cash prize for the most wins that night. I claimed the prize for the most losses.

The leader of the Captains' wives was thrilled to hand me the loser's prize—a large pink flamingo. I was told it had to be displayed in the front yard until next month's game.

Maggie made sure to follow it up with a quick jab about ruining the look of my giant front yard.

I actually thought the flamingo would look perfect next to my resin statue of a dog peeing on a hydrant.

By the end of the evening I was glad to head home. I hadn't felt so bullied since the seventh grade.

We found out later that some of these higher-ranking wives (egged on, I'm sure, by Maggie) had dubbed us "butter bar" wives. This nickname is based on our husbands' rank and the gold bar symbolizing it on their uniforms.

To some of these women the evening had not been a nice neighborhood get together, but an effort to make sure we knew our place.

I wished they had simply peed on us to mark their territory.

This was not the fun gathering Mary had encouraged me to attend. Still, I refused to give up hope. For some strange reason, I looked forward to next month's game.

BETTER FRIENDS IN ONE MONTH OR LESS

The evening had left me drained, but determined. I now knew there were women to avoid, but some good ones to get to know. It pulled me out of my funk and got me proactive.

I had made two friends that evening—Natalie and Kathleen (who we called "Kat"). Since our husbands were in the same battalion, we began to plan get-togethers on the nights the boys were in the field.

We became known as "The Three Amigos." We had such great fun together, getting to know each other and sharing all the new experiences of living on base. At last, I was no longer alone.

My new friends had very different personalities.

Natalie is so laid back; I love her relaxed, chilled-out temperament. She is tall with the most beautiful long brown curly hair. She loves to just hang out, drink a beer, and laugh.

Natalie walks softly, but carries a big stick. She does not chatter on like Kat or me, so when she speaks, you listen. And when Natalie speaks, it is with carefully chosen and wise words.

She would, in the years to come, be my voice of reason and the only friend willing to set me straight when I was out of line. She would also set others straight when they messed with me.

One time she went to bat for me before I learned to stick up for myself. I had purchased a ball gown, but had gained weight as it got closer to the ball. I took it to the cleaners to have it altered, but when I picked it up the dress didn't fit.

I could barely zip it up and when I did, I couldn't breathe.

The seamstress refused to fix it. In broken English, she insisted, "It looks good! Sexy time!"

Still young, I hadn't learned how to be assertive, so I left without getting the dress fixed.

When I got home, I started crying to Natalie. I was upset I had wasted money getting the dress fixed and now I was going to have to buy another one.

Natalie went nuts. She got me into the car and drove us back to the dry cleaners. Within a few minutes Natalie had gotten a full refund and had made the seamstress alter the dress again.

She gave me strength when I didn't have any.

Kat, on the other hand, is taller than Natalie and has the greenest eyes I had ever seen. She and I could talk so much our tongues had to stop before our brains would.

We are both very outspoken, but in completely different ways. I'm more prone to yelling out something vulgar, while she is likely to yell at me for saying it.

She would claim that her delicate ears could not handle hearing such words. However, a glass of wine later and she could match me tit for tat with "F" bombs.

I was, on the other hand, a lightweight when it came to drinking. One drink and it was lights out for me. I was a social drinker and smoker.

Kat is what I would call an "I'll have one of yours" drinker and smoker.

I sensed she was struggling with her Catholic guilt and trying to find herself.

I tend to attract people who are afraid to express themselves. They can sin vicariously through me. In fact, I tease my husband, who is Catholic, about my Methodist beliefs.

We don't believe in purgatory, so I tell him that he better die first because he will need a head start since he'll be in purgatory for years before I die.

I, on the other hand, will go straight to heaven.

You could say that Kat and I are opinionated, but that would be an understatement. Natalie would sit back and shake her head whenever the two of us got going on political, moral, or Biblical topics. We thought we knew everything.

Kat had gone straight from her parent's Catholic upbringing to a Jesuit college, and then into marriage.

I had attended Christian schools for twelve years and knew a little bit about that type of education as well as complete immersion into a religion.

Although Kat had fewer "real life" experiences than Natalie or me, she often gave me the best advice.

I could really get worked up over issues, but Kat would calmly and rationally see the best way to handle a situation.

The three of us connected completely after that first Bunco game. We balanced each other out. I had finally made connections and found good friends.

Mary had been right after all. Bunco did open up doors to find good friends.

BEENIE WEENIE

I was still looking for my best friend—that one special girlfriend. The one that I could say anything to and wouldn't be judged by her. I found her in Beenie.

Jon tried to introduce me to as many wives as possible. Luckily, he got a call from some of his TBS buddies who invited us to Del Mar beach. It was there I met Beenie.

She looks like Betty Paige with black hair, bangs, and long legs. She giggled non-stop and always has a smile on her face. She also smoked and had a cooler filled with Miller Lite.

I was drawn to her laid back spirit. She was confident and didn't appear to care what others thought of her.

Sitting next to her that day on the beach, I realized we had so much in common. We both had poodles and had lived for years in the Carolinas. (Beenie was not raised in the South, so she was not truly "Southern." There is an expression for people who live in the South who aren't born there: "Just because the cat has kittens in the oven doesn't make them biscuits.")

She had been a schoolteacher and was an amazing artist. Like me, she had married her Marine within months of meeting him. Like us, they had eloped much to the dismay of some of their family and friends.

She said she met Lloyd at a party in Wilmington, North Carolina. He was so charming, fun, sexy, and wild that she just had to marry him. She said she wanted a husband who could party with her. And it worked for them. They loved to party and had friends over all the time.

Beenie's energy was just what I needed at that point. She wasn't bothered by my loud mouth attitude. If anything, she spurred it on by laughing at my outrageous behavior.

When I started doing stand up comedy, I would run jokes by Beenie and she would laugh and laugh. I'd say, "did you get that one?" And she would say, between giggles and tears, "I think so!"

When you do stand up you are supposed to imagine you're speaking directly to someone. My someone is always Beenie. She's my Ed McMahon without the cheesy sweepstakes.

Beenie also does the same thing my dad does. She pronounces McDonald's as Mac Donald. Or Kimora Lee Simmons as Kamero. She also tends to drop the 's' at the end of a word and adds an "s" to words that don't have one. Sometimes people didn't understand what she said, so I'd have to translate. After a while, I started to talk like Beenie, which tripped everyone out.

It was also great to meet someone who had a lot of things fly right over her head. Neither of us "got" half of what our husbands said. We weren't exactly simple-minded. We just didn't catch onto some things quickly.

When my father developed prostate cancer I called to share the news with Beenie. She and my dad had shared many a Miller Lite.

I assured her my dad would be fine, but that he would have to have minor surgery to remove the cancer.

Beenie was naturally concerned for me. "Oh Mollie, do you think you should go get your prostate checked?" she innocently asked.

After we met that first day we chatted on the phone constantly. I was glad to finally have someone to talk to in between "Lifetime" movies on days Jon was at work.

Beenie became the gas to my fire. She seemed to be happy and operated on a plane of existence I have yet to discover. Best of all, she keeps her life uncomplicated.

It's something I wish I could do. I am so high strung, while Beenie lets it all roll off. Nothing gets under her skin.

There was only one time when she popped. For some reason, Beenie's husband could never do anything right. He's one of the smartest guys I have ever met, but he had this lawyer attitude that he couldn't leave at the office.

Here's the thing: Lloyd absolutely worships Beenie. He goes nuts trying to get her attention—even competing with me for it. He would even get jealous if he called home and found she was talking on the phone with me.

It wasn't a "beat your wife" type of jealousy, just a guy up against a challenge. The more Beenie would ignore Lloyd, the wilder he would get. And does Beenie know how to work him!

Anyway, in his efforts to get her attention, Lloyd would mess up—often. In fact, he seemed to like it when she was mad at him, as if he had more of a challenge to overcome. They would have these huge blow-ups and she would lock him out of the house. I would call two hours later only to hear they had just had wild make-up sex.

I secretly came to believe that Lloyd did his best to make her mad just to get her in bed.

A SENSITIVE SUBJECT: POGUE VS. GRUNT

Jon and Lloyd were great pals as well. Irish Catholic, charming, goofy, party animal, USMC lawyer—that was Lloyd.

Lloyd and Jon had been in TBS training together. Lloyd went on and on about how Jon had been the only one to beat him at puggle stick fighting. Jon didn't really remember the incident, but Lloyd recalled the match in perfect detail.

He insisted on a rematch. He kept going on and on about losing to a "Grunt." It was a "Grunt versus Pogues" issue. While I knew my husband was a Grunt (an infantryman or "ground pounder" Marine), I didn't know about Pogues.

Evidently we were surrounded by Pogues that day because they all kept chiming in on the rivalry between Pogues and Grunts.

Jon later explained there is a long-standing rivalry in the Corps. Being a Pogue or a Grunt is based on your MOS (job).

According to Pogues, Grunts are stupid, barbaric ground-pounders who are too dumb to be Pogues.

According to Grunts, Pogues are intellectual, soft paper pushers and too weak to be Grunts.

The joke to me is all Marines have to be Grunts at one time, while nearly every Grunt becomes a Pogue at some point or other. Yet they have this need to tease each other constantly.

NEIGHBORS

Our first neighbors had finally moved out. They had been a nightmare. He was in the Navy, had cheated on his wife, and had given her every sexually transmitted disease known to man. And she had shared all of this with me on a daily basis, making us both miserable.

Each time I ran out the front door to jump on my husband and greet him with a kiss when he came home, she shot me an evil look. She constantly tried to scare me with on-base gossip about Jon's upcoming deployments and rumors about when or where he was going. She took every opportunity to frighten me.

Her husband deployed soon after that and she decided to move off base. I prayed to the Lord that He would bless our next neighbors. After all, we would be sharing a driveway and a bedroom wall.

By the time our new neighbors moved in, I had made friends and was no longer feeling depressed.

When a car pulled up, I peeked out the window and ran out the front door.

There stood Michelle—beautiful and blonde with her tiny tow-headed baby David on her hip, and four-year-old Jacob holding her hand.

She told me she and her husband Kevin were from Cherry Point, North Carolina. I was on Cloud Nine—another Southern girl!

Michelle looked like a combination of Dolly Parton and Anna Nicole Smith. She had the big blonde hair, wide smile, and large boobs. She also had a big Southern personality.

I can only imagine what the neighbors said about Michelle and me. The sight of two blonde-haired and big-boobed Southern girls chatting incessantly probably sent some people over the edge.

Michelle also had a funny way of talking—wide open about everything. She talked about all body functions and all things private. If she didn't have anything nice to say, or if she wanted to say something mean, but couldn't because the kids were within earshot, she would just say, in a high pitched voice, dragging the word out, "Weeeeeeeelllll!"

This one word became our thing. We would use it when others were around and we wanted to talk smack about another neighbor.

"So and so stopped by. She is so lovely, but her husband, he sure is . . . different."

She would reply, "Weeeeeeeeelllll!"

Or I'd say, "I saw Jacob playing with that brown-haired boy across the street. He certainly does have a rough way about him."

To which Michelle would reply, "Weeeeeeelllll!"

We could say it all in just one word. In a truly Southern fashion we managed to be ugly without hurting anyone's feelings.

I was elated to be sharing my driveway and bedroom wall with Michelle and her family. We became so tight that we were constantly in and out of each other's houses. We were like peas and carrots.

MOLLY, YOU'RE SUCH A BITCH!

Ironically, our new neighbors had a dog named Molly.

Throughout my life, I had had to deal with dogs with the same name as mine. I have met people who pop right out with "I have a dog named Molly!" Like this is supposed to make me feel warm and fuzzy?

Depending on my mood I might retort with "What a coincidence! I'm a bitch, too!"

Or this: "Great to hear it. Do you want to tell me your name or shall I sniff your ass to see if I recognize you?"

Having a neighbor named Mollie and a dog called Molly can be down right confusing for the children, especially when someone says, "Molly scooted her butt on the carpet again."

The kids would fall down laughing when Kevin would rant, "Damn it! Molly pooped in the neighbor's yard again!"

In an effort to prevent some embarrassing moments, they came up with a simple solution. They decided I would be known as "Miss Mollie," a title of respect straight out of the South. The golden cocker spaniel, on the other hand, stayed simply "Molly."

While the name change helped the kids, I still got looks from our other neighbors whenever Kevin would yell at the dog. "Damn it, Molly, quit humping!" Or, "Molly, stop licking your ass!"

DAVID THE MENACE

Michelle's youngest son had a devilish streak. And he would get this twinkle in his eye just before he would strike.

At eighteen months, David would sit at the end of the driveway with a pacifier in his mouth and wait for his four-year-old brother. When Jacob whizzed by on a skateboard, David would push a skate into Jacob's path, causing him to crash.

Jacob would cry and we would run to see what was wrong. There we would find baby David—quietly laughing.

David also loved boobs. He would look at me while Michelle was holding him, grab a handful of his mom's boob and giggle. If I held him, he would rest his tiny hand on my breast and laugh.

If you caught him in the act he would shrug and lift his hands up.

David was our little "Dennis the Menace." When he got that certain look in his eye we'd said, "Here comes Dirty Dave!" He was a stinker, and I wished he were mine.

Jacob could be incredibly brave and quite sensitive. Shortly after they moved in, I found Jacob crying in the garage. I approached and asked him if he was OK. He said he was, but became embarrassed that I had seen him crying.

I told his dad, who explained Jacob was crying because a boy had been mean to another boy on the playground. Jacob had been so upset he went off to cry in private. I was so moved that a four-year-old had the capacity to feel such empathy for another.

I was impressed at what Jacob could accomplish. He was a natural athlete. The fact that he could crash and burn on a regular basis and come out unscathed amazed me.

One day I saw him playing in the backyard when a large tumbleweed blew by, picked him up and the two went rolling away. They finally crashed into a trash can.

I envisioned Jacob becoming a stuntman. He could master all sports: skateboarding, roller skating, bicycling—anything. He simply had no fear.

What stole my heart, though, was that he would always ask if my daddy would let me play with him. I assumed this was because Marines look pretty much the same in uniform. In this child's mind, guys in uniform equal daddies.

Still, I guess many of the kids on base thought I was a kid just like them. It wasn't just because of my size (I was only five inches taller than Jacob). It was because I could match them tit for tat when it came to screaming, farting, and yes, fighting over toys.

Most days we spent in the driveway or backyard running amuck playing together on swings or going down the slides.

Jacob never really understood that Jon and I were married. If Jon came home from work and Jacob and I were playing, he would ask Jon to join him.

"Mollie made me dinner, Jacob," he would reply. "I have to go in and eat."

"Oh, your mommy wants you to come in for dinner?"

I was as proud as his parents when Jacob learned to ride a bike without training wheels. Michelle and Kevin asked Jon and me to come out and watch. There was Jacob on the tiniest bike I had even seen in my life.

He proudly announced he was going to demonstrate riding without training wheels. We all made a huge fuss. "Why, you are only four! If you do that, you must be so brave!"

To insure Jacob's safety, Michelle held David in her arms. She wanted to avoid one of David's sneak attacks.

Off Jacob went—soaring at top speeds down the driveway. We all cheered.

He yelled: "Look at me! Look, Miss Mollie, look at me!"

We all cheered some more as he peddled into the street. As we stood there bragging about his accomplishments, my analytical husband asked, "Isn't there a car parked on the side of the road in the direction he was headed?"

We stopped talking just in time to hear a loud crash. A second later we heard Jacob's wail, followed by David's giggle.

Crash and burn. Jacob's first bike ride without training wheels had been only a partial success.

Michelle and I took much joy in talking about things that made our Catholic husbands very nervous.

Because we shared a bedroom wall, much of our privacy was sacrificed. Since we were Southerners, we decided to nonchalantly disclose details of our sexuality instead of worrying about being embarrassed.

Michelle is what you could call hyper-sexual. Where some neighbors would call on their way to the commissary to see if you needed a gallon of milk, Michelle would call whenever she was doing a sex store run to see what I wanted.

This is just the person I wanted living next door to me if the power goes out. More importantly, I could count on her to have the right supplies when my husband was gone.

CHRISTA AND THE SCHWANN'S MAN

I met Christa at a scrapbooking party. I didn't scrapbook. I just went to meet friends.

She was a Captain's wife, younger than me, and had the cutest baby boy named Silas.

Christa towered over me with three inches of brown curls. Best of all, she cursed like a sailor. If only we had had her at the first Bunco evening to break the ice. I knew this type of higher ranking officer's wife existed and thanked God I had found her.

She also lived in a bigger house than everyone, in a newer part of the Del Mar Housing. I asked her if the other Captains' wives hated her because of it. Her response? "Fuck um!"

Like Beenie and a few of the other Captains' wives I had met, I now saw that not all higher-ranking wives were jerks. Nor was I any longer intimidated by them.

Christa wanted to know if I had met the Schwann's man yet. I had no idea what she was talking about. That's when she sat me down for "the talk."

According to Christa, you knew you had finally arrived at a level of wifedom when you started ordering dinners from the Schwann's man. He delivered delicious gourmet ice cream and frozen dinners in his big yellow truck.

The convenience of pre-made meals was something the new generation of military wife celebrated, Christa told me. It was a way for us to express our independence from making everything from scratch.

Would my grandmother approve of the Schwann's man's unconventional practices?

Christa promised if I developed a relationship with this man, all my problems with meals and party food would disappear.

I begged her to enlighten me! I wanted to know "The Way"! She gave me my first Scwhann's brochure and showed me the pages of bestsellers.

That Thursday I waited with anticipation as the yellow truck made its way around the neighborhood. Some of the neighbors' faces appeared in their windows as they saw his truck pull into my "Butter Bar" driveway.

Yes, folks! The Schwann's man is coming to my home. I'm breaking free of constant trips to the commissary!

Over the next four years, my Schwann's man and I developed a very intense relationship centered on chicken Cordon bleu and orange push-ups.

Ours was a discreet relationship, though. Josh gave me what I needed (frozen dinners and ice cream) and I left him a check.

I knew the older generation of wives talked, but I didn't expect them to understand. The relationship I had with Josh allowed me to become a better wife.

BUTTER BAR BUNCO

By the next Bunco party the "butter bar" wives had become tight. Our husbands had been gone for nearly a month, which gave us lots of time together.

Now half of the neighborhood children would be jumping on my trampoline while eating ice cream. We would go to the beach, take walks together, or just hang out at Natalie's or Autumn's.

At the first Bunco party, I had agreed to host the next one. Maggie had insisted that my house was the biggest, an ideal place for the next game.

Since it was going to be on "butter bar" territory, we decided to call the shots.

First of all, rather than serving Brie and the usual appetizers, desserts, and table snacks, we decided we would spice things up.

I called my "Butter bar girls" and started making plans. The invitations went out with specific instructions: No kids or military talk allowed. Please bring your favorite dance music CD.

We also had new food assignments: who would bring the beer, the margaritas, and the wine coolers. We decided who would bring the different flavors of cigarettes: lights, flavored, and ultra-lights.

Table snacks changed from raisins, Goldfish, and carrots, to Combos, hot fries, and M&Ms.

Finally, instead of having a purple dog bone for the winner of the most Buncos, Michelle provided a "Bunco boner." It was a pink, sticky penis made of a material that could stick to the wall and crawl down it like a Slinky.

Instead of being outnumbered by higher-ranking wives, I thought the evening should be full of enlisted and officer wives. We had a fun girl's night planned!

About an hour into the evening, we realized most of the Captains' wives had not shown up. As more guests arrived, they brought regrets. So and so couldn't make it because she couldn't find a sitter. So and so couldn't come because her child was sick.

We began to realize we were in trouble. You need twelve people to play Bunco. And if you can't attend a Bunco night, it's your responsibility to notify the host or find someone to fill your spot.

Christa looked at me between drags on her cigarette and said, "I know Maggie's not coming. She told me last week."

The one wife who had insisted that I host a party because I had a large house was not even coming. Glad she told me to my face.

Worse still, she was supposed to bring the Bunco kit. When I pointed out that Maggie was supposed to bring the kit, Christa stared blankly at me. Maggie had told her she did not have the kit.

This is insane, I thought. I bet her perfectness couldn't stand the thought of being in the home she thought she deserved.

I figured the fact we had changed the rules of etiquette had also gotten under their skin. They wanted to let us know they were above our beer-drinking, cigarette-smoking, junk food-eating party.

After my anger wore off, I became hurt and sad. I was obvious to me that she had called the handful of her cronies and told them to boycott my party.

It was not enough that they ignored the invitation, but they also tried to ruin our fun.

What was ironic is those wives had decided not to attend because they thought our behavior was inappropriate. And yet, they were the ones being rude. They were the ones acting like snobs.

But without the game kit, how were we going to play Bunco? I couldn't think of what to do.

Christa saved the day. "Let's play something else! This is really just supposed to be a time that we all get away and be girls. It's not about the Bunco. It's about hanging out, without kids or husbands!"

The women looked up at me and smiled. My anxiety melted away.

Another wife chimed in, "Let's just stay out here on the patio and talk. Screw Bunco!"

So we sat on the patio, laughed, drank, ate junk food, smoked, farted, teased, and bonded. A few wives who heard the commotion from down the street joined us.

It was the best night of my life.

Thereafter, my house became known as the party house for the new clique in town. Of course, none of the uptight wives were included.

It became a mix of wives of Captains, Lieutenants, enlisted men, officers, and even Marine and Navy wives living on and off base.

At least once a week you could find a group of women on the back patio hanging out. We kept the extra fridge there stocked with popsicles and wine coolers. And there were plenty of comfortable couches.

Later that week, Christa helped me make a new Bunco kit, complete with the "Bunco boner." The butter bar wives now had their own Bunco kit.

One Captain's wife named Melanie hand-painted Bunco Christmas ornaments for all of us one year. I think of our close knit group every year when I hang it on our Christmas tree.

Even the guys tried to crash our parties.

One night we sent the guys off to play poker while we played Bunco. But Beenie's husband and one of his JAG friends tried to crash our party while pretending to look for more beer.

Splat! One of them ended up with the sticky Bunco boner crawling down his cheek. "No boys allowed!" we screamed.

But they still didn't want to leave. They said our party was more fun than their poker game!

I found out later that one guy declared, "those girls are worse than a bunch of guys at a bachelor party."

I take that as a compliment. Butter Bar Bunco evenings acquired the reputation of being wild and fun. Bunco had done for us exactly what Mary had promised. And we had become the greatest of friends.

PARTY AT THE GROSS HOUSE

Jon and I didn't plan to have children until the deployments were done.

Still, we had become attached to the neighbors' kids and wanted everyone to feel welcome at our home. So . . . we bought a huge trampoline at Wal-Mart. (Just in case you think I am totally nuts, I was a gymnast for twelve years so I knew *a little* about what I was doing.)

My husband got a little too excited and started jumping on the trampoline before I had finished putting the safety padding on.

"Jon, wait. It's not ready!"

He refused to heed my warnings. A minute later he was cutting a flip when he ripped his ankle open on an exposed spring. After we stopped the bleeding, Jon quietly helped me finish attaching the liner.

It was at that point I realized I didn't need a child; I had married one.

You get used to having kids in your home when you live on base. I can't tell you how many times we came home from church to find a random child sitting on the sofa eating our food.

"Hi there," I would say.

"Can your son play with me?"

"We don't have any children."

The child would think about it, shrug, and reply, "Well, can I play your XBox?"

Only when the child found out that we did not have an Xbox or a Wii would he venture home.

If you don't want kids in your house, don't bother putting a "No Trespassing" sign in your yard. Just put out a sign that says, "We have no Wii."

Like a magnet, our trampoline drew kids in from every corner of the neighborhood. When kids spotted our heads bobbing up and down over the privacy fence, accompanied by screams and giggles, they figured out what was going on and asked to come over and jump. On any given afternoon there would be four or five kids eating Schwann's ice cream and jumping up and down on the trampoline. Their mothers and I would sit on the back patio chatting and sipping Cokes.

I was grateful for the company of these amazing women and their kids, especially when Jon was in the field.

THE GO CART

Jon was off to Combined Arms Exercise, a month of desert training at 29 Palms, California. I was sulking.

I had finally settled in. My home was my own and I had friends. I no longer freaked out about CH 46 helos flying overhead or tanks driving past my car. I no longer flinched when I had to show my ID, or felt odd when the sticker on my car was saluted.

I had come to grips with the fact that I was no longer a career woman. I had accepted my role as a housewife. I had worked since I was fifteen, but now I had to be a supportive spouse.

Not all jobs come with a salary. You can't put a price tag on the important roles you play in life. I had started to learn new recipes and was cooking a few new things. I was enjoying myself, but I was still struggling with not working as I thought and felt I should be. I had a lot to learn about partnership in a marriage.

The pouting started when Jon left for training. I had been daddy's girl and was used to being spoiled. I had not seen my Marine often when we dated, but when I did, I had all his attention.

Now that we were married, it was different. We lived together, but the Corps called all the shots. The Marine Corps provided our home and the commissary kept us filled with affordable food. Health insurance was free. Still, I had no income.

Financially it was difficult to go from two salaries to one. I had never been a designer girl, but I did like to have fun and was used to buying something when I wanted, or going out to eat. Now we had no money for extras.

I struggled with the possibility of getting a job. Some of my girlfriends did work. When their husbands were gone for three days, they were grateful for their jobs. When he was home for a week straight, they were miserable because they had to leave him to go to work.

I was not ready to make that commitment. I wanted every minute with Jon.

I could no longer afford acrylic nails, so Jon treated me to a pedicure. While there, I met a lady who had her own business and needed an assistant. She offered very flexible hours and wanted to pay me in cash.

I was so excited! I now had a job and I felt great! I would be working, but would still be able to support my husband.

On the drive home I saw a motorized go cart at a tire shop. A flashback of high school days whirled through my head and happiness flooded over me as I remembered the go cart I had had and all the joy it had brought me.

My mother had won a green 3.5HP Indy model go cart with a fiberglass shell at a convenience center convention. I spent many afternoons with my girlfriend Shannon riding the high-powered machine. It was a blast.

We had driven it all over my parent's property, thrill riding for hours up and down the driveway and through the woods.

Now, here in front of me, was another go cart and it was for sale! And this go cart looked just like the one I had had in high school.

It was love at first sight and it was only $1,300. I bought it on the spot, reasoning that I had a job.

When the Indy cart was delivered the next day, the children on base looked at me like I was their hero! They wanted to take turns sitting in "Miss Mollie's real race car."

When Michelle saw it, she just said, "Weeeeeellll!"

The other mothers just stared at me.

Beenie, always my partner in crime, thought it was awesome. She couldn't wait for her next visit so she could take it for a spin.

Autumn just laughed when she saw it.

The husbands gazed at it—talking like it was a hemi, considering its specs and its engine.

One even tried to buy it. "NO WAY!" I replied. I would never part with my happiness. (I was such a dumb ass.)

Natalie proved to be the only voice of reason. She yelled at me when she found out. "What are you doing? Are you nuts? What are you going to do with that thing? Get a paper route? How much was it? Do you think you are going to hide this from Jon? Are you insane? Do you really have a job? How did you pay for this? Have you even told Jon what you have done? What does a grown adult do with a go cart?"

At least Natalie loved me enough to tell me the truth.

As she spoke I realized what a horrible mistake I had made. I hadn't even discussed the huge purchase with my husband. And it was not even for something that was practical, like a $1,300 grill or new tires for the car.

I became defensive. I wasn't ready to admit my error, but I knew I was being selfish and unfair to Jon.

I had complained about Jon not knowing about bank accounts, how to do laundry, or how to eat well-balanced meals. I even whined about the fact he didn't pick up after himself.

But it was nothing compared to what I had just done. I was the one who was being irresponsible and disrespectful.

We were partners and still working out our roles. I was responsible for our meals and the house, but I continued to bitch that he should know about that stuff.

Instead of yelling at me not to overspend, he had thoughtfully treated me to a pedicure. I, in turn, had purchased a $1,300 go cart.

When he called that night, I asked him if he wanted the good news or the bad news. This always freaked him out because he thought that I was pregnant.

"The good news."

"I have a job!" Once I explained all the details and the flexible hours Jon was stoked. He didn't care if I worked or not, if I made five dollars or five hundred. He just knew I wanted to keep busy when he was in the field.

"What's the bad news?"

I told him about the go cart. He went silent.

"I have a job now," I continued, "so I can pay for it myself."

"But you haven't made any money yet, Mollie, so really you haven't paid for it."

Jon was so patient. I didn't deserve his kindness. How many times had I started raving over something before he even got the whole story out? Now my husband was "disappointed" in me, which was tough to hear.

He never yelled; he never really got angry. He had so much guilt about being gone all the time that he felt he had no grounds to be upset about my purchase.

However, his guilt didn't justify my bad behavior. I had lost perspective. I needed to spend more time finding positive ways to develop my friendships and be productive with activities instead of whining about his absence.

If I could not go without his attention for a few weeks, how would I make it through an entire deployment? It was time to show Jon I could be trusted not to make bad decisions in his absence.

It wasn't long before I lost interest in the go cart. I was so embarrassed and ashamed of my impulsive purchase.

Finally, Jon told me to snap out of it. We invited the husbands over for a big go cart race. We timed each other, did donuts, and had a lot of fun.

My husband forgave me and made me forgive myself.

Now and again, we would pull the go cart out of the garage and wreak havoc throughout the neighborhood. Kids would pour out of their houses and follow me back home to get some Schwann's ice cream and a jump on the trampoline.

There was forgiveness and we moved on. I know now you can't buy happiness. Nor can you behave badly and expect to be forgiven.

After the go cart incident, Jon and I settled on a fair dollar amount that we could each spend without the other person's "permission." We agreed any purchase over $100 had to be discussed with the other spouse first. And we each got $40 a week to spend on whatever we wanted.

It was a respectful compromise.

I GET IT NOW

A few times when I complained about military life to civilian friends or family they replied, "Well, you knew what you were getting into."

Did I really know what I was getting into?

I think the point was not what I knew, but what I did with the knowledge.

Once I did, I found I enjoyed my new role as a military wife. To make a military marriage work you must accept that you are number two in your husband's life—behind the military. The key to keeping the marriage together and the home happy is keeping him number one in your life.

This is a really tough pill to swallow. This means living for someone else and recognizing his life is not about you.

Some wives never accept this fact. I admit I struggled with it as well.

In a civilian marriage, a husband and wife decide where the family lives and where the family will vacation.

When you're in the military, however, the government decides all that.

It's hard to surrender that power, but you learn to roll with it. If you both love each other and keep in mind you are serving a greater calling, you will find acceptance and peace.

One day Jon came home from work, gave me a huge hug and said, "Thank you."

"What was that for?" I asked.

Jon told me that while he was enjoying the lunch I had made for him, one of the Marines asked what he was eating.

"Leftovers," replied Jon.

A huge discussion followed. Other Marines gathered around Jon and said things like, "Your wife cooks for you?" "Your wife packed you a lunch?" "How did you get your wife to cook for you? I can't get mine to heat me up some soup!"

One told him his wife didn't like to cook. I thought, "Well, who likes doing chores?"

Still, I like the pride my husband shows me when I cook, clean, and care for our home.

I was happy to know that Jon was proud of me because of what I was doing at home. My husband took comfort in the fact that I was finally happy.

Our home had become a peaceful place that Jon could come to after being in the field knowing he was not obligated to do anything.

Chapter Four

LIFESTYLES OF THE MILITARY

Military life is a culture unto its own. We have different priorities, values, time management schedules, rules, and even language. We also answer to a higher calling. We answer to God, family, and country (sometimes in that order).

More specifically, our loved ones answer to the Commander-and-Chief, as chosen by the people. We have respect for our leaders and serve without complaint and with humility.

Military spouses follow their men wherever service takes them. We serve beside them quietly. That's why we are known as "the Silent Ranks."

My feelings about military life and the bond that forms can be summed up in a bumper sticker given to me by Mustang Major Lou. It says: "Marines welcome anytime; family by appointment only."

The people in the military become your new family. Doors are always open. Blood willing to be shed for another is thicker than blood that runs through veins.

Little differences can be found between military families and civilians. For instance, military wives are pretty "Chatty Cathys" all day on the playground or on the phone. When 6:00 p.m. rolls around and the men start heading home, that becomes family time.

It better be life or death if you call another wife when her husband is home on a work night. And don't get me started on what she will say to you if it's pre-deployment.

No matter where they live, military families share the same bond. We silently serve beside our spouses—providing stability at home.

It is hard to be the strong one when you know war is a reality. We are second in our marriages. This fact can be difficult to comprehend and accept, but it's the bond we share. It is not one easily understood by civilians.

Those of us in the Silent Ranks wear that badge of honor proudly.

This section of the book is meant to offer a tiny bit of insight into how we shop, celebrate, and relax.

MILITARY HOSPITALITY

Nothing is stronger than the bonds of the military. Its hospitality is over the top.

When a Marine falls in action, women from all over provide meals for the widow, offer to clean her home, and help out wherever they can.

At the same time, children may stay at a neighbor's house while their mother goes to the doctor or needs a few hours by herself.

Doors open when one is in need of a cup of sugar or the use of a washing machine. There are no limits and no favor is too big to ask. Hospitality in the military is accepted when needed and given without hesitation.

Jon and I didn't have children, but we kept our fridge stocked with juice boxes, popsicles, and all kinds of snacks for the neighborhood children.

At any hour of the night or day, we knew no matter where we were stationed or if our husband was home or not, we had family and people to help us.

WATCH YOUR MOUTH

Gossip can be destructive on base, especially in base housing neighborhoods. Military branches are relatively small. You may live next to someone on your first duty station and then again eight years later.

I learned to watch my mouth when it came to expressing how I felt about another wife. Our actions can affect our husband's career or influence their commanding officers.

My mom and I attended Jon's graduation from IOC. At the social after the ceremonies, I began chatting with Jon's roommate and his fiancé. Jon stepped away to introduce my mother to someone.

While Jon was gone another graduate and his fiancé were standing behind me. She was loud and obnoxious. Whatever it was about her, it turned me off instantly.

I turned to my husband's roommate and fiancé and said, "That girl chaps my ass."

Right then Jon showed up, grabbed my arm, and pulled me away. He gave me the lecture of a lifetime. Keep in mind that not only does Jon rarely talk, but he also never tells me what to do.

"You better watch your mouth. The Marine Corps is very small. You don't know her or her fiancé. You also don't know my roommate and his fiancé. You never know if they're friends. What if we're stationed with that couple? What would you do then if she heard you or if one of her friends told her what you said?"

I was embarrassed and realized I had to learn to start biting my tongue. My husband was right. That couple ended up getting stationed at Camp Pendleton with us, and her husband was assigned to my husband's battalion!

PCS: PRETTY CRAPPY SITUATION

In the military an average stay at a duty station is three years. In my personal experience, the wives are usually the ones in charge of the Permanent Change of Station move. We end up packing and organizing, or providing donuts and pizza for the TMO movers.

In the end, I think it is only fair that the wife picks if she wants to manage a TMO or a DITY move.

I recommend a TMO (Traffic Management Office) over a DITY move.

Men always want the DITY move because the military pays you to do it yourself. But the DITY move requires you to weigh your vehicle, rent U-hauls, pack boxes, and drive your belongings to the next station. It's a real headache and very stressful.

When you select a TMO move, you arrange for the military to pack your belongings and move you to your next duty station. And they do it as inexpensively as possible.

If you go through TMO, follow the rules, particularly when it comes to what you leave to be packed. If not, they will pack up your garbage and move it. Seriously, I found a still-full bathroom trash can in a box after one move. It had been on a truck for more than a week.

What's in your bathroom trash can? Do you hear me on this?

I have experienced both DITY and TMO types of moves and I have to tell you they both suck.

With a TMO, I had things stolen, broken, and lost. I packed anything I could not live without, like curling irons, make-up, and medications in my car.

In fact, I recommend you pack and move your own family heirlooms, photos, and jewelry as well as your intimate apparel.

Let's just say this: it was quite a treat to see a "gentleman" from the moving company with his hands in a pile of my black leather and lace lingerie. I also suggest you move whatever you keep in your "night stand."

Besides, if something from your private collection gets stolen, I doubt you will want to request reimbursement. So, ladies, make sure you personally pack those boudoir photos, if you get my drift.

When PCSing, pick the lesser of the two evils. It depends upon where you are moving as to which you choose, but do keep your private, expensive, or special items with you.

I learned a benefit of PCSing every three years. It's another opportunity to forget to tell your mother-in-law your new address.

THIS BASE SUCKS!

So many wives have told me the bases their husbands have been stationed at sucks. They'll whine that there's nothing to do at 29 Palms (or any other base).

And yet, some wives in similar situations have a totally different perspective. They'll tell me they're going to functions every week and are planning other activities with their friends.

I know that certain stereotypes exist for some bases. Certain regions in the States, as well as in other countries, have very different weather. In Okinawa, for example, there's a lot of rain. New residents often come down with island fever.

So, it's all about being willing to embrace the differences and taking the time to explore your new home. It all boils down to perspective. Your attitude determines what your living situation will be like.

When I first got to Camp Pendleton, I hated it. I didn't understand because this was the base everyone wanted. But when I changed my attitude and started getting involved, I started to like it there.

Set a goal and explore. Make it an adventure.

LIFETIME

One of Jon's Marines once sought him out for some advice. Newly married, he came to Jon to ask, "Sir, what is this 'Lifetime?' All I know is when I come home at night my wife has been watching it all day on the TV and she is really mad at me."

Jon explained what he had learned from my co-dependent relationship with Lifetime. I think I spent my first three months on base watching Joanna Kerns and Valerie Bertinelli starring in "Raped Again."

I remember getting up at ten to catch "Unsolved Mysteries." By eleven, I was completely freaked out and it was not even lunchtime! That music would get me completely tweaked.

After hiding under a blanket for about an hour and jumping out of my skin at every sound, I would turn on "Lifetime" for a little ER.

After my delicious lunch of tuna in a can, I would settle in for an afternoon of Tracy Gold and TV's Dean Cain starring in "Too Young to Be a Mom When You're Anorexic."

The next thing I knew Jon would be home and I was sure he would rape me or that he had stolen my credit cards and knocked up a teenage babysitter.

A full day's dose of those stories can really mess you up. I had to learn to ration my "Lifetime" so it was more enjoyable, instead of it becoming an "all women are victims of evil men" brainwashing session.

Jon explained all this to the young Marine. Don't worry, he assured him. His wife's "Lifetime" obsession was just a phase. He just needed to be patient with her.

Jon suggested introducing her to the Enlisted Wives Club, or one of the many volunteer groups on base. He assured him that once she made some friends, she would let go of "Lifetime."

PARTYING

When you live hard, you also have to party hard. The military does a lot of celebrating and hosts lots of speeches by people who are less than motivational.

In fact, I remember the speech during Jon's graduation from TBS. Some crusty colonel stood up and said that a Marine's job was to, "Destroy things and kill people." I was not ready to hear that.

There are "Hails and Farewells" welcoming someone coming into or switching out of a unit. There are celebrations when someone is promoted and then there are the "pinning on" or "wet down" parties. These are very classy events to which family and friends are invited.

The "dining ins" are what the men look forward to all year. They're also referred to as "mess night." This is an evening full of tradition where the Marines feel free to cut loose and make fun of their superiors. Many were the nights that Natalie and I had to pick up our drunken husbands after these events.

But the best party of all is the Birthday Ball. It's like prom night for military women.

THE BALL

I will never forget my first Marine Corps Birthday Ball.

I could tell Jon was very much in love with me just by the way he looked at me from across the table and smiled. He was watching me charm the other Marines and guests. I could tell he liked that I was gregarious and entertaining.

And I was proud to see him stand at attention as the band played our national anthem.

I had spent the entire day getting ready for the ball at my grandmother's house. She loved seeing Jon in his dress blues and me in my gown.

I think at one point she tried to push me down the steps so she could go to the ball with Jon herself. She had such a great time reminiscing about balls she had attended with granddaddy.

My dad took 800 pictures of us. It really did feel like prom night.

The anticipation of the night is all tied up in buying the dress, getting my hair and nails done, and even buying some sexy lingerie and good perfume.

The couples with kids would stay in a hotel that night. This was the one night of the year they would get away.

Of course, this led to another phenomenon: Ball Babies. These bundles of joy arrive exactly nine months later. Ask a military wife when her children's birthdays are. If it's July, I'd avoid borrowing her gown.

THE BELLE OF THE BALL

I had a humiliating experience at my third ball. Let me explain.

I purchased my gown while Jon was deployed. At that point, I weighed about seventy pounds because I had not been eating.

Once he came home I became fat and happy again. That also meant the dress no longer fit.

So I bought an industrial strength girdle from Sears to get my "mother's hips" into the dress. I had had some technical difficulties with the girdle earlier in the evening at Natalie's, where I had nearly passed out trying to get it on.

In fact, it had taken two people to get me into it. How in the world did Scarlet O'Hara pick cotton in one of those straitjackets?

The girdle went from just under my breasts to the top of my knees. It cinched me in pretty tight. In fact, it was so tight that when I sat in it and farted, the farts would slide up my back, shoot out the top of the girdle, and make my hair fly off the back of my neck.

If I changed position to allow room for outgoing gas, the air would blow down the girdle between my legs. Without warning, my legs would kick out in front of me.

How was I going to pass those farts off on someone else all night? There was only a tiny hole in the crotch to allow you to pee without taking it off.

At first, I figured I would not drink anything all night. That really wasn't feasible because it was one of the few times when I could allow myself to cut loose. In the end, I figured I would have to risk a bathroom disaster.

I could also barely breathe and kept taking shallow breaths, which left me feeling lightheaded.

Before we left home, my hair had already started to fall apart. I decided to pull it into a bun high on my head and attach one of those fake hair things that look like a nest of cute curls. I slapped a tiara on my head and was good to go. I had my weave, my girdle, and my tiara. I was ready to party!

This ball fell between deployments. Jon had just returned from Iraq and we were gearing up mentally for his next deployment in two months. There was a lot weighing on our minds, but we kept smiles on our faces. I started to drink and it didn't take long before I was feeling wild.

What happened next may not come as a surprise to you. Let's just blame the girdle. It squeezed all the sense right out of me.

I had not met Jon's new company commander, Captain Rodriquez. All that my husband had told me about him was he was very big and very quiet. My husband is a man of few words himself, so I had to push for more details. I needed to know what he looked like, so I wouldn't act like a total idiot in front of my husband's CO.

Jon paused and finally replied, "He looks like a big black Arnold Schwarzenegger."

That's all I needed. He sounded good to me, real good, in fact. Arnold had been my total teen heart throb.

I was cutting jokes and telling some silly stories to a captive audience of single Grunts when Jon asked me to come with him to meet his CO.

I put my game face on, but it was too late. There was a large handsome man with a huge smile, great dimples—sexy-looking and baldheaded. And he had the most gorgeous, petite woman on his arm. Her black hair went down to her butt. She looked like a Hawaiian Tropics model.

I started in. "Oh my God, my husband was right! He said you looked just like a big Black Arnold Schwarzenegger and you do! Look at you two! Stop everything! Give me the camera!"

I told his wife to come and stand by me to look at our two men. I went on and on about how handsome they were and how they should do a calendar together.

She was laughing. He was laughing.

I asked her if she "Bunco-ed" and she said she did. She lived near Christa, so I assured her she would be attending the next party.

Meet and greet accomplished. I thought I was so cute and charming.

Later that night, Jon and I tried dancing. We had taken a few swing lessons and thought we were "hot to trot."

By that time, however, we were both tipsy. To make matters even more interesting, I had not eaten. I could barely breathe or move because of my girdle.

The next thing I know, Jon shoots me under his arm knocking off my nest of fake curls.

I screamed, "My weave, my weave!" as it flew through the air and landed on the ground. I was on my hands and knees crawling around looking for my weave when I found it next to Captain Rodriquez's shoe.

I jumped up and said, "My weave got snatched off. I gotta go to the bathroom."

And I took off.

The next morning I was horrified to realize I had made a total fool of myself in front of my husband's CO and his wife.

Then I started thinking that Rodriquez is not an African American name. It's Spanish in origin. I had made comments about this man's ethnicity, but what if he was not black? My husband had been born and raised in Idaho and didn't see a black person until he was in college!

Why had I listened to him? I had been raised in the South and knew black people. In fact, a black woman had taken care of me until I was 12.

I cried all morning.

Clearly, the Rodriquez family thought I was a freak and a racist. Or that I was a Southern country bumpkin who had never met a Latino, Puerto Rican, or Mexican, and so thought anyone with tan or dark skin was black.

I bawled all weekend. I could not believe I had screamed in front of this man that I had lost my weave. I made Jon promise to apologize for me when he went back to work.

Jon talked to his new CO that Monday. He said it went something like this: "Sir, may I please speak to you about something my wife is upset about. It concerns your ethnicity. She is afraid she offended you."

Captain Rodriquez laughed in response. He said that he actually is a little bit of everything and that being African American is a big part of his heritage. He told Jon to tell me not to worry.

We ended up becoming great friends and later laughed about the incident. His wife and I still encouraged the boys to do a calendar, but they never did.

RANKISM

There is an issue in the military that can get very ugly: "rankism." This is discrimination against someone based upon their own or their spouse's rank.

The rank system is part of the military's core structure, which is fine for the service men, but not so fine for the dependents.

Excessive fraternization among the ranks is just not acceptable. You don't want to spend weekends drinking beer, cutting farts, or watching your boss and his wife get into a fight. When you do that, you can't maintain a certain level of respect at work.

There have to be boundaries, especially when you're talking about leadership roles in life and death decisions.

However, some dependents take this to mean they have a license to act like they are better than others. Some dependents think their husband's rank means they do not have to be accountable for their actions.

Neighborhoods on base are divided up by rank. As a result, certain people always socialize together. Clubs are also set up by rank to avoid fraternization.

And yet, the tension about rank between dependents goes both ways.

Del Mar housing included Navy and Marines living on the same base. At that time we had Warrant Officers, 1st and 2nd Lieutenants, Captains, Navy Captains, and one Marine Corps Colonel (who had the house with the best view).

I had already experienced serious grief from other wives when we were assigned a higher ranking house, but the neighborhood was about to be turned on its heels again.

There were a slew of Captains who were "selected" to pick up Major within the next eighteen months. These families were still living in the smaller town homes.

You-know-what hit the fan when word came in that Staff NCOs would be moving into the neighborhood.

I could have cared less, but a slew of those higher ranking officer families that were due any minute to pick up higher rank threw a royal fit. They refused to live in the same neighborhood as enlisted families.

I thought this was "rankism" at its worst.

In the end, a handful of families moved out of the neighborhood. They "pulled rank" with the housing office and found themselves in the four-bedroom, large backyard housing in Field Grade neighborhood next door to all the Colonels.

Why would you want to live next to a Colonel? No offense, but you could never have any fun.

I think the way some of those ladies went around the neighborhood gossiping, "Did you hear? The enlisted are moving in!" was disgusting. They should have been ashamed of themselves.

If they qualified for bigger houses, great—more power to them. Move on up! But running around gossiping and slandering others is uncouth and so low class.

I had also been a victim of rankism (probably) while living on base.

As a Key Volunteer, I had to call wives married to all different ranks to give them updates on the battalion. There was one enlisted wife on my call list I enjoyed chatting with whenever I called. I helped her with a few things here and there whenever she called or if I saw her at functions.

The first time she saw me with Jon was at the Ball. We were laughing and talking. But when Jon walked up to me, the expression on her face changed completely.

Her husband grabbed her arm and they stopped talking and just stared at us.

After Jon introduced himself, the wife said nothing. She simply walked away. I was shocked. I asked Jon if that Marine was in his platoon, and Jon said he was not.

I slowly realized that they had walked away when they saw my husband. She no longer wanted to talk to me.

Maybe it was her husband who did not want her talking to us, or it was some irrational fear of fraternization. Maybe it was rankism. I will never know for sure.

I do know it hurt my feelings as I felt deep down that she was avoiding me because of my husband's rank.

Another run-in had to do with an officer's wife and an enlisted wife. I had injured my back and could not get a doctor's appointment. After two days of unbearable pain, I finally went to the ER.

Half of our doctors had been deployed to Germany. Add a heaping spoonful of moms, who were freaking out over their child's every sneeze, which resulted in a trip to the hospital. Finish this fine mess up with a dash of retired vets arriving by ambulance every thirty minutes, and you have won yourself a fifteen-hour wait in the ER.

I made friends as I lay on the floor of the waiting room. We bonded over the treatment and long wait. Some had been there before me; many others arrived after. It appeared to me as if no one in the waiting room was being admitted.

After hour number ten—about two in the morning—a few of us went looking for snacks.

Someone said something that shocked me: "You know, they are only seeing officers and officer's wives. They check your rank."

I knew for a fact this was not true. I realized this person and some of the others were enlisted because they had been talking about their neighborhoods. They went on to complain about the special treatment officer wives get all over base—from the hospital to the commissary.

I guess one of them saw the dazed look on my face and asked how long I had been waiting. When I told them, they all gasped. It had been at least seven hours longer than them!

"Yeah," I answered, "and my husband is an officer! Can you believe they have made me wait so long?"

They all stopped and stared at me. They were sooooo embarrassed.

I changed the subject as we headed back to the waiting room. As we continued to chat, I acted like I was not even bothered by what they had said. But not a one apologized to me.

I should also add they were all seen before me, including the wives who came in later. The few who had made those nasty comments earlier looked ashamed as they left the ER before I had even laid eyes on a doctor.

Maybe God had me wait so long so those ladies could see that they were wrong. I don't know, but I hope that they remember that night before they spout off about rankism.

PARTYING WITH POGUES: BRING A LIFE VEST

For all the rivalry between Grunts and Pogues, we had some of our wildest parties with Pogues.

One time Beenie and Lloyd asked us to join them at a hot tub party at their house along with USMC lawyers (Pogues) and their wives. We were the only Grunt family.

Marines are a breed of their own, and I personally think the craziest of all the military. They love to party and drink beer. We knew enough to pack an overnight bag. Nobody would be driving home.

The guys were playing horseshoes and Beenie and I were enjoying a wine cooler when I was introduced to Beenie's four-pound poodle.

I started crying because in our move across country I had left both of my poodles with my mother, as Jon put it, "until further notice."

This tiny black poodle was all character. In fact, Willy smoked cigarettes! Beenie would take a drag and when she put her hand down, the dog would sneak up behind her, bite the filter, and run off into the yard with it in his mouth! You should have seen a bunch of Marines chasing a poodle around trying to get the cigarette away from him!

The barbecue was great. Lloyd prides himself on his grill specialties. In fact, you just might see him on the Food Network one day.

At sunset, it was time to fire up the hot tub. Beenie and Lloyd decided because it was a "hot tub" party that we should play 70s R&B mixed with today's best rap. We cranked up the volume and popped the tops on the appropriate beverages.

Some Pogues left after the hot dogs and hamburgers just as the girls put on their bikinis and the first rap song started blaring. The rest of us—four couples—were in it for the long haul.

Now, Lloyd is the most non-Poguey Pogue and my husband is the most non-Grunty Grunt you will ever meet. Neither one of these guys really lives up to the stereotypes associated with their nicknames. In fact, Lloyd is really tough and my husband is really smart.

Still, there was this silent competition that had started with the infamous puggle sticks battle. I am not even sure if my husband was participating in this competition or if he was just a bad drunk. But he and Lloyd were in rare form. We were drinking Alize, which tastes like liquid sugar and goes down like Kool-Aid.

Alcohol upsets my stomach. We did a lot of partying while living on base, but I was very selective about what I drank. Many times I was the sober one of the group. As I've gotten "older," I've stopped drinking alcohol as it causes debilitating migraines. Besides, I act stupid enough without adding alcohol to the equation.

But that night the Alize tasted like candy, so I took a few sips here and there, pacing myself like a mature lady.

What they don't tell you about alcohol is that you're not supposed to consume large amounts of it while in a hot tub. Evidently the alcohol and the heat work together as a toxic combo that can dehydrate you.

At one point during the party Beenie could not find me and began asking around.

One of the JAG's wives said I was in the hot tub with Jon and another couple. Still, no one could find me anywhere, nor did they see me in the hot tub.

The other wife in the hot tub finally said to Jon, "I think she's under water, I think I see her under your arm."

Yes, I was drowning.

As Michelle would say, "Weeeeelllllll!"

I think my husband had been using the top of my head to rest his beer bottle on. I had been under the water for at least a minute. Luckily, I was so wasted that I had stopped breathing.

After the party there were pictures circulating that showed me sliding below the surface of the water as my husband looks off into the distance—probably listening to one of Lloyd's many stories.

Thanks, Lloyd.

POKER NIGHT

After Beenie and Lloyd had their first child and Lloyd returned from his first deployment to Iraq, they decided to move into a terrific house about three doors down from ours. It soon became our weekend hang out.

Lloyd was the master at poker parties and spots filled up quickly. Natalie and her husband Carl, Jon and I, and Beenie and Lloyd were regulars at the Texas Hold'em table. We'd take the money of our regular guests at these all-night parties.

Beenie and I had a foot up on the competition because we did not drink. She didn't because she was pregnant again and I didn't because I am a lightweight.

Not only that, I am the master at bluffing at poker. I won't give away my secrets, but there was many a night when either Beenie or I would claim the entire pot.

It was so much fun to do these normal neighborhood functions since so much of our time on base had been spent without our husbands. We went out of our way to plan fun events when everyone was home.

CAREER OPTIONS

Many military wives complain about not being able to find the right job.

I was fortunate to be offered a job practically my first week on base. My first day on the job I was delegating, multitasking, and shaping future lives of America. Who knew babysitting could be so rewarding?

Sometimes PCSing every three years can limit your career options. Your priority has to be to support your spouse.

I personally struggled with it. My husband's schedule was so sporadic that I never wanted to be at work when he was home. It was also important to spend time with him before he deployed.

Some wives were lucky to find flexible jobs or work from home opportunities.

I remember wives who had decided to further their careers being very disappointed they had to work when their husband had leave.

During my husband's time in the military I was a housewife, a volunteer, returned to work, and even attended college.

I went back to work full time toward the end of Jon's military career. I was lucky to have a sales job, which was based out of my home and allowed me to make my own schedule. I did not have to miss Jon's down time. Best of all, I was still able to take care of our home.

CHILDREN

In many ways the lifestyle of a military family looks like a step back into the 1950s. Most moms stay home with their children. In fact, housewives are highly respected in the military. Women are praised for volunteering during the day and cooking their husband's meals at night.

Are the feminists from the millennium freaking out right now? Well, with your husband deployed, do you think you are needed behind a desk at a company, or at home being the only parent your kids have? Military moms are the cream of the crop. They have to be; often they are the only parent around.

My girlfriends who were moms taught me the benefits of raising kids without dad around. They joked that it was the perfect opportunity to instill core family values like, "Mommy is always right!" And, if anything goes wrong, "it's Daddy's fault!"

My girlfriends also loved to instill this rule with the kids: "When Daddy gets home, be sure to go to him with all your homework, dirty diapers, and boo-boos. He wants to make up for all he missed!"

Sometimes, though, a mom needs reinforcements when her husband is deployed.

One day Michelle called to ask Jon to stop by after work while still in uniform. I thought it was a bit odd, but told her we would be over as soon as Jon came home.

We walked over to Michelle's garage and saw David, who was two at the time, holding a spray bottle of cleaner.

Michelle saw Jon and exclaimed, "Thank God, you're here! David has had that bottle all day and I can't get it away from him. If I go near him, he sprays me!"

We asked her to demonstrate. Sure enough, David sprayed his mother with cleanser. I stifled a laugh, but Jon was puzzled.

Michelle was convinced that David would not obey her. She believed children respond better to a man's voice.

I set out to debunk her theory. I looked Dave straight in the eye and said, "David, give me that bottle!"

He looked at me, laughed, and sprayed me in the face.

Michelle begged Jon to do something. Now, you have to understand that my husband is about as good with kids as Arnold was on his first day in "Kindergarten Cop."

Seeing this poor mother at her wit's end, though, he decided to help out.

"Jon, David will think you are Kevin," Michelle explained. "Just keep your cover on and tell him to give you the bottle."

When Jon approached him, David took aim.

Jon looked down at him and calmly said, "No."

David instantly dropped the bottle and began to wail. Michelle rushed to David and began to coddle him.

I guess Michelle was right. Her son needed a strong male role model.

LET'S MAKE BABIES

Now let's discuss the phenomenon of how military wives get pregnant. Perhaps you're thinking I'm going to give you a lesson in the birds and the bees. That's not what I'm talking about. Remember Ball Babies?

Well, there are also pre-deployment babies, reunion babies, and "Okinawa surprises." That's what you come back with after being stationed over there for three years.

I was constantly warned to watch out for certain events or places that resulted in pregnancy (as if coitus had nothing to do with it). I met a wife at a Battalion BBQ who introduced her children like this: "Well, the 6-year-old is my pre-deployment baby, the 4-year-old is my reunion surprise, and the toddler, my husband calls him a 'negligent discharge.'"

Many of the wives I met on base associated their pregnancies with specific events. I was even told the B-billet was tied to pregnancies.

After your Grunt does four years in the "fleet" (a deployable billet), he goes to a non-deployable billet for four years—a "B-billet." (In this case, the "B" stands for "bullshit.")

Many veteran wives encouraged me to get my husband stationed in Hawaii or to do recruiting in my hometown so I could be somewhere comfortable when I had my children.

Look at the ages of the children in a Grunt's family. Many of them had two kids within a four-year time period. Then there's a four-year gap and more children.

I can tell you the majority of wives I knew during that first deployable cycle started their families during the B-billets.

Many wives will plan their pregnancies around their husbands' deployment. Some want to be six months pregnant when he returns so he can be there for the birth. Not as many wives plan on having a baby while hubby is deployed, but it does happen.

Beenie had her first child this way and said it was not so bad. She said it was better to take care of the new baby alone, and then to incorporate her husband into the routine when he returned.

Everyone in the military makes "family plans" a little differently—planning around billets, deployments, duty stations, and let's face it, Balls.

PLAY GROUPS

Mommy/child play groups are very common on base. We had a very active one in the community playground in our neighborhood. These groups encourage moms to build up a real sense of community with the other moms on base.

These moms also look out for each other's kids, and would lend a helping hand whenever someone needed a last minute sitter.

I also heard my neighborhood play group made some pretty good margaritas.

ADVENTURES IN BABYSITTING

During my first two years as a military wife, I did a lot of volunteer work for the Key Volunteer Network, as well as for the battalion.

I also did a lot of babysitting since I had a trampoline, endless supplies of ice cream, kid's movies, and toys.

There were always children at the house. Often Michelle and I would be with the kids on my trampoline or in her baby pool when moms and their kids would join us. Sometimes they would just drop them off while they ran an errand.

One afternoon Michelle was entertaining the neighborhood children in her blow-up pool. I suggested they come over to jump on the trampoline and have popsicles.

I remember thinking that David, who was just two, was getting so strong and sturdy for his size. He was jumping up and down on the trampoline as I watched with admiration. After a few minutes, I saw liquid flying through the air. I walked over and saw the liquid was all over the trampoline.

"Who has chocolate milk?" I asked Michelle. "They should not drink and jump. Someone will get sick."

She shot me a puzzled look. "No one has chocolate milk," she replied.

Then I saw the liquid leaking from David's swim diaper. While it wasn't chocolate milk, it certainly was a treat. With every leap and bounce, the liquid flew higher and higher into the air.

I think David knew all about this "chocolate milk" treat streaking down his legs, but he was enjoying this session on the trampoline too much.

We finally got him off the trampoline, stripped him bare (he thoroughly enjoyed this as well) and proceeded to spray David down with the garden hose.

(Yes, I sprayed the trampoline down as well.)

Whenever Michelle and Kevin had a date night, they'd leave David and Jacob with me. Since Jon was deployed some of those times, it was just me and the boys. They were such gentlemen.

Jacob would kick my butt at Nintendo. I had taught him how to play Mario Brothers, but he killed Kumba within half an hour. Was there anything this kid could not master?

For some reason whenever I took care of David, his body fluids would reject my authority.

I remember one night Jacob was happily playing Nintendo when David began to look a little pale. "My tummy hurts," he told me.

David had been born with a stomach problem, so it was not unusual for him to get an upset tummy.

I didn't think anything of it until he looked at me and barfed strawberry yogurt all over my bare legs. I could not move. My legs and feet were covered with warm strawberry yogurt vomit. I almost puked myself.

As I stood there in shock, he barfed again.

Jacob started yelling, "Eeeeeeww, it stinks! I'm going to puke! Eeeeeww, Miss Mollie, your dog is eating it!"

By this time I am gagging while grabbing David for a run to the bathroom.

I put him down in front of the toilet. "Puke in the bowl," I commanded.

I was reaching for a wet washcloth to put on the back of his neck when I realized he was thoroughly covered with puke, so I picked him up and we both climbed into the tub.

I got the nozzle down and started spraying us as I peeled off our clothes.

That's when I began to panic: I was half-naked in the bathtub with a half-naked three-year-old!

Freaking out that I would be arrested for child abuse, I put David on the floor with a washcloth and a blanket.

Even though we had tracked puke through the house, the dogs had taken care of most of it. Still, the house stunk to high heaven. Let me put it this way: no one will be making this lovely scent into a candle fragrance anytime soon.

Anyway, I got myself some clean shorts and a T-shirt, then made David a nest of blankets on the floor and gave him an all-fruit popsicle. I called Michelle, regretfully asking her to end their date early. As it turns out, David had the flu. In fact, the whole family ended up getting sick. I didn't, thank God.

But to this day I can't eat strawberry yogurt.

GROCERY SHOPPING

I developed this love/hate relationship with the commissary. You really can find the best deals there—if you can handle the experience.

I will never forget one night my husband and I went off base to buy a frozen pizza. That's when we discovered that pizza costs $4.00 more off base. The point is that when you're young and in the military, every dollar matters.

There are some definite rules to follow if you shop at the commissary.

One of the most important is to avoid the commissary on paydays. In fact, I had the day before payday marked on my calendar. It wasn't to prepare for payday, but to remind myself to go to the commissary before the payday insanity hit.

Payday at the commissary is like a slow death. Think the lines at the post office are bad? Well, it's like a day at Disneyland compared to the commissary on payday.

Paydays mean every mom is there with all of her children and two carts overflowing with her purchases. She is usually screaming in an effort to keep control of the children that dangle off her cart like spiders. Try to escape her, but she'll be down the next aisle. She's red-faced, miserable, and trying to pick out cereal as her children sneak candy bars into the basket.

I want to help her. I do, but I am repulsed by the high-pitched screams coming from her offspring, so I slink away.

I honestly have pulled into the commissary on payday and just as quickly driven away. I would rather eat soup for two days than deal with the one-hour line at checkout.

I also urge you to stay away from the commissary in the early morning hours. This is the time when the retirees shop.

I love America's vets and I appreciate their sacrifices to our country. But I don't like shopping with them.

There is usually this 80-year-old man with a HUGE hat on his head proudly proclaiming "Pearl Harbor."

He appears clueless as he pushes two carts around. His wife is this tiny Asian lady about 20 years younger than him, and dressed to the nines. But she is constantly screaming at him: buy this, don't buy that because it is too expensive, etc. She argues with his choices of snacks complaining, "Jerry, you fat!" One time she pointed out that the doctor said he could not eat this or that because of his "high blood." On and on she goes—telling him not to buy something because he can not digest it or reminding him he has acid reflux and gas problems.

Normally I would say they are fighting, but I think this man gave up years ago. She screams at him; he pushes the cart. She won't let him buy anything and yet, they have trouble navigating two carts through the small aisles.

All the while she's yelling, "Jerry, you wake up last night! It take you four hours to pee!"

When you try going around without bumping into them, they scream "Watch where you're going! You young kids today are always in a rush!"

I want to yell back, "No sir, I don't mean to rush to get around you, but I am choking on your farts. Please excuse me."

Don't even think about picking up your vitamins on "Veterans' Day" at the commissary. You will see a serious "Hover Round" scooter backup right around the Metamucil.

OK, WHERE'S THE HIDDEN CAMERA?

A very pregnant Beenie and I had an experience at the commissary that we will never forget. Our husbands were deployed, so one night Beenie and I headed down to the commissary for some food.

The minute we walked in, we knew we had entered upon a freak show. It started in the produce section when an 80-year-old veteran approached me as I picked out some tomatoes.

He started to reach toward my selection saying, "Let me tell you if they're ripe!"

It seemed a bit bizarre, but I figured he was just being nice. Just as his hands closed around two big tomatoes, his wife came up behind him and started screaming.

She was glaring at me yelling, "Hussy! Keep your tomatoes to yourself!" She knocked them from his hands with her purse. He lowered his head and walked away.

Beenie and I quickly exited the produce section.

As we turned down the snack aisle, I saw the tiniest Marine I have ever seen in my life. I seriously thought he was a child wearing his father's uniform. Now, let me remind you that I am five feet even. My dad is 5' 3"; my mom is 5' 4". So, short people don't usually surprise me.

However, I know the Corps has standards and I was taller than this gentleman and he was wearing boots.

I knew better than to turn to Beenie and yell, "Yo, check it out! Did you just see the midget Marine?"

Instead, I made eye contact and we moved down the aisle.

As we did so, we heard this tiny Marine shout out, "Hey! Hon! Is this what you were looking for?"

Apparently he was not someone's child after all. Around the corner comes this six-foot, 300-pound woman pushing a baby in a stroller.

I'm embarrassed to admit what images flashed through my mind. I could no longer contain myself. I left our shopping cart right there in the aisle and ran.

I refused to even look at Beenie, who had grabbed the cart and was following me. I knew she was thinking the same things I was.

I had to avoid making eye contact or I knew I would lose it and yell, "The carnival is in town! Freak show on aisle seven!"

We waited till we were in the checkout line before we looked at each other. We started to bust up with laughter, so we looked away.

Finally, we paid and the bagger offered to take our groceries out to the car. We could not get out of the commissary fast enough.

As the bagger put the groceries in the car, I noticed the license on a car driving by. It read, "3 TTs."

I yell to Beenie, "Oh, my gosh! Look at this character's license plate! What's that about?"

We exploded with laughter—releasing everything we had kept pent up while inside the commissary.

Then we get a good close look at the bagger. We hadn't really looked at him until then. He had just four teeth, but they were all rotten. His crossed-eyes were hidden behind one-inch thick glasses and his face was riddled with acne. Worst of all, he must have been nearly 40.

"I should give him a big tip," I thought to myself. I felt so sorry for him.

Just then he started laughing and pointing at the car's license plate and screaming. "Three Titties, yeah, that's what I'm talkin' about! Three titties, This is what I would do with three titties!"

Then he began this juggling/miming action demonstrating what he would do if he ever got so lucky.

That's when I threw money at him and climbed into the car with Beenie. As we drove off, he was still playing with three invisible titties and yelling, "That's what I'm talking about!"

The entire trip was so bizarre we tried to convince ourselves that it had all been a put-on, and that we had been on Candid Camera. Unfortunately, it was all too real.

PARTNER IN CRIME

I met Erin (who would turn out to be a lifelong friend and source of advice) on a trip with Jon to Charleston, South Carolina.

Erin was a kindred spirit from the second we met. You would have thought we were twins if you knew our personalities, but physically we were a little different. We both had blonde hair and light-colored eyes, but I am all boobs, while Erin is all leg. She must have a foot on me, at least.

We are both Southern and loud as hell. We can keep each other laughing with our unique sense of outrageous, shocking humor. Not only that, we have a knack for attracting drama and bizarre occurrences that you'd think were scripted by Candid Camera.

In addition to giggling over farts for hours, we each have a deep faith in Christ and always pray for each other.

Her fiancé, Mike, was my husband's college wrestling partner. Both had planned on joining the Marine Corps upon graduation from the Citadel. However, Jon graduated one year ahead of Mike so Jon started TBS while Mike was finishing school.

We met up at Tommy Condon's, an Irish Pub in Charleston that was notorious for hosting many drunken Citadel cadets. That's where Erin and I hit it off instantly.

Since Mike's father was in the Marines, Erin had already become very familiar with the military lifestyle. She explained much of what I'd be encountering as a military wife and became the person I'd call when I had a question or needed someone to soothe my fears.

Over the years we would be there for each other—helping each cope with military challenges. We would comfort and advise the other about elopements, church weddings, deployments, in-law trouble, pets, PCSing, our fathers' cancers, and then children.

I would tell her everything I learned and give her advice. We flip-flopped like this for years, helping each other out with one military experience or another. It seemed at times that we were the only two people in the world who understood each other. We told each other everything without passing judgment.

Meeting Erin that night in Charleston changed my life. Although we were never stationed together, we have remained incredibly close. She was my first military sister.

Erin also had her share of mishaps at the commissary. Like most women, she would put her purse in the cart and then roam the aisles grabbing various products. In the produce section, she was picking out some cantaloupes when she got into a friendly conversation with an elderly retiree's wife.

When she got to the checkout line, Erin realized she had someone else's purse in her cart. That's also when she realized the items in her cart were not hers.

Just then she heard a voice yelling, "That's her! She stole my purse!" She turned and saw the lady she had met in the produce aisle standing with an MP who had Erin's purse in his hand.

After a few minutes listening to the elderly woman's claim that Erin had tried to distract her in order to steal her purse, the MP allowed the women to switch carts and proceed to the checkout counter.

Apparently, the valuable contents of the elderly woman's purse consisted of an entire box of tissues, 60 throat drops, $13.00 in change, a military ID, and a checkbook.

I have to take some responsibility for Erin's next disastrous trip to the commissary. I discovered that when Jon was deployed, I could not listen to the radio. Whenever a love song came on, I became a puddle. I would be driving down the road, crying and swerving all over the place.

So I started burning my own CDs so I could control what I was listening to, and that's what I mailed to Erin to help lift her spirits.

One day her car was in the shop and she was forced to drive her husband's truck, which we dubbed "the White Whale." It wasn't a huge truck, but it had an extended cab and bed. Because of its size, Erin would only drive the White Whale when she was forced to.

Anyway, it was almost closing time when Erin realized she needed something. She jumped in the White Whale and off she went. At the commissary, Erin parked at the far end of the lot because the truck is so hard to maneuver.

She was feeling a bit bummed about being alone, so she popped in one of my burned CDs. Gloria Estefan's voice filled the cab.

Immediately Erin's spirits lifted and she began to "conga" as she backed out of the parking space. After a few feet she saw a red flash in the side mirror and a man running toward the truck.

She screamed and sped up, but he kept after her, pointing to the back of her car.

She silenced Gloria, rolled to a stop, and cracked the window. The man ran up to her. "Lady, I'm sorry I scared you. I'm not going to hurt you, but you need to get out of your truck and come see this."

Although she was still frightened, she stepped out of the truck and walked around to the back. That's when she saw a grocery cart wedged under the back bumper.

The man looked at her. "Ma'am, you hit it full force. You dragged it about 50 feet. I have never seen sparks fly like that before in my life! I tried yelling at you to stop, but you were dancing and carrying on, so you couldn't hear me. I had to stop you before you got out of the parking lot."

Humiliated, but grateful, Erin and the man wrenched the cart out from under the truck. The cart had seen better days, but the White Whale emerged unscathed from the incident.

The CD was put away for a while. While there are rules banning texting while driving, I wonder if there ought to be a ban against Conga dancing in the car during deployments.

NAVAL HOSPITAL

There is a reason military medicine is free: no one would pay for it.

During our stay on base, most of the doctors had been shipped either to Germany or Iraq. That meant the ones left behind were overwhelmed and overworked.

It also meant I saw a different doctor every time I went in.

My main doctor was this young looking man, probably about 28 but he looked all of 18. He was so timid and nervous that he barely would make eye contact. He shook my hand like a Nancy Boy. All my visits were strained and weird.

I was dreading my annual pap smear because I was sure he had never seen a real vagina before (well other than in a textbook, or on a computer screen, if you catch my drift.)

I was scheduled for a pap about two days after Jon deployed. When I went in, the doctor was polite, but obviously uncomfortable.

When he examined my breast for lumps, he acted like he was poking a jellyfish to see if it was alive. I think he may have even used a stick.

At one point I swear he was flicking me. I wanted to yell, "Look, buddy, it's not a booger!"

Thank God, there was a nurse in the room during the pap exam. That was taking way longer than usual, so I figured he didn't know what to look for.

Finally I asked, "Is everything OK?"

He answered, "Ah, well, I can't seem to locate your cervix."

Without thinking, I replied, "Well, my husband deployed two days ago. Maybe he knocked it out of place."

The nurse howled with laughter, but the doctor left the room, obviously embarrassed.

After our second Marine Corps Birthday Ball, I became very ill. I have never been in such pain in my life. I lay in bed, unable to move or straighten my legs. I would scream in pain followed by explosive diarrhea.

Jon was supposed to leave for 29 Palms in two days and I was freaked.

Eventually I started sleeping on the potty. Jon put a TV tray with a pillow in front of me so I could get comfortable.

By the time he left, I had been in the bathroom for two days straight. I called the Naval Hospital, but they had no appointments. They suggested I go to the emergency room.

I could not leave the bathroom for more than five minutes, and yet I had to get to the hospital, which was half an hour away.

I called Michelle, who told me she had to take the boys up there to get shots so she offered to drive me. She suggested I put a maxi pad on my butt and bring an extra pair of pants. On the way, we stopped at a McDonald's so I could poop.

As soon as she dropped me off at the emergency room, I ran in and pooped again.

I explained what was going on to the receptionist, who informed me there was a 12-hour wait.

At that point I broke down in tears. She offered me a doctor's appointment for the next morning if I was willing to come back.

I took it and a case of Pedialite. I pooped again and got in Michelle's car and headed home—cheeks tightly clenched.

The next day I put on a makeshift diaper as well as an extra pair of panties to drive myself to the hospital.

I found out my appointment was with Dr. Lund, who was gorgeous and about 28.

I had the great pleasure of explaining to this hot Navy man that I had been blowing my ass off since the Birthday Ball.

He had the great pleasure of sticking his finger up my butt.

After checking my medical records, he pointed out that I had had my wisdom teeth out two months earlier.

At that time, I had been given a certain type of antibiotic that can attack the intestines. As a result, I had caught clostridium difficile (or "C-diff" as its victims have dubbed it).

It is typically something that can be passed around to residents of convalescent hospitals. One gets it and passes it on to the next person who uses the toilet. It causes your stomach and intestines to fill with bacteria.

At the youthful age of 24, I had caught the C-diff.

Dr. Lund sent me home with massive amounts of pills, but informed me that I would have to return the following week with a sample of my poo and undergo another manual exam.

The next week I showed up for my appointment with my poop in a jar.

However, it was not Dr. Lund who saw me, but Dr. Land.

He tried to put me at ease by saying, "Oh, you're the one Dr. Lund was talking about."

Now what did that mean?

Here's an equally gorgeous, young Navy doctor ready to give me the ole' "one in the stink."

So, he sticks his finger up my butt in and exclaims, "The good news is there is no anal spillage!" This is doctor talk for hemorrhoids.

Then he smiles and winks at me.

Could life be any crueler? His opening comment keeps playing in my head. "You're the one Dr. Lund was talking about."

Was he going to tell Dr. Lund about my lack of anal spillage?

I was convinced that I was developing a reputation in the internal medicine department. Every young doctor there had seen my privates and had had their fingers up my butt.

I was becoming paranoid. What were they talking about behind my back? Did they compare notes? Did my primary doctor tell them about my husband "knocking my cervix out of place?"

I whipped myself into such a tizzy that I did not go back for several months. I suffered two bouts of the flu with no assistance; I just could not face them again.

Not only that, every time I drove by the hospital my butt would begin twitching.

HOLIDAYS

Holidays can be tricky, particularly for the military. You are usually stationed far from home and your husband is deployed or away training. In fact, you usually have to start new traditions that can adapt to your new duty station.

It can be easy to feel sorry for yourself because you're spending the holidays without your loved one.

While guys sit around sharing war stories, the wives take turns bragging about all the things we had to do without our men. In fact, we would play the "one up" game comparing the anniversaries and Valentine's Days we had spent alone.

It's our way of proclaiming the sacrifices we had made in our marriage, thanks to Uncle Sam. The more a wife had suffered, the better her chance of winning.

Wives are proud of what they have given up for their country, and all points awarded in "One Up" game are worn like badges of honor.

Here's how we play. One wife begins with, "Well, my husband has missed every Valentine's Day and wedding anniversary for the first three years of our marriage."

Remember no sympathy is awarded in the game. This is a competition for bragging rights, not compassion.

Her comment is an invitation to another wife to challenge her suffering at the hands of the American military.

The next player proclaims, "I had my first baby when my husband was deployed and it was on Christmas."

The crowd goes quiet as eyes dart back and forth waiting to see who can "One Up" the last play.

Another wife finally counters with, "My husband did an unaccompanied tour last year and missed Christmas, our wedding anniversary, Valentine's Day, and our son's first birthday! This past year he was home for Christmas, but we found out he had duty on Christmas EVE!"

A collective gasp can be heard. Many wives nod—obviously impressed. Who could possibly one up that one? Lips are tight and nostrils flare as everyone waits to find out if she would be crowned champion.

Silence fell as we all process this last proclamation. The one who suffered the most wins? But do you really?

I was so blessed to have Jon home at Christmas. And yet, even if they are not deployed during the holidays, certain ranks still have to stand duty.

This can create a serious uproar at home. Imagine planning an entire Thanksgiving feast for your husband only to find out he will be on duty.

To balance it out, you have to make the best of the holidays you do have together.

I tried to make it easy for Jon when he was standing duty by bringing him a home-cooked meal, or at least sitting with him for an hour. One night we found a way to have a little fun with it.

Jon's good buddy, Carl, was standing duty, which meant he had to miss poker night. We decided to prank call him at 2:00 a.m.

I called up to the duty desk and pretended to be a woman looking for her baby's daddy.

When Carl answered, I started in. "I am looking for Lance Corporal Jones. He's my baby's daddy. I am up here at the gate and they won't let me in! I need some diapers for my baby!"

"Ma'am, ma'am, please slow down," replied Carl, who was obviously beginning to panic. "Who is your child's father?"

I started again. "I said Lance Corporal Jones. He hasn't given me no money in three weeks. My baby needs some food. I am going to call up the newspaper if you don't get his ass down here right now."

"Ma'am, I want to help you," continued Carl, "but I need . . ."

I cut him off yelling, "Shut up fool! I need some diapers for my baby!"

At that point, I could no longer contain myself. We all started laughing.

"Ma'am? Ma'am?"

It was then that Carl's wife Natalie got on the phone. We took turns making fun of Carl.

About a month later, Jon was on duty while Carl and Natalie were having a barbecue. Carl's brother, Joe, was there as well. Around midnight Carl decided it was payback time. He had Joe call the duty desk. When Jon answered, Joe starts in.

"Sir, I messed up. I really messed up. Please. You have to help me."

"Just slow down," replied Jon. "What's your name and what company are you in?"

Joe interrupts, "Sir, I am in Mexico—Tijuana. I was arrested."

This is every Officer of the Day's nightmare. I could just see Jon beginning to sweat. When a Marine gets arrested in Mexico, the Corps' Officer of the Day has about twelve hours to bail the Marine out before he disappears in the Mexican prison system forever.

Joe starts up again, "I'm in jail here and I messed up, I'm sorry . . ."

I could see Jon's face. I knew he was beginning to freak out! And that's when we started laughing. We knew we had really gotten him.

I am not encouraging you to play pranks on the Officer of the Day, especially if it's your husband. Remember, this is the government we are talking about. Still, those were hysterical pranks.

VALENTINE'S DAY

The stores are stocked with candy and cards. Movie channels play chick flicks back to back. Everywhere you go you see pink and red. Love is in the air on the universal day of romance.

But this day had no special meaning to me. That's because for five years straight I have not spent a Valentine's Day with my husband.

For me, VD had become a day spent watching thriller movies and eating a box of candy I bought for myself—all the while trying to think about anything but love.

Why? Because Jon was either deployed or in training every February 14th from the day we met.

Still, that day was harder to get through when he was deployed. I guess what made it worse was that we could not even talk.

What can be worse than spending a Valentine's Day alone? Well, I discovered it.

During my husband's first deployment I woke up feeling sorry for myself since there would be no candlelit dinner or kinky sex that evening. By two that afternoon I was still wearing my nightgown, eating raw cookie dough, and watching "Maury."

Then the doorbell rang. It was a flower delivery! My mood changed instantly.My husband had remembered me! I was thrilled! My heart soared as I gazed at the arrangement of roses. I tore open the card anticipating my husband's love note.

This is what I saw: "Happy Valentine's Day from your mother-in-law."

What's worse than being alone on VD? Getting a bouquet of roses from your mother-in-law—especially when you're expecting your husband, who is on the other side of the world, to remember you. That's right, I got a romantic delivery of roses from my mother-in-law on Valentine's Day! Of course, it was at the point in the deployment when every kind gesture hits a nerve. And I officially lost it. I knew she meant well, but to a wife in the midst of her husband's deployment, the gesture was quite inconsiderate. I couldn't bear to look at them.

My mother-in-law's gesture had crossed the boundaries of communication between a husband and wife. She had done what he was supposed to do.

I thought I was used to civilians doing random acts of kindness for me knowing it was really for their own benefit. I could just hear her telling her friends, "I sent Mollie flowers today because I wanted someone to remember her on Valentine's Day."

It's the same when civilians pay for military folks' dinner or drinks. It's really cool, and appreciated, but we also know they like to talk about it later.

When you're going through a deployment, marriage is defined differently. There is just so little to be shared between husband and wife.

Sending flowers on Valentine's Day is a romantic gesture. If Jon had not been deployed, I would consider the gesture weird, but I wouldn't have flown off the handle.

However, during a deployment we all have short fuses. Somewhere in her mom mind she had imagined she was doing something good. Bless her.

I stewed as I thought about calling to thank her for the flowers. I knew this would be an uncomfortable conversation. I could imagine having to report I had not received flowers from Jon, but thanking her for hers. The conversation would eventually lead to her wanting to compare notes on how many letters, emails, and calls we had each gotten from Jon.

I thanked God when Kat called to invite a slew of us over for an impromptu girls' night out.

Once we had gathered in her living room, the gossiping began. I knew my girlfriends would bring me out of my funk.

Then her doorbell rang. It was a delivery of flowers! Unlike mine, Kat's romantic arrangement had been sent by her husband, who was also serving overseas.

Kat's husband Craig may have been gone for this romantic holiday, but Kat had not been forgotten. As we all cooed over her flowers, the chatter began on who had received what for Valentine's Day.

The wives who had not received anything began to get defensive and a game of "One Up" started.

They thought the game was over until I said, "My mother-in-law sent me a bouquet of roses today to wish me a Happy Valentine's Day."

Everyone gasped. I could tell that my "gift" had set new standards of holiday blues without a husband. For the first time in the history of "One Up," a wife actually received a few sympathetic nods.

Kat walked over and encircled me in a hug. I had somehow "One Upped" them all, but it didn't make me feel proud. I actually felt worse. A few wives offered their condolences.

I walked home feeling defeated and depressed. I was thinking about my husband and our time together. We had not spent a single Valentine's Day together. Valentine's Day no longer meant candy, flowers, and romantic dinners.

We had never thought we needed a particular day to express how we felt because we did it all the time. My husband often surprised me with flowers on random days.

As I walked home, I thought about how my husband had showed his love on so many other days of the year that this specific day no longer mattered. I was allowing myself to get upset on a day the world determined love had to be shared. I knew my husband loved me and showed me his love on a daily basis.

I was feeling stronger as I turned the corner and saw a bouquet of roses on my doorstep. The card read: "Go look in the laundry room on the top shelf behind the bleach. Jon."

I pushed through the front door and ran inside. I had to put a footstool on top of the dryer just to see inside the cabinet. Behind the bleach I found a card from Jon. It was then I realized he had hidden it there before he had left!

Tears poured down my face as I read my husband's precious love note. It felt good to know that Jon had remembered me!

I thought about what the Apostle Paul had said about love: "Love is patient. Love is kind. Love is not easily offended."

I placed both sets of flowers on the table with Jon's card in the middle. I felt truly loved as I looked at them both.

I then went to the computer and sent an e-mail genuinely thanking my mother-in-law for the flowers.

FIREWORKS

Our first Fourth of July on base was spent on the beach at the north end of the base with Jim and Jessica. Jim is a Pogue/JAG who had gone through training with my husband and Lloyd.

His wife is an excellent cook, very chatty, fun to talk to, but a very nervous person. She has a darling 10-year-old daughter from a prior marriage.

Jim and Jess had a rather humorous (some would call it odd) relationship. She fretted all the time. He ignored her. She would make bold statements like, "You take all the joy out of my life!" He would just look away and smirk.

Beenie and Lloyd joined us at the beach. Good people, good holiday, good times.

And yet, we were bummed when we found out there would be no fireworks display. Still, there were plenty of things to do—roast marshmallows in the fire pit, play volleyball, or swim in the ocean.

Beenie and Lloyd had rented a tiny cabin at the beach. It was actually a trailer, but it was a place to go to the bathroom and change clothes.

This holiday also fell at the time of the month when Beenie was the most fertile. She and Lloyd were trying to conceive, so several times during the festivities they would "excuse" themselves and go off to the cabin.

For some reason this got under Jess' skin. She apparently wanted some afternoon delight as well! We could hear her badgering her husband with, "Why don't you even want to take me away like that?" "We never go off and do it like that!"

After listening to a full 30 minutes of her whining, I had a feeling there were many other reasons her husband had not taken her away for some love making.

Jim had started to play with a scanner that some other Marine had brought down to the beach. He was listening in on the various frequencies and became lost in his own world.

Jess continued nonstop. "Why aren't you playing with my daughter? Why aren't you whisking me off to make love in that flea-infested trailer? Why won't you get in the water? Why won't you build me a rocket ship?" And on and on she went.

Her husband simply turned up the volume on the scanner.

She finally told her daughter that she would play with her. Lloyd had played with her in the ocean most of the day, but he was now ready to sit next to the fire pit and relax with a beer and a hot dog.

So Jess and her daughter went off to play volleyball while Jon and Lloyd got into a discussion about surfing. Beenie and I settled back to cheer the players on.

Volleyball nets had been set up all along the beach. About fifty feet away were large cement fire pits set deep in the sand. They had been used heavily that day. Although it was July, the weather was overcast and cool.

Anyway, someone volleyed the ball to Jess, who hit it out of bounds. You guessed it. It went off in the direction of the fire pit.

She yelled, "I'll get it!" We watched as Jess, who stands all of 4'9", ran straight toward the fire pit. The ball had rolled past it.

No one said a word of warning because we figured no one could miss a giant fire pit. No one flinched until she flipped ass over elbow into the damn fire pit! Her tiny body disappeared beneath the surface.

Beenie and I jumped up screaming, "Oh, my God! Jess is on fire!" As I ran toward her, I yelled back at Jon, "Get a towel. Get it wet. Jess is on fire!"

By the time we got to Jess, she was climbing out of the pit. She looked like a Phoenix rising from the ashes!

While there was no fire in the pit, Jess had landed on hot embers, which had burned her entire hand.

She was brushing away tears as we began to fuss over her. Even the strangers she had been playing with gathered to check on her. Jon and Lloyd rushed over with wet towels while her daughter tried to hug her.

Her husband, however, remained sitting in his chair, listening to the scanner. I screamed at him, "Jim! Your wife was just on fire!"

He looked up, looked her over, and went right back to the scanner.

The rest of the evening was awkward, to say the least. Jess was trying to make jokes about falling into the fire pit. I actually think she was embarrassed that her husband had ignored her.

Beenie and I were doing our best to distract her. Since she hadn't even yelled at him, we were holding our breath waiting for the inevitable explosion.

Jess started poking fun at herself when we checked the ice on her hand. I told her she would be fine, that "Johnny Tremain" had turned out OK and so would she.

I was referring to a popular book for elementary school students. It's the story of a Colonial-era youth who became disabled when he burned his hand.

I guess she had read the book, but didn't see the humor in my comment. She abruptly stood up and asked her husband to take a walk with her. It was obvious she needed to talk with him.

There was a moment of uncomfortable silence. We thought she was finally going to let him have it.

As they walked up and down the beach, we could hear her screaming. Her poor daughter just sat in her chair. No one said a word.

We could see Jess's tiny frame in the distance—waving her hands and gesturing. As her volume rose, we did our best to try and ignore it.

Then she pointed at me and I heard the words, "Johnny Tremain." Right then Lloyd, who had gone to the restroom (alone), showed up. "Mollie, she's mad at you for calling her a cripple," he explained. "She's been going on about it for ten minutes."

That did it. Jon and I grabbed our chairs and left. The base may not have provided fireworks, but we had gotten a "fire show" and enough "explosions" to last us for a year.

INDEPENDENCE DAY

Naturally, the Fourth of July is a big holiday on base. And we had some amazing Fourth of July parties. However, Jon never made it to another after Jess caught on fire.

Since many of the men were deployed during the summer, the wives went all out for this celebration. It was the last holiday before the men came home!

Our Navy neighbors across the street invited us over to their backyard to watch the spectacular fireworks. We would pile in, grill out, eat cupcakes, drink beer, and watch the fireworks.

At one party I managed to get wasted while playing horseshoes. A five-foot tall, 100-pound spouse going through a deployment should not be given heavy metal horseshoes to throw around, especially if she is drunk.

There are pictures circulating of me wearing a tiny Uncle Sam top hat while drunkenly throwing horseshoes at people. How anyone avoided serious bodily injury is a miracle.

It was not my best moment. Good thing I limit drinking to parties. After that day, I started to think that even that was too often.

HALLOWEEN

We always had the fall months together and thoroughly enjoyed them.

Halloween has always been a favorite holiday. With all the kids on base, I was so excited about trick-or-treat time. Jon and I went all out carving pumpkins and putting costumes on them. One year we had Hajji pumpkins with full headdresses.

Jon was usually in the field during trick-or-treat hours, so Michelle and I would sit in lawn chairs in the driveway and hand out candy.

One year a Marine family dressed up as members of the band KISS. Even the three-year-old was in full KISS gear. We got the biggest kick seeing these big masculine Marines dress up in costumes along with their kids.

Jon and Beenie's birthdays were near Halloween, so we would plan huge costume parties. We had music, cake, and prizes for the best costumes. It was excellent to see all these Marines cut loose and get dressed up.

One year, Christa and I dressed as Sigfried and Roy. Another couple was Clementine and Dangle from Reno 911—tiny shorts and all. All the couples really got into making their costumes and trying to outdo last year's design.

We would hold the party in our garage—moving couches out there and putting up lights and decorations everywhere.

The fall and winter holidays came right before scheduled deployments, so they became a way for all of us to blow off steam. We enjoyed them to the fullest.

GIVE THEM THE BIRD

Thanksgiving has turned into my next favorite holiday and I owe it all to the Corps. It is the one holiday that nearly all military families spend together.

Our tradition is centered on the turkey. No one can fry up a Thanksgiving turkey like Beenie's husband. Once you have had a fried turkey, you won't want it any other way. You will risk burning a hand or even your entire home just to have a turkey fryer out back.

My husband had to serve duty on our first Thanksgiving together. I remember taking Jon a plate and sitting with him in a tiny office as we ate our dinners. We sat and watched a movie together, then I headed home.

Beenie's dad, who lived in Las Vegas, would sometimes join us. Boy, was he a treat! His hobbies included gambling, undergoing plastic surgery, and dating as many young ladies as possible.

I would tease Ed: "Oh, Ed if I wasn't married, and just a few years younger!" He loved it. No one really knew how old he was because he looked amazing—a bit like Ricardo Montalban, but with this great mustache. He was really debonair, and a huge flirt. Ed would take turns socializing with everyone while nursing his Crown Royal.

At our second Thanksgiving together we had just said the blessing over the meal. Beenie's first child, Grace, just six months old, was sitting in a walker beside the table. I was next to Autumn, who was next to Ed, who was next to the baby at the end of the table.

Ed stood up after the blessing and started to say something. The next thing Autumn and I knew, Ed looked at us and then seemed to leap backward like a cheerleader at a football game prepping for a back flip.

As he was flying through the air, I saw that the baby was directly in his path. Nor could I do anything to stop what surely was going to happen.

He went flying through the air and bounced off the baby in her walker. Once he landed on the ground, we saw that not one drop of his Crown Royal had spilled.

Grace was screaming, but more from fright than pain. Apparently he had missed her by inches.

The men pulled Ed up off the ground. As they did, he exclaimed, "My leg atrophied." I have never seen an atrophied leg, but I had just seen a 70-plus-year-old man cut a back flip at Thanksgiving dinner. Who knew a little Crown Royal could do that?

Beenie missed the entire incident, but Autumn and I being Aries and horribly immature, had to excuse ourselves and go into the garage for major giggle fits several times during the evening.

To this day Jon and I have kept our military tradition of frying a turkey at Thanksgiving. We will either spend the holiday with members of our military family or invite friends over who are unable to go home for the holidays.

Our prayers of blessings and thanks are always focused on our military family wherever they may be in the world.

CHRISTMAS COMPETITIONS

Base housing neighborhoods go wild at Christmas. The competition starts when the first dad climbs on the roof to put up lights. The obsession of "yard of the quarter" hits its zenith in December. The designated parking space at the commissary is awarded to the house with the best holiday decorations.

However, the spot is not as prestigious as the respect from the other men in the neighborhood when your home has the best holiday decorations.

I have to say Del Mar housing had some bizarre decorations. Maybe it was because we were in California and everyone was trying to be politically correct, or maybe it's because there were just more options for decorations at Wal-Mart.

Some of the houses were adorned with Mexican Santas—very tan, very festive Santas. Neither white, nor Black, but definitely Latino.

One of our neighbors had this bizarre blow-up reindeer that was over nine feet tall. He would climb up on his roof, complete with night vision goggles, and scope out the competition in the neighborhood before blowing up his monster reindeer.

This made the wives nervous. Here was someone with night vision goggles looking in our yards at night. (Keep in mind that I had a trampoline in my backyard that neighborhood parents were just as fond of "playing" on as the kids!)

My personal favorite decoration was the one in the Colonel's yard down the street. He had a light-up Santa seated in a wheelchair. I wondered if Santa had had an accident while trying to get down a chimney.

It was great fun to drive around base housing checking out the lights. Some houses were just over the top.

One of our Bunco ladies, Sally, had lost her husband in Iraq and it was her first Christmas without him. Whenever she would come down to the base to play Bunco with us, she often stayed at my girlfriend Karen's house.

At night those two would go wild. The Officers' Club was just behind our neighborhood, so those two would take a shortcut by cutting through the tall grass.

Every time Sally came down for a visit, two things would happen: they would "drunk dial" me at two in the morning, and the reindeer decorations would be rearranged to make it look like they were humping each other.

The coital reindeer raised some eyebrows in Del Mar housing. The few teens in the neighborhood were getting blamed, but I knew it was all the work of one woman: Sally from the Valley.

Look, she had lost her husband in the war against terrorism. I think she should be allowed to blow off a little steam.

Sally became an inspiration to us. Humping reindeer aside, she showed us that life goes on, and it is all about attitude.

HOLIDAY WISHES FROM A DRUNK POGUE

Our first Christmas on base started off on the wrong foot. With the holidays approaching we looked for an opportunity to share a little Christmas cheer before we traveled to see our families throughout the United States.

Jon's first deployment with Second Battalion, First Marines, was in January. This was going to be our first Christmas on base and our last holiday before deployment.

The deployment was getting close so we wanted a festive gathering. Jon and I decided on a holiday "wine and cheese party."

No offense to Grunts, as I am deeply in love with one, but my attempts at a sophisticated, elegant party stopped at the invitation. Even the fact that I had sent out invitations was, by the guys' standards, "gay."

I should have known better and planned a beer and pretzel party instead, but hindsight is 20/20. I tried really hard for the sake of the women. We had had so much fun getting dressed up for the Ball. I wanted another chance to feel elegant.

I even attempted to make fondue. Here's my recipe for Grunt family fondue: heat up Cheese Whiz.

I did get a bunch of gourmet cheeses and Brie (whatever that is) from a grocery store off base, but I didn't have matching wineglasses. But I did have glasses I had collected from the restaurants I had worked at over the years.

I told everyone to bring his or her favorite wine, which translated to the wives bringing their favorite wine coolers and twelve packs of beer for the men.

Mostly, I just wanted the evening to be fun. The women had hung out with each other while the guys had worked together for nine months. But this was going to be the first official gathering we had had in our home.

We were proud to have the 2nd Lieutenants from the battalion in our home. The Christmas tree was up and I thought it looked darling. It was our first Christmas tree together.

There were many things to be proud of that night, but the disaster that happened was not one of them.

Beenie was about six months pregnant with her first baby. Although Lloyd was not in my husband's battalion, she had spent so much time with us at the beach and playing Bunco that it seemed natural to include them. Besides, Lloyd had gone through TBS with all of these guys.

Beenie drove down early to help me prepare for the party. She and Lloyd also planned on spending the night with us.

As I was getting things ready, I noticed she kept calling Lloyd on his cell phone. She told me that he had gone golfing with a bunch of higher-ranking Marine Corps judges.

I was not concerned about any "Grunt/Pogue" rivalry during the party because these guys had gone through TBS together. That rugged Marine infantry training can result in some serious bonding. Some of it borders on what wives call, "Brokeback TBS." We have heard stories of guys sleeping as close together as possible (cuddling?) while in the field during the long Virginia winters.

To these stories, Marines respond, "What happens in the field, stays in the field."

Beenie was getting more and more concerned as the afternoon wore on. Lloyd finally arrived, but he was drunk as a skunk when a friend dropped him off.

I had a feeling it was going to be a long night because Beenie was HOT! After some arguing, she made him take a nap in the hope that he would sleep it off. I did not want to embarrass her further, so we didn't tell Jon or any guest that Lloyd was passed out drunk in the guest room. Big mistake!

The party was going along smoothly. We were talking about the last few months of training and were starting to get to know the single Marines a little better.

We were well into a gag gift exchange when we heard a racket at the back of the room. There was Lloyd standing on one of my kitchen chairs. He was waving a fondue stick and had a mouth full of cheese.

He started yelling, "Any of you Grunt motherf*****s think you can take a Pogue, why don't you just?"

And then Lloyd fell off the chair.

We all looked at each other. Can you say "uncomfortable moment"? Keep in mind, most of these guys had no idea that Lloyd was even at the party since they had not seen him since TBS.

They all had looks plastered on their faces that said, "Who was this random stranger at the Gross' threatening to fight?" I felt bad for Beenie, who by this time was starting to cry.

Jon jumped up to help Lloyd, who had landed in the Christmas tree water. Jon and Carl pulled him out and carried him back to bed.

I have to say my house full of Grunts handled the threat very well. There could have been a rumble. On the other hand, maybe it was the Christmas spirit that kept them in check.

After Lloyd's appearance, the party took a wild turn. The next thing I knew, my theatrical wigs had been pulled out of the closet as well as my hats and fur coats.

Before I knew it I had about seven drunk 2nd Lieutenants in drag posing for pictures on my couch. I have been sworn to secrecy, so I won't tell you who they were. I will tell you this: my husband was wearing a pink cowboy hat. These Grunts know who they are and they each have copies of the photos—*but I have the negatives.* :)

I'm not so sure that what happens in the field really does stay in the field.

HOT BUTTERED RUM

The harbor is just outside the gates of Del Mar. Every Christmas we would bundle up in coats and blankets and go down to watch the Harbor Lights Parade. All the boats are decorated with lights and carry men dressed as Santas.

For this event, Autumn would fill a thermos with hot buttered rum using a recipe she'd gotten from her mom. It was supposed to keep us warm and feeling festive. There is nothing more sweet or warm than her hot buttered rum, which tastes like warm butterscotch.

My husband fell in love with this beverage. I watched him finish two cups while standing in her kitchen. After that he filled his thermos and mine up to the top with this buttery grog.

However, I decided to switch over to hot chocolate because I didn't want to have to find a bathroom while we were watching the parade.

At the harbor we watched the yachts and tiny tugs decked out for Christmas. As everyone was enjoying a light buzz from the buttered rum, I noticed my husband starting to turn a little green. It was then I figured out that Jon had polished off both thermoses of hot buttered rum.

I alerted Autumn. We did the math. Jon had ingested about four sticks of butter, six cups of sugar, and at least one cup of rum! We told him we thought it would be best if he stayed away from the Christmas fudge and cookies.

When he absorbed the reality of all he had ingested, Jon agreed to lay off the sweets and then walked off to puke.

Hot buttered rum and "butter bars" don't mix.

DEALING WITH EXTENDED FAMILY

This is an extremely touchy subject. When dealing with your extended family, married couples need to remember that it's OK to do things differently from your families. In fact, Jon and I had to come to terms with the fact our respective families' traditions were not wrong, just different.

Every family has its own quirks, traditions, and priorities. The beauty of being married is that you get to start your own family traditions. Define your new family by looking at your families of origin and deciding what traditions, values, and priorities you want to repeat, and which you want to ditch.

I believe the biggest challenge in the first year of marriage is defining your new family. It is especially difficult in the military because the government makes the priorities for you so you and your spouse have to work with what's left. If you don't focus on that little bit that is your own, you can get very lost—quickly.

One of the big mistakes Jon and I made during our first years of marriage was to devote our vacations and down time to our extended families. I think the shock of living so far from both families coupled with the stress of the war made us think we needed to spend all of our time with them.

In hindsight, I think we overdid it. We should have taken time for ourselves and created our own family traditions. Honestly, at that time none of us knew if Jon would come home from these deployments. We all wanted every minute with him.

So many problems with the extended family arise in military families. Those problems included in-laws unwilling to support the marriage, wanting to be on hand for farewells and reunions, showing up uninvited, and arguing over where everyone would spend the holidays.

It seems to be a trend in the military to see disconnects or strife between the service man and his family.

A lot of military personnel come from a family tradition of military service. However, I really think a lot of men and women join the service to have a sense of belonging and to be a part of a new family. Joining the military is a way to create a new family, find a sense of belonging, and serve your country.

It seemed during our time on base that nearly every other couple was experiencing some turmoil with extended family. Family squabbles on top of prepping for war is just too much unnecessary stress.

I saw Marines who came from unhealthy homes try to reach out one last time in an effort to make things right. More often than not the effort blew up in their face and caused a lot of grief for their wives during the deployment.

Whether you're military or not and you're having issues with your extended family or friends, start by setting boundaries. Be polite. Put yourself in the other person's shoes before reacting to a situation. Try to understand what they are thinking or feeling. And take responsibility for what you may have done to create the strife.

Finally, and most importantly, you and your spouse must preserve the sanctity and respect of your own family. When facing the reality of war, you do not need other distractions.

Military wives can act as the filter, deciding what their husbands need to deal with during their deployments and career. These women have made great sacrifices to be with their men on this journey. Military wives need to remember, when dealing specifically with a mother-in-law, that you both love this man. It is not about your husband or son choosing who he loves more. It is about making life for the service member easier as he prepares for a life of duty to his country.

Wives, what a great gift you give your husband to keep peace in the family by being polite and kind the few times a year that they visit. If there is an issue with your mother-in-law, your husband should take care of it for you.

Extended family can be like civilians in the sense that they may not understand your lifestyle, priorities, and values. It is up to you as a family to handle what you can control. It will take some time, but as everyone adjusts to the lifestyle and becomes aware of everyone's stresses, you will, hopefully, be able to get along.

Bottom line: nothing or no one should be allowed to act in a destructive manner to your family. You and your husband have to set boundaries appropriately. It can take years to build a relationship with the extended or civilian family, but once you do, it can be very rewarding. Maybe you won't be the best of friends, but you could at least get to the point where you sincerely enjoy each other's presence and enjoy a true love.

JARHEADS

When I first met my husband I noticed that his head was partly shaved, which signified to everyone that he's a military man.

It was not until I questioned why he always cut our weekend visits short that I fully understood the grooming necessities of men in uniform.

Jon explained that he had to get his hair cut every week. He assured me that if he did not, he would be subjected to the wrath of his commanding officer.

This fact did not really seem like a good enough reason for him to leave me so early on a Sunday. I mean he is a Marine. He could deal with a little yelling. Wasn't I worth it?

That's when he confessed that a certain barbershop inside Quantico run by women from Okinawa closed early on Sundays. That's why he had to leave early, so he could get back in time for one of their haircuts. I kept pushing and discovered that after the haircut they would give him a head and shoulder massage.

I went wild with jealousy and hit the roof. "A six-dollar haircut and massage was worth leaving ME!?" I screamed.

So we went to the Wal-Mart and purchased a set of clippers so I could give him his Sunday evening haircuts. Now you ask yourself, "How can a person mess up shaving another person's head?" Easy—I was what you could call a beauty school drop-out.

For the sake of love, my soon-to-be husband suffered through my bad haircuts, gave up massages, and got even more heat from his commanding officers over his hack job haircuts.

But, I was not the only person who thought they could master becoming a barber without training.

Beenie told me stories of Lloyd trying to shave his own head. He insisted he could do as good a job as any barber. One Sunday he managed to electrocute himself and nick his ear—all in an effort to save six bucks.

You can usually tell a person's MOS, the branch he serves in, or sometimes his rank, by the Jarhead style he sports. Many Marines had a unique style of Jarhead based on their personal preference.

There is the "Low Reg," which is usually sported by Navy and Air Force personnel. This is clean-cut short hair with a very light buzzing around the back of the neck.

This haircut is also grown by a service man approaching his End of Active Duty Service date. And it is favored by retirees who do not want to let go of the glory days. When worn by a Marine, it is viewed by peers as a little slack.

The "High and Tight," a Marine Corps standard, is an aggressive haircut—intimidating and non-approachable. It is the antithesis of the "low reg." The High and Tight is also how most Marines like their women's private parts, which is a little ridiculous. Like the Marines, it can only be pulled off by the few and the proud without looking extremely threatening.

My personal favorite is the "Med-Reg," which my husband wore for years and is quite handsome. It's a stately haircut, with definite substance on top and around the sides. It's all about the fade with this style—clean and crisp sides and smooth shaven in the back.

It's a less intimidating haircut than the high and tight. It's approachable, friendly and yet it still demands respect.

Those working closely with civilians or the media usually wear this style of Jarhead cut since it makes the man appear approachable.

There is one style that I believe is out of control. It's typically only worn by the most militant of service men—either Majors or above or those men who aspire to wear medals on their dress blues.

In the "Horseshoe" cut, the head is shaved from the base of the skull all the way up—stopping just past the crown. What remains is a horseshoe shape of hair around the front of the face. It looks like they placed a horseshoe on a Marine's head and shaved around it.

This hair cut is technically forbidden in the manuals, but that doesn't stop the fierce commitment to style sought after by those wanting their look to be "squared away" and "locked on."

All Marines who have a Horseshoe cut are the same. Don't shake their hands. They will crush your fingers with their grasp. Horseshoe Marines are a force unto themselves. They only speak in acronyms, so don't even try to communicate with them. Horseshoe Marines think nothing is funny—unless they said it. It's all business with these fierce fighters. Indeed that haircut could scare away the enemy from miles away.

The shaved head is sported by men on deployment who either cannot deal with stopping to get a haircut or men going bald. This is a focused Jarhead style and, to me, it's a no-nonsense look.

While it's not favored by wives, it's much better than a Horseshoe. One last thought: make sure you have a nicely shaped head before you shave your hair off.

Now, when picking your style of jarhead flare, it's also important to consider the barber. You may not be able to control this, particularly if there's a long line and a "churn and burn" system on the weekends.

Men, if you choose to have a delightful Asian woman cut your hair and give you a massage, you better keep it to yourself or that arrangement won't last long once your wife finds out.

I have also heard horror stories of husbands taking the matter into their own hands. As we learned earlier from my failed attempts, it's better to pay a professional. It's only six bucks, for God's sake!

One last tip: beware of the 98-year-old barber in Oceanside who has a large moose head in his shop. I suspect he is legally blind. I watched him shave off my husband's widow's peak. Jon ended up with a shaved patch on the front of his head, while the rest of the hair was an inch and a half long.

Maybe this was an attempt by my husband to return to his beloved Asian masseuse. It didn't work.

BIRTH CONTROL

Let's talk about other grooming and appearance challenges for military men. I got the shock of my life when my future husband came for a visit and got out a pair of reading glasses.

Urckle had nothing on these military-issued glasses! They were the ugliest, squarest, brownest glasses I have ever seen.

He explained they were his BCGs and had been issued to him. When I asked what "BCG" meant, he responded, "birth control glasses."

Indeed, that is one way to keep our military personnel out of trouble during training.

Thank God he had not been wearing those dorky things when I first met him. If they would just issue those glasses to the entire Marine Corps on the night of the Ball, we might not have so many Ball Babies.

MOLEST-ACHE

Let's talk about a bizarre desire that sweeps over our husbands when they deploy. I'm talking about the decision to grow a mustache. Or, as I like to call it, a "molestache."

Navy men can wear mustaches. They are given a cultural dispensation to have fashionable facial hair. In fact, they are practically issued one with their uniform. And I think Navy guys look good with them.

Unfortunately, our Devil Dogs, Army soldiers, and Air Force men just can't seem to look good with facial hair. On the rare occasion when they do, it looks offensive. Those who try will pay the price. They'll be made fun of behind their backs, even by their own wives.

I use the term "molestache" because as the second day of the peach fuzz above the lip starts to darken, the men take on the look of someone who should be on a list of registered sex offenders.

Now there are some men who wouldn't look right without a mustache: Burt Reynolds, Will Smith, Magnum P.I. But let's face it, most Marines don't look like Tom Selleck with a Hawaiian shirt, gold chain, and fully permed chest hair. Marines, soldiers, and airmen need to face the fact that they are not on the list of acceptable people who can sport a mustache.

When the men deploy, they figure this is their time to bask in their testosterone. Misguided, they think the best way to exert this power is to flaunt the potential of their "stache."

When I received the photo of Jon in Iraq proudly sporting a molestache, I was appalled. All sexual desires for him vanished. It looked like the nastiest caterpillar crawling on his lip.

I had a flash back to junior high when a creepy guy in a Camaro followed me home from the bus stop. I rushed inside to check if Jon was on the registered sex offenders' list.

Now, ladies, your Marine will tell you it is imperative he grow a mustache while deployed. Those headed for the Middle East will claim the locals have more respect for men with moustaches.

This is all a bunch of bologna. They are simply driven by their desire to have facial hair. So, let them.

For some reason this "molestache" gives them something to look forward to every day. I think they like to caress it and watch it grow. It's like having a forbidden friend.

When they get home and realize there will be no kissing until it's removed, they will make sure to shave it off before the reunion. You can also fight fire with fire. Tell your man that you will shave your legs once he shaves off his molestache.

PETS: OUR DEVIL DOGS

Pets are an absolute necessity in a military family, especially to the ones left on the home front, but only if the family understands the responsibility of owning a pet.

I believe that because the military wife is the one in charge of the military home, she should pick the pet. I saw too many military families get in way over their head with these huge aggressive dogs that were supposed to protect the family while dad was deployed.

In reality, it is the wife who the dog listens to and who does most of the training. She should pick what type and size of dog she wants to handle. The family pet should be more of a companion than a protector.

When my poor husband married me, I had two cats and two dogs. However, this package did not mean two really cool, masculine dogs like bulldogs or even miniature pinschers. Nope, I had two six-pound, white teacup poodles. The female is CoCo (her friends call her MeMe). Her husband (yes, they are married and have had babies) is Monsieur, which is French for Mister.

When we made our initial move across country, my parents took the dogs. We were not sure what we would get for housing or if we would be able to have dogs. When we were settled in and Jon's deployment date was set, I told him it was time to send for the dogs.

He fought me tooth and nail until I started crying. I told him that I would need a companion while he was gone. He finally agreed, but I think it was more out of guilt than anything else. My parents brought the dogs out a few months before he deployed. Those dogs, in fact, saved my sanity while Jon was gone.

Sadly, my poor husband would have the humiliating task of taking them potty before he left for work. Imagine this big handsome Marine walking these two six-pound Devil Dogs around our base. The looks he got from the other Marines were priceless!

I took every opportunity to remind him of the companionship they would provide me while he was gone.

Monsieur and Jon got off to a rough start when we were dating. One time Monsieur peed on Jon's undershirt while he was visiting from Virginia.

Monsieur jeered at Jon. When he did, I could hear him telling Jon in a French accent, "Monsieur Gross, you are taller than me, no? But you see, proportionately my pee pee is bigger than yours. I have also fathered many children with my wife CoCo. What have you done with yours?"

I probably should have stepped in, but I felt like one of those women who brings a man home when her kids are still in the house. I believed I had to let them work it out.

The dogs required regular grooming, which usually resulted in a fluffy hairdo adorned with bows. I had extensively detailed instructions for the groomer.

CoCo got a "muffin"-like shape on the top of her head accompanied by "Dorothy Hamill" ears adorned with a bow. CoCo also wanted her toenails painted red. All this was essential for her feminine image.

Monsieur has one very specific requirement: he had to have a mustache. That was vital to his masculine image.

Many groomers tried giving him a different style over the years. For a while he had a fierce Foo Man Chu, but my favorite was a simple French look with a full mustache and small goatee. Yes, my dog could pull off a mustache, while my husband could not. I think this fact deepened the divide between Jon and Monsieur.

On one particular trip to the groomer, I dashed out without leaving my full explanation. When I remembered, I called the shop and described what was supposed to be done.

When I picked them up a few hours later, I was horrified at the results. They had gotten my dogs mixed up! I guess it was much too much to check their genitals. Anyway, Monsieur had painted nails and a shaved face, while · CoCo had a huge handle bar mustache.

Once home, I tried my best to repair the damage. I shaved off poor Coco's mustache, but her self esteem had already suffered.

Monsieur seemed to enjoy his painted nails, which disgusted Jon. The morning walks were now ever more unbearable as Monsieur happily lifted his painted toes to pee while Jon held the leash.

It goes without saying that I switched groomers. Some things are unforgivable.

SHARK ATTACK

While Jon (barely) tolerated my dogs, it took years for him to actually love them. Now Jon enjoys their company.

I think he was at first embarrassed that they were so unmasculine. He felt ridiculous having these fu fu dogs around.

Add to that the fact we had a very tight budget. Jon didn't understand why I had to get them groomed, nor did he appreciate the money being spent on them. So I used the money from my part-time jobs and my savings to cover their care. Vet bills were something we tried to avoid.

We had a neighbor dog we dubbed "The Shark." This thing was black, sleek, and an evil predator. Like a shark, he stalked his prey, which usually meant my little six-pound poodles.

"The Shark" barked at everything, lunging in an effort to attack if you got within fifty feet. Needless to say, I was scared of this dog. He only weighed about twenty pounds, but it was twenty pounds of pure terror.

If I was walking my poodles or if I even saw him when I went to the mailbox, I would run back to the house as fast as I could.

"The Shark" would usually threaten Monsieur with a barrage of barking and growling. In his nasty Brooklyn accent, "The Shark" would often make nasty comments about CoCo.

"Yo, Frenchy! I like your wife's little bows. Why don't you walk over here so I can sniff her butt? Yeah, you stay over there or I will rip you a new asshole!"

All I can say is, thank God Monsieur does not understand English.

To make matters worse, "The Shark's" real name was Molly. Yes, the irony was so thick it dripped.

One afternoon my dogs and I were playing in Kevin and Michelle's backyard. When Kevin came home, he took the boys to play at the community playground behind our street.

As they were leaving, Monsieur squeezed through the gate following Jacob to the playground and ran directly toward the children.

As they turned to greet Monsieur, I saw "The Shark" just behind them. I screamed and started running for the playground with CoCo on my heels.

"The Shark" was running directly for Monsieur, who immediately changed direction and started running back to the safety of Kevin and Michelle's backyard.

Unfortunately, the gate was now closed. I screamed. CoCo was barking. Monsieur was panicking because "The Shark" was inches away from his tender little behind.

I thought Monsieur was running straight for me. I even crouched down prepared to pick him up, but he ran right past me. He was heading for the now closed gate.

Kevin and I stood and watched as my tiny dog dove head first into the chainlink fence. He looked just like a baseball player sliding into home plate. I guess he was trying to fit through one of the tiny holes.

As Monsieur's face made contact with the fence, "The Shark" bit his butt and CoCo bit "The Shark's" butt.

The force of the impact sent all three dogs flying through the air.

It was literally the funniest thing I had ever seen in my life. I knew Monsieur was OK because he immediately jumped into my arms.

A few days later, however, Monsieur began to act strange. He wouldn't let me pick him up nor could he sit down. I examined his bottom and hind legs and found what appeared to be a blister the size of a silver dollar next to his butt hole.

I took him to the vet and learned the stress of the attack had caused Monsieur's anal gland to rupture. He would require surgery and a drain, advised the vet. "The Shark" had torn Monsieur a new asshole.

I just couldn't tell Jon that the surgery would cost us $700. I used the last of my savings to cover it.

Poor Monsieur had to wear a plastic collar around his neck. Not only that, he had a shaved butt and a drain hanging out of it for two weeks.

Imagine how Jon and Monsieur felt as they went on their morning walks. I don't know what was worse for my family—Jon walking a poodle with a shaved butt and an anal drain, my now empty savings account, or Monsieur knowing his wife had beaten up his bully.

WHO'S YOUR DADDY?

Individually, our two cats weighed more than the dogs combined. However, they gave us equal parts of trouble.

Darius, a black male domestic short hair weighing in at fifteen pounds, had lived with me since high school. My brother had named him after Darius Rucker, lead singer of Hootie and the Blowfish. His reasoning was the cat was black and I was attending college in the band member's hometown.

While I was attending the University of South Carolina, I lived in a quadplex during my freshman year. One time Darius got out and I was forced to get my fat ass outside to find him.

Yes, I was fat. I had gained the freshman fifteen pounds. OK, not to brag, but I am an overachiever; I had really gained twenty-five.

Anyway, I am outside screaming, "Darius! Darius! Come here! Come here right now! Come here to your mom!" Finally, my black cat crawls out from under some bushes and leaps into my arms.

As I turn to go back inside, I see a man standing beside his two-seater BMW staring at me. At that moment, my knees went weak: it is THE Darius Rucker.

And he's looking at me with this, "You are a freak, lady. I thought you were screaming at me, but now I see you are a stalker who named your black cat after me. Where the "F" is my pepper spray? Don't come near me, you irrational obsessed fan."

I later found out he was going to a party with the girls living downstairs. I was so humiliated I ran back upstairs and hid in my apartment the rest of the night.

I should have said something like, "Hey jerk, remember after that concert in Virginia when you took a bunch of groupies backstage? Does this cat's face look familiar?"

CAT ON A HOT BASE HOUSING ROOF

Our other cat is Tipple, a name that means absolutely nothing. I have been asked if her name was a cross between a "tit" and a "nipple," which I guess it technically is, but I picked the name because it just sounded funny and I liked the way it rolled off my tongue.

Now, let me say this up front. This cat is an asshole, but I love her in the same way a parent loves a child that regularly disappoints them.

The attitude of this cat flabbergasts me. It's like she wakes up every morning and declares, "I choose hate. I do not choose love. I choose to hate everyone." That's Tipple's attitude toward life and toward me.

While she has a rotten attitude, she is soft and beautiful on the outside. She is a Siamese mix with white hair, gray points on her ears, feet, face, and tail, as well as the most beautiful blue eyes. She acts like one of those women who knows she's pretty, but acts mean because people want to be around her.

We always want to hold and kiss her, which she hates. She has never wanted me to pick her up, nor has she EVER sat on my lap.

She freaks out and starts to cry whenever I pet her for more than twenty seconds. She never hisses or attacks us. She simply doesn't want human contact. If you leave her alone, she leaves you alone. But if you touch her, you're asking for trouble.

This drives my husband wild because he wants to squeeze her, hug her, and call her George. Jon loves to pick her up and try to cuddle her, which usually results in huge scratches down his chest and stomach.

They have developed a bizarre relationship that included some strange games. Those games started with Tipple and Darius going outside to hunt gophers, birds, and squirrels. When it got dark, we brought the cats inside to keep them safe from the coyotes and skunks roaming the base.

On the nights my husband would come home late, Tipple would crawl onto our roof and scream in an effort to compel Jon to get her. We had a one-level house, but to get her down he would have to jump on our trampoline and then land on the roof of the garage. He would then scrabble across the roof to get to her.

Once he had her in his arms, though, she would scratch and hiss at him. The blood would follow, as would a loud hiss and frantic struggle until my Marine and cat landed on the trampoline.

This only happened when Jon came home late, and never on nights when he was in the field. This beast wanted his attention, and knew on which days to get it.

I could only imagine the neighbors saying, "Look at those two. Thank God they don't have any children. They can't even control their cat! Look at him on his roof! How ridiculous! How can he control a platoon if he can't get his cat to listen to him?"

CAT CRAP FEVER

At the very end of my husband's second deployment, a funky smell began to emanate from our bedroom closet. I wanted to concentrate on Jon's homecoming by getting back to the life we had before he left. You know, like buying real food for the house, practicing getting dressed every morning, and shaving my legs.

However, the smell coming from my husband's side of the closet kept distracting me. The closer I got to the closet, the worse it smelled. It was the most foul and rank stench I had ever encountered.

I searched everywhere but could not find the source. Jon only had a handful of clothes in the closet since he wears the same sets of utilities every day. I checked the armpits of his shirts to see if one of them had turned ripe after six months, but found nothing.

I wondered if there could be a dead rat in the wall. Was it the fabled "base housing mold" that seasoned wives talked about? You know, where you breathe the mold spores for years and then your kids grow up abnormally tall or develop horrid skin rashes?

I didn't have time for this drama. I was on a countdown. Jon was due back in three days and I had this awful reek in our bedroom. I needed to find the problem and eliminate it ASAP. This was not the type of ambiance I wanted in our love nest.

By the second day when I hadn't found the source, I had a horrible thought. Maybe I was the cause of the stench? Could it be that over six months of neglecting my basic hygiene that I had begun to rot?

I had to admit that not only did a few days slide between showers, but I had also been known to wear the same outfit (OK, pajamas) several days in a row. And I had lost my toothbrush—several weeks ago.

While I thought the smell had been coming from the closet, I now wondered if it was my nasty breath bouncing off the clothes and back into my face! I went nuts thinking the stench was coming from me!

I used a travel toothbrush I found in a suitcase to brush my teeth three times. And, yes, I even flossed. When I was done, I dashed back to the closet. The stench was still present—but not accounted for.

Although I had managed to shower—OK, every other day—I had stopped most waxing, pedicures, hair dying, and shaving of excess body hair. It had to be my body hair that was holding onto the odor, right?

While I knew I would have to shave my legs in time for Jon's homecoming, I had figured that like everything else it could wait until the last minute.

Now I was sure it couldn't wait. I showered and shaved down, which left me a pound or two lighter.

The smell in the closet remained.

I was at the height of my hysteria when I spotted Tipple exiting the closet. When she saw me looking at her she dashed off with a rather guilty look on her face. Ah, I thought. That's it! The cat had left me the gift of a dead mouse in the closet.

When I looked inside the closet, however, there was no dead mouse to be found. When I stuck my head deeper into the closet, I was hit with a stink more potent than before!

That's when I noticed one of Jon's shoes had been turned on its side. I picked it up and almost passed out from the smell. The shoe was definitely the problem, but Jon had not worn it in six months. Did my husband have some kind of alien athlete's foot that had sprouted latent spores in his absence? I looked inside and found the answer.

Tipple had pooped in one of Jon's favorite pair of shoes! It's bad enough that my husband only had two pairs of shoes besides his combat boots, but Tipple had used one as her toilet.

She had somehow backed her bottom right into the toe part so you couldn't see the poop until you looked inside the shoe. Upon further inspection I found she had left a surprise in both shoes. How about that as a welcome home present?

I had to ask myself if this was the same as a gift of a dead animal left by the bed. Does the poop mean she wanted him home or was it her silent protest about having to share the house with another person?

It didn't matter. I washed out the shoes—twice—and started locking up the closet. Even though he was not home, Tipple was still letting Jon know who was boss.

THE BIRDS!

Both of my cats are excellent hunters. In Del Mar we had countless varmints wreaking havoc—lots of moles, gophers, mice, rats, skunks, and endless numbers of birds.

As I left for work in the morning, I would see my cats in a neighbor's yard, stealthy watching a nest of feathered creatures. When I came home hours later, they would be in the same position still waiting to strike.

While Jon was gone, their little "gifts" arrived more frequently. It was quite unsettling to find half of a bird or a pair of gopher's legs in my bedroom—especially since I had no one to get rid of them for me.

I knew when to be on alert for their gifts. They would announce it with a particularly chirpy type of meow. That's when I knew I would have to check under the bed, in the closet, or in the bathroom.

One day in particular, Ms. Tipple was in my bedroom acting strangely. She was carrying on and chattering, pacing and meowing—a sure sign she had brought me a present.

Then I saw the large black feathers scattered around the bedroom. I checked in the closet, the bathroom, and under the large canopy bed.

Nothing.

Then I noticed Tipple was staring at the top of the canopy bed. I couldn't deal with it. I figured the dead animal could stay there until my husband returned in two weeks to clean it up. This cat had already put me through enough with the shit in the shoes and dead animals everywhere.

For three days Tipple sat beside my bed chattering, meowing, and pacing, but I ignored her.

One afternoon, Autumn stopped by to return a pan. We were standing in the hall when we heard a loud fluttering and felt something swooping overhead. We both looked up to see this huge crow coming out of my bedroom, straight down the hall, and straight for our faces!

I knocked Autumn to the floor. We were lying flat with arms over our heads in a protective stance. "Cover your eyes!" "Oh, God, where did that come from?"

I leapt up and found the bird frantically flying around my living room. I ran to the sliding glass door leading to the backyard and flung it open. The crow flew out, landed on the power line, turned, and stared at me.

That crow had been perched on top of my canopy bed for three days just waiting for the right moment to fly my coop! How my fifteen-pound cat had managed to get that giant black crow into my room will always be a mystery to me.

I do think it was part of Ms. Tipple's plan to have the crow peck my eyes out. I'm convinced she wanted her daddy home and me out of the picture!

BARREN BY CHOICE

The worst gossip about my pets started when CoCo hurt her hip. Every night Michelle and I would speed walk about two miles through the neighborhood. We wanted exercise and fresh air. It was also an opportunity to get out of the house, chat, and burn off a few calories.

Michelle would push her youngest, David, in the stroller and walk her cocker spaniel, Molly. I would walk CoCo and Monsieur.

CoCo had had two litters of puppies and was now in the empty nest/ retirement phase of her life. She was glad to have her children out of the house, which was near the beach. Never mind the fact that she still lived with her parents.

Giving birth will change a woman's body. Ever since the birth of her last litter of twins, Coco's hips had not been the same.

Sometimes on our long walks, CoCo would simply stop walking and I would end up carrying her. Although six pounds is not a burden, Monsieur would get jealous and demand to be carried as well.

Sometimes if David was in high spirits, Michelle would suggest that CoCo ride with him. Many times David obliged, but he was also three years old. Without warning, David would throw CoCo out of the stroller.

Other times they would be quietly riding along when Monsieur would get jealous and dive into the stroller landing on a sleeping David and CoCo.

Of course, David would react by ejecting both dogs from the stroller.

One evening we saw a stroller on the side of the road left by a family that was PSCing out of the neighborhood. Michelle urged me to take it to use for the dogs on our walks. It was a brilliant idea. I loaded the poodles in it and took off.

I enjoyed those walks with my children in their stroller, waving at neighbors. Then I started hearing the rumors flying around the mail boxes and commissary: "Poor Mrs. Gross, such a shame. Her husband couldn't give her a real baby before he deployed. Now she has gone crazy and thinks her dogs are babies!"

Or better yet: "Poor Mrs. Gross, I heard she is barren. All she has to live for are those dogs!"

I didn't mind the rumors until they reached my husband in Iraq. Once my husband's CO heard I was trying to breast feed my poodles, he thought it had gone too far. I had to park the stroller and get the leashes back out.

ADDICTED!

I credit my pets for being my main support during both of Jon's deployments. I know I had friends and family, but a pet's unconditional love cannot compare. Keep in mind that many of us were war brides, newly married with no kids. Our pets became our babies.

My girlfriend Erin, who was stationed with her husband at Camp Lejeune in North Carolina, had a yellow lab named Ashley. She's become Erin's number one companion.

Like kids, pets can go a little bonkers when their "daddy" is deployed. Maybe it's because they miss him or they sense their owner's nerves are on edge. For whatever reason, they usually end up in serious trouble.

Erin had noticed that Ashley was not acting like herself. She had become excessively hyperactive and was chasing her tail all the time. The dog was spending more and more time outdoors as if she was looking for something in the grass.

Eventually, Ashley would start barking like mad and run up to the door with a crazed look in her eyes and foam around her mouth. Erin knew it couldn't be rabies since the dog had been vaccinated. Ashley continued to spend her days nipping at the air and barking at nothing. It was truly bizarre behavior.

After a few days Erin found a toad on the porch. She watched as Ashley followed it around, licking it.

Erin called me to ask what I thought was going on. I told her what any parent with a husband away on deployment did not want to hear.

"Erin, I think she is addicted." I went on to explain that some toads secrete a hallucinogenic. If you lick one, you can get high.

Erin screamed, "No, not my child! How did I not see this coming! I ignored all the signs!"

She was blaming herself, yet how could she have known? Her child was getting high right in her own backyard! I suggested she take Ashley to the vet to get a professional opinion.

The vet confirmed that Ashley was addicted to toads. He informed Erin that she would have to immediately separate the two. Since Ashley was addicted, the toad would only peer pressure her into continuing to abuse toads.

It was up to Erin to kill the toad. Even worse, Erin would have to tell her husband, who was in Afghanistan, that their child was an abuser. It was not a good call, but Erin and her husband loved each other and they loved Ashley.

The family eventually got through it and Ashley recovered. The toad, on the other hand, mysteriously disappeared.

I WANT A PONY!

Beenie and I played this fun game with our husbands. The thing was they didn't know it was a game. We had both married our spouses after very short courtships. As a result, much of our honeymoon phase was spent getting to know each other.

Beenie and I had already had four pets each when our husbands said, "I do." But we would often go on and on about the exotic animals we wanted for pets.

It really made Lloyd and Jon nervous. The thing Jon and Lloyd had in common was they found it hard to say no to their wives. Their best hope was that no new strange ideas would creep into our minds.

The one thing Beenie and I shared was a love of animals, and we both always wanted more.

During Jon's first deployment, I decided I had to have a turtle. Jon freaked, particularly since I had already picked out a name—"Frere Jacques."

One day Jon called from Iraq just after Beenie and I had been checking out turtles at the local pet store. I had no intention of buying one, but Jon and I had been apart for so long that he was starting to think about the go-cart incident.

Jon started pleading. "Please, Mollie, don't buy a turtle while I am deployed. They look cute now, but they get really big."

I pretended to cry. "But this one loves me! He is the size of a silver dollar. He runs up to me every time I walk by his cage!"

Beenie is in the background screaming, "You have to buy him, and get another one so he's not lonely."

Then Beenie gets on the line, "Hi, Jon. How is the desert? Yes, well, my mother had a pet turtle when she was a girl. They are quite fascinating. It got so big she would ride it to school! Mollie is so tiny, I bet she could ride a turtle all over Del Mar housing!"

We started giggling and screaming just as the phone cut out. Suddenly it was not so funny. It occurred to me that Jon would now be sitting in Iraq thinking he was coming home to a circus.

Poor Jon. He probably didn't know we were kidding. I felt horrible that I had created a distraction at a time when he needed to stay focused.

Thank God he called back right away. I assured him I learned my lesson with the "go-cart incident" and promised I would not buy a big item without first consulting him.

He told me he loved Beenie, but that she was an instigator. He made me promise not to buy a turtle—not even a cute one in Chinatown. Especially not a cute one in Chinatown! I promised.

When Jon came home, he brought me a tiny hand-carved wooden turtle from the Seychelles Islands. Of course, I named it Frere Jacques.

By the second deployment, though, I had a new obsession: miniature horses.

One night while watching TV in bed, Jon called my attention to a show featuring a tiny horse (about the size of a lab) wearing shoes and serving as a guide for a blind woman.

I decided then and there that I had to have one. When I told Beenie about it, she decided she had to have one as well.

We searched online every chance we got. We printed out pictures of ones offered for sale and put them on our fridges.

The one I really wanted was a tiny black and white miniature I named Pygmalion. I talked about him non-stop—how I would buy him shoes and train him to help the blind. Beenie thought this was a riot.

Jon, though, had had enough. He made me promise not to discuss miniature ponies for six years. If I did, he would consider getting me one if we ever lived on a farm.

I readily agreed. He was going on deployment anyway, so I knew I could talk about it all I wanted; I would just have to wait until after he left. He would never know.

My birthday arrived after Jon deployed. Natalie, who knew how much I loved Pygmalion, had his photo scanned and put on my birthday cake. It was the best surprise.

The wife of Jon's CO asked me to explain the story behind the pony on the cake. When I explained, she thought it was a hoot.

When her husband called from Iraq, she told him about the birthday party. Then she told him all about the pony on the cake and the fact Jon wouldn't let me have a pony. Unfortunately, the conversation got a bit mixed up.

"Karen, I am staying out of this. If a wife got a pony for her birthday and it is going to upset her husband, I am staying out of it," he said. "I need my men to stay focused right now."

Then the phone cut out.

She called to warn me that her husband was going to say something to Jon about my pony.

I acted quickly. I was sure Jon thought I had a tiny pony in the house—shoes and all. I e-mailed him a picture of the cake telling him, "Look, the ladies got me my pony!"

I was hoping he would see the cake and put two and two together.

Jon called to ask about my birthday party. Thankfully, the CO had not said anything to him.

Chapter Five

PRE-DEPLOYMENT

Pre-deployment leave is the time to tie up loose ends, as well as to emotionally and physically prepare for the long separation.

In the military, you sometimes get that call that your husband is going on an unscheduled six- or seven-month deployment, which means you have no time to prepare.

Since my husband was in the infantry, we knew that war or no war, he would leave for two six-month deployments in a four-year block.

The military schedules so much intensive training up to that point that you feel as though he's already been deployed since he is gone so much.

It feels like a roller-coaster ride. He's home one week and gone for two weeks. These "work ups" go on for six months. After that, the military gives you a little leave.

This is the only time you know for certain that no one will have to stand duty or go on a weekend hump. It's a time when you're finally free to go about your business and relax.

HA! HA! How can you relax knowing your husband will be gone for seven months? What an oxymoron!

Not only that, but many families have the added level of stress of the extended family's desire to say, "Goodbye" to the service man before he deploys.

This is totally understandable. However, a military family needs to be preparing its own family, including children, emotionally as well as physically for the absence. Instead, military families often end up taking a huge family vacation or hosting a huge family reunion.

Who does all the planning, partying, and packing? That's right, the military wife. What joy! All you want to do is have some quiet time with dad and the kids and maybe fit in a romantic date or two.

Then the doorbell rings and there stand the in-laws, grandma, and the extended family. They're anxious to visit, while you end up playing hostess instead of spending time alone with your sweetheart.

The other problem is you end up feeling guilty for resenting them and selfish for feeling that way. You know what? You're normal. Your feelings are justified.

I couldn't understand how some extended family could go for months, or even years, without visiting. But the second the service person is scheduled for deployment, they schedule a visit during the week before he leaves.

It's important to keep in mind you are the matriarch of the house. And, as such, you must set the boundaries.

The extended family is important, so you should make time for them— but not the week before he leaves. I would go as far as avoiding visits from extended family during the pre-deployment leave.

Everyone needs to recognize that your family's day-to-day life is about to change. The extended family should be alerted to this fact. It's up to you and your husband to gently and mutually set boundaries for pre-deployment calls and visits from outsiders.

If you can't manage this, I can promise that one of you (the wife) will be blamed for "keeping him away from the family."

Pre-deployment leave is meant for the service member. Don't burden him with guilt by forcing visits with family and friends as well as making time for you.

Make it easy on everyone by setting boundaries and sticking to them. This is the time for last minute trips to the orthodontist or to get the car's tires changed, as well as to go on family outings without outside interruptions and distractions.

Do those errands that are easier to do when hubby is home. If you do not take the time for them during pre-deployment leave, you will be upset you have to do it when he is gone.

My advice is simple. Plan a family gathering a few months before the deployment so everyone gets their time.

SECOND MARRIAGE

For our pre-deployment leave, Jon and I had a little matter to address before he went off to war. We needed to get married. I know, you're thinking we eloped.

Yes, we did, and so we didn't have a traditional church wedding. And some people had made me feel guilty about eloping with Jon.

It's quite common for military families to elope, then have a formal wedding. As I got to know other military wives, I realized I had nothing to be ashamed of. If other people had a problem with our decision to elope, then it was their problem.

While Jon and I had considered ourselves husband and wife from the second we said "I do," we faced a new dilemma. Jon had been raised Catholic, but I had been raised Methodist. Being married in the Catholic Church was important to Jon and his family.

Both of us are Christians and our faith is very important to us both. We consider spirituality a huge part of our relationship. Our faith holds us together.

Still, I realized that being married in a church was important to Jon and his family. And that's why we planned to have a church wedding before he deployed.

SIGN HERE

Even though we were already married, the Catholic Church required us to participate in premarital counseling.

My girlfriend Erin, who was converting to Catholicism, had already gone through the counseling program in preparation for her marriage to Mike. She called to warn me about an agreement the priest had asked her to sign.

Apparently, the paper spelled out various martial agreements. Erin said she didn't read through them thoroughly—just quickly went down the list and initialed each one.

When she went back later and read them, Erin freaked. She said some of the agreements were harmless, like saying she would accept children graciously from God and would raise them Catholic. But another stated she would "give herself to her husband physically in marital relations whenever he desired!"

She could not believe what she had signed.

Now her husband was carrying the agreement around in his pocket so he could torment her with the fact that she had agreed to be submissive sexually! Every chance he got, he teased her mercilessly.

It was hysterical, but I knew I would not sign anything like that.

When we got to the classes, I think my priest quickly realized he better not ask me to sign that statement. He probably figured it was pointless since Jon and I were already married.

Regardless, I carefully read over the paperwork before signing it. Thankfully, that statement had been omitted.

MY SECOND WEDDING

We finished up counseling and decided to marry at the beautiful Ranch House Chapel on Camp Pendleton.

After nine months of living as husband and wife, we got married again, but this time we did it with class and sophistication. The priest was sober. Nor was there a line of folks in matching sweat suits waiting in line to get married.

I will admit it felt silly to be going through this ceremony since everyone knew we were already married. Still, it was great to have my new military family watch as Jon and I affirmed our love for each other.

I don't remember the date of our second wedding because Jon and I prefer to celebrate our "real" wedding (the elopement). Still, our church wedding was magical and we have the pictures to prove it.

All of Jon's friends from training and his battalion were dressed in full uniform. All of my wonderful new military girlfriends joined us as well. I had my two matrons of honor—my very best girlfriends, Erin and Beenie—

who had a huge responsibility. They were supposed to be on nipple watch. But they both failed, miserably.

PEEK-A-BOO

Before Jon and I moved to California, Erin and I had gone shopping for a wedding gown at a store near her hometown in South Carolina.

I wanted the dress so my mother-in-law would know we had every intention of getting married in the church when the military gave us time to do so. It was my way of reassuring her.

Anyway, I fell in love with this strapless dress. I knew I looked adorable in it—like an upside down teacup. And it was ivory because . . . Well . . . I obviously could not wear white.

But there was another matter to consider. I am five feet tall and weigh about 110 pounds, and thirty pounds of that belongs to my boobs. And yes, they are real. My mom believes they came from the hormones in milk. I certainly didn't get them from her.

The problem is they make me top heavy. They also present a problem when I'm going down stairs. Picture a Slinky.

Needless to say, when your legs are as long as your boobs stick out, you're facing a challenge to find clothes that fit.

Anyway, this dress was a perfect style for me, but it was eight sizes too big. I decided to try it on just to see if it would look good with my skin tone. Erin was on the other side of the store looking at shoes or veils or something when I saw my reflection in the mirror.

I started screaming and running through the store looking for her. I have to admit I caused quite a commotion.

Erin remembers it happening in slow motion, complete with the theme from "Chariots of Fire" playing in the background.

As I was running toward her, I stepped on the three yards of material that was too long. It snapped me forward like the metal on a mousetrap. My head flipped forward. With my momentum propelling me forward and my foot on the fabric, I pulled the dress down in front. Did I mention it was strapless?

I fell flat on my face and then rolled over on my back. My bosoms were released, exposing my nipples. As I lay on the ground topless, I told Erin, "This is the one. Doesn't it look great?"

I had no idea my "girls" were playing Peek-A-Boo.

You'd think that my embarrassment would have been tempered by the fact that there were only women shoppers in the store. But some hussy had brought her boyfriend–fiancé with her, and he had witnessed the entire scene.

According to Erin, this guy just stared at my milk white breasts while his girlfriend pitched a fit. I may have caused their break-up.

I ordered the dress in the correct size, but I think my nips remembered that incident. After that, it seems that every time I put the dress on, my boobies tried to poke out and say "good day!"

I realized this in the fitting room and again at my house while I was posing for photos with Erin and Beenie before the wedding. It was at this point that I asked them to watch my "girls" and keep them in their place.

My photographer, who did an amazing job of capturing that day, assured me she could touch up anything out of place in a photo. I took comfort in knowing that for a small fee she could eliminate pimples, make sure eyes were open, and even move someone around.

Once I saw the initial set of photos, I was overwhelmed by the loveliness she had captured. I called the photographer to order a few photos and asked, "You said it was $20 to remove pimples, but I need a quote on the cost to remove nipples."

We laughed and laughed at the fact that in about five different shots one of my "girls" was poking out trying to get a bit of sunshine.

I laugh every time I look at the photos. No wonder the priest avoided talking to me during the reception.

SWORD FIGHTS

I am here to tell you, the sword swat you get on the butt as you walk through the sword arch is painful!

The stories of women padding their bottoms before going under the arch are no joke! I wish I had. My bottom was stinging for about an hour after I got whacked. No one would tell me which of Jon's friends did the smacking, either. I had to wait until the photos were developed to find out.

If you're having a military ceremony, buy those panties with the padded butt. You're gonna need 'em!

Top: Grandma Ruby took this picture of me at age 2 about 10 seconds before I got a spanking. I locked myself in her bathroom and refused to let her in to "wipe me." Clearly I did not have the situation under control. She must have heard the commotion from outside the door, and got the camera. As you can see, the toilet paper was everywhere but on my bottom! Above: Hanging out with my favorite cousin Kevin at age 4.

Jon and I went out to 5 points in Columbia, SC for Halloween when we were dating. He's the goofy Marine with the BCGs and I am the hooker who is refusing service. Sorry Marine, those BCGs (birth control glasses) are a total turn off!

I didn't find out who whacked my bottom with his sword at the end of the sword arch until the photos were developed. I thought it was Carl, but the evidence pointed the finger at LLOYD!

Right: Jon was shocked to see what he found hiding up under my dress when he went in for the garter! My wedding night surprise was ruined!

Below: Jon and I at our church wedding, "renewing of the vows" October 2002. The Ranch House Chapel, Camp Pendleton

Erin and me fighting over the first dance with JJ at my church wedding. Who can resist "Kid Dynamite!"?

Michelle, me, and Beenie (left to right) during one of the "Mommy and me playgroups." The guys are gone so Michelle is copping a feel.

Beenie and me at the secret beach. When your BFF becomes your "spouse" during a deployment . . . sometimes you can get into some misunderstandings. Watch out Paris and Nicole!

Above: Us wives at the 80s-themed roller skating birthday party. Oh no, where is David the Menace? And do I really look 15? Top, left to right: Melissa, Julian, Natalie, Lauren, Autumn, Dawn, Beenie, Grace. Bottom, left to right: Nick, Michelle, Jacob, me, Alek, Kianna, and Karen.

Below: My dad, Erin, and Mom visiting the weekend of my church wedding. The east coasters are freaking out over the chilly Pacific Ocean! I am freaking out over my mom and dad wearing their sweatshirts like that!

Jon and I out in front at grandma's doing some paparazzi poses before attending the Marine Corps Birthday Ball. Dad was there taking pictures, mom and grandma were fussing over my hair, make-up, and girdle.

Sorry for the fuzzy picture, but I love this one. Jon and I enjoying a rare trip to Del Mar Beach, Camp Pendleton the summer before he deployed. We are newlyweds here. We would not spend a summer together for another 3 years.

Grandma Ruby and I at Christmas 2003 between Jon's deployments.

Top: This is the kind of goofy picture I would mail to Jon to make him laugh while he was deployed. Tipple and I are having a little dress up mother–daughter time. No wonder this cat hates us.

Right: Grace and I, two Aries girls.

Top: My favorite photo of my neighbors, David and Jacob. Michelle had them in desert cammies for a photo shoot when daddy was deployed. Above: The infamous go-cart, with the more infamous JJ the yard boy.

Above: My KVC and great friend Karen took this photo of Jon and I when we first saw each other after his second deployment.

Inset: Imagine my shock when I developed this role of film mailed to me by Jon from Iraq. Jon and all his 2/1 buddies had grown the "moleste-ache." Although respected by the local Iraqis, women back in America hid their children and did a check online for registered sex offenders.

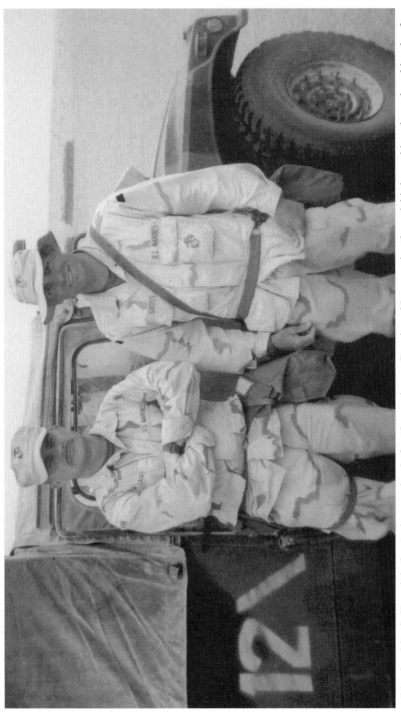

Lloyd and Jon in Kuwait in the staging area just before the war began. Beenie and I were going through birth coaching class when this role of film reached us. Our men were about to go to war! This picture made us both very emotional. And Lloyd had to ruin this perfect photo by growing a molest-ache!

Jon and I at the birthday ball. I was so gassy I could not hold it in. My girdle was too tight, and I am trying to cover my HUGE "gas baby" with my hands. I could not wait to go home, strip, and let out a big toot of relief!

I have been told that on stage I am quite animated. I never fully "get it" until photos are developed. Then I invariably turn to Jon and say, "I looked like that!?" Here I am in Beaufort, South Carolina, performing "Mollie Gross, Military Wife Comedy."

But, that was just the beginning of my sword problems.

Before we cut the cake, I gave a speech to our guests. I spoke about our love for our birth families as well as our love for the military family with us that day. And I talked about the deployment we were facing.

Let's just say this. I have a degree in speech. By the time I was done, we were all crying. The mood became intense and powerful, so in an effort to lighten the mood, I yelled, "Let's just eat some cake!"

Jon used his military issue sword to cut the cake. He gently fed me a tiny bite and I did the same in return. As I was nibbling on the cake, I saw Jon starting to scheme.

NOT GOOD.

He was looking at his sword, which is now covered with chocolate icing. (Yes, I had chocolate frosting on my wedding cake!) I could see him thinking, "Gee, what do I do about this?"

To my shock, he opened his mouth, stuck the sword in, and closed his lips over it like you would with a spoon dipped in cake batter. Then he pulls the sword right out between his lips.

Every woman in the room gasped. I was mortified. "Oh, my God!" I yelled. "What are you doing? Open your mouth! Let me see your tongue. Did you cut yourself? Are you insane? I may need that later!"

Between my swollen butt and my husband nearly cutting his tongue off, I had had enough of swords that day.

Still, the whole affair was really lovely. It was not something I thought I had wanted, but I'm happy we did it.

A GIFT BEFORE YOU GO

Before Jon left, I gave him two gifts.

The first was a handmade patchwork quilt I had worked on for months. I thought he could use it on his bunk on ship.

The second was a tiny leather album with photos of us. At the back of this family album, I stashed some sexy boudoir photos of myself. He was very happy, and especially pleased with his "bonus" gift.

I had heard stories from "veteran" wives about rampant amounts of porn on deployment. This didn't sit well with me. My husband was not the type of man who liked to look at those magazines. (We didn't even keep that garbage in our house.) However, I knew seven months would be a long time to go without "marital relations." I was surprised to learn that some of these "veteran" wives didn't care about the use of pornography and even encouraged their husbands to look at it.

I decided to take matters into my own hands. I spoke with the photographer who took pictures at our second wedding.

She offered me a "boudoir" photo session. These are "tasteful" nude or partially nude photos taken in a studio. I figured since my nipples had to be airbrushed out of several of our wedding photos, why not let them have their moment in the light?!

The photos turned out beautiful and were very classy.

WORD TO THE WISE: If you do boudoir photos for your man, be sure to give him the photos before he leaves. Do not mail them. Remember, packages can be searched and confiscated. Unless you want to be a "pin-up" for the entire battalion, hide them in a photo album you give him before he leaves.

It's also a good idea to keep track of any copies you have at home. I had an eight-by-ten of myself standing in front of the American flag. I was wearing a red bra and panties along with Jon's dress blues cover.

My Marine mother, Mary, stopped by one day with her fifteen-year-old son, JJ. I was so pleased with the photo that I decided to show it to her. As I flipped through the photos, I had her stand close to me so JJ would not see it. But I couldn't find it. I stared at this cardboard backing muttering that I had just seen it the day before.

Then I looked up to see her son's eyes were bulging out of his head. I flipped the cardboard over and realized the photo had been facing him the entire time.

I guess JJ got a gift as well.

THE CLAW

One day my husband told me he had a gift for me, too. (No, not a baby.)

Jon explained that he had thought of me when he saw this and knew that I would need it while he was gone. This way, he continued, he could still be with me even when he was gone.

I was giddy with excitement! I knew it was going to be good!

Jon went into the kitchen—and brought out this bizarre contraption that can only be described as "the claw."

I thought it was a joke, but my husband doesn't know how to be funny. He has a good sense of what is funny, but no talent when it comes to delivering the punch line.

We have this rule in our family: Jon is not allowed to be funny because when he tries too hard it comes out really mean and sarcastic. He just does not possess comedic timing. I am the funny one, and he is the sensible one with all the brains. It works for us.

Anyway, I had no idea what this gift was. It had a handle that extended out about two feet. At the end was a pair of pinchers with rubber stoppers. When you pulled the "trigger," the stoppers pinched together.

I still didn't get it.

What did this claw have to do with me?

My husband stood there beaming from ear to ear. "Look, this is amazing," he said. "Now, you can reach anything while I am gone. You won't have to worry about not having me around to reach for something."

Granted, I am five feet tall and fall constantly as I climb the base housing counters trying to get a dinner plate down, but this wasn't what I expected from my husband about to leave on deployment. I started to cry.

Maybe I was crying because on some level I realized how much I really depended on my husband to reach things for me. Or maybe it was because I expected something romantic and I had gotten something . . . practical.

Ok, I was pissed and refused to use the claw.

My anger was not directed at this crazy contraption. It simply symbolized how much I needed Jon. Worst of all, it made the deployment too real.

My husband was devastated by my reaction. He had put so much thought into this gift and I was acting insulted.

In my pre-deployment state of mind, I could not see that Jon was simply being practical. That was his way of being thoughtful. He was thinking about how to take care of me, even when he was gone.

Jon became defensive—like he needed to prove how amazing this gift was. Over the next few days anytime I asked him to reach for something, he would bring that damn claw and use it.

I went nuts! I threw the claw in the garage and vowed NEVER to touch it or depend on it EVER! Every time I banished the claw, it found its way back into the house. Once Jon left, however, the claw remained in the garage.

About two months into the deployment at one of my infamous Bunco / patio parties, someone was jumping on my trampoline and threw a pack of smokes on the roof.

It was dark, but we could see the cigarettes. But no one could reach them. We were all freaking out. That was the only pack of smokes for five girls. No one was crazy or drunk enough to climb on the roof. Still, we needed to find a way to snag those smokes.

You guessed it. I gave in and used the claw to grab something out of my reach. I did find solace in the fact that I had to use it to retrieve cigarettes and not something . . . practical.

LEAVE ALREADY!

The clock is ticking. Your husband has completed all the work up training and has taken his pre-deployment leave.

You did the trip to see the family and now it's quality time for the two of you. You stare at him sitting on the couch next to you, or maybe in bed beside you. This man is caressing you gently, lovingly staring into your eyes.

This thought keeps coming into your mind. You want to scream: "Get out! Leave already! JUST LEAVE!!! Let my countdown until you come home begin!"

At the same time, you feel shame and guilt because you've started to pull away. And you begin to hate yourself for reacting to him this way. You just can't seem to connect with him.

Please understand. This is a normal reaction! It's your self-defense mechanism. You are starting to detach and mentally prepare for life without him. I know because I felt the same way before both of Jon's deployments. Fortunately, my husband understood.

Right before Jon's second deployment we had a really rough day filled with fighting, crying, and tension. We were afraid these would be the last days we would have together.

We prayed together. We asked God to get us through these next months.

That day we saw the biggest rainbow. Here is the thing. It seldom rains in Southern California. And there in front of us was God's promise.

We hugged each other and I cried again. The tension was finally gone so we could enjoy our last few moments together.

Just know that you can think or feel anything, but it's your actions and words that matter. Even if you don't want to be close or intimate, do it anyway!

Eventually, you will be able to let your guard down and enjoy the tenderness of those moments.

While it takes more effort to connect during this time, you will regret pushing him away. Savor each moment.

THE CONVERSATION

There's another topic that needs to be addressed: SGLI, which is government-issued life insurance automatically provided to military personnel.

In the event of death, the next of kin can receive about $500,000. But you need to ask yourself if this insurance policy is enough. You have to decide based on the dynamics of your family.

Here's the point: you need to discuss it.

I know you don't want to release such thoughts into the universe, but you need to be realistic and prepare for the worst.

Whether your husband is deploying to a war zone or just a MEU (Marine Expeditionary Unit, deployment served on ship), you need to prepare a will as well as discuss what you would do if he does not return home.

I heard one tragic story about a widow who discovered her husband had not purchased additional life insurance before he left. In addition to learning this, she found out he had made his alcoholic, compulsive gambling mother the beneficiary of half of the funds. The widow was left with only $250,000 to take care of their four children.

Do not let this happen to you. Have the conversation.

One day during his second deployment, Jon was thrilled to hear the words "mail call!" He had been in a very dangerous situation throughout the day and was finally feeling safe. Although he was miserable and starving, Jon was happy to have a letter from me.

He ripped it open expecting to find my comforting words that would lift his spirit and sweep his heart back homeward. Instead, the letter was one line with another sheet attached: "I think you need more life insurance. Sign here and mail back."

Jon was devastated. "Well," he exclaimed, "my wife's betting against me!"

He showed it to the other Lieutenants, who thought it was hysterical.

Now, as in today, I think it's funny, but I can only imagine how Jon must have felt when he opened it. I realize now we should have had that conversation *before* he left.

If you do have to mail a similar letter to your lover, at least include some homemade cookies.

Here is another serious issue that needs to be addressed: children.

If you have kids, it's best to involve a neighbor or your closest living relative when you decide what to do with the kids in an emergency. You need to discuss with them what to do with the kids if you are involved in an accident or are killed while your husband is deployed.

And be sure to put in writing your wishes about who will be responsible for your children in your absence.

It is also important to explain to your extended families the procedures to be taken in the event of a death or injury of a service member. That way, you won't have to deal with panicked emails and phone calls each time the news reports are bad.

I find it difficult to believe I was twenty-four when Autumn and I talked about what we would do if our spouses didn't return. We realized some of our civilian friends with children didn't even have wills. Nor could they understand why we were preparing for war or that I could even consider life without Jon.

For my part, I couldn't fathom how they could be so irresponsible as to not prepare for their children.

I am proud that my husband honored me by having these uncomfortable, brutally honest conversations.

Every night and day of Jon's deployments, I imagined riding our motorcycle together and going to the beach when he got home. I saw it in my mind's eye and felt it in my heart.

This is my advice. Prepare for everything you can, then continue to think and dream about your life together.

Chapter Six

DEPLOYMENT

Every family has its own way of saying goodbye. No way is easier than any other. It is all up to you and your husband to decide what's best for you.

Some families want to go with their service man to the departure site and wait till the last bus rolls out. Some prefer to say goodbye at home.

I had heard stories of wives who would take their husbands down to the ship where these stupid reporters would surround them. As they said their last goodbyes, some dipstick reporter would shove a camera into the wife's face, look into the camera, and say, "Ma'am, your husband is going to the Middle East to face guerilla warfare. He may never come back. What are you going to do while he is gone?"

Later you see this mortified woman's face plastered across the TV screen looking so frightened. What did the reporter expect her to say? "GEE, I think I'll go to Disneyland!"

These reporters can be such idiots, turning this final intimate moment into a complete nightmare.

On the other hand, I have also heard amazing stories of friends waving to their husbands from the dock as their husbands stood on the deck of the ship waving back. They blew kisses and watched the ship float off into the horizon.

I sought out the advice of Mary, my Marine Corps mom, for my husband's first deployment "goodbye." Her advice resonated with me.

"Mollie, say goodbye at home as if it were any other work day. Do not treat it any differently. This will help with the regularity of the day. When he gets to his departure point he is a Marine, and he needs to be a Marine. Let him focus on what he needs to be doing and the deployment ahead. Let him say goodbye to you at home, and leave that memory there with you."

My husband did one deployment on an MEU and one when he flew straight over.

I handled both our goodbyes the same. Both times we said goodbye in the bedroom early in the morning. Then a friend would drive him to the departure site.

He left his pack by the front door where I would not see it when he left. With his uniform on, he kissed me goodbye in bed just like he did every other morning before he left for work.

I vividly remember the stage of deployment when I hit rock bottom. I was eating raw cookie dough, shopping on QVC, and hitting on the toothless bagger at the commissary. And that was just the first day!

Honestly, I was in shock that first week.

It finally sank in as I was doing the laundry at the end of the week. I washed all his clothes, folded them, and put them away. That first week I left his shoes around the house. Then there were papers and magazines. I was still picking up after him.

But after I put everything away, I realized I was done picking up after him for seven months. There would be no more little reminders of him in our home.

I finally crashed after I washed our bed sheets. I would hug and smell his pillow. For the first week I would sleep on his side of the bed just so I could smell him. I put off washing the sheets for the longest time.

That was always the saddest part of both deployments. When the clutter that I had bitched about everyday was finally put away, I was face-to-face with the reality that he was gone from our home.

WAR BRIDE

The war got underway around the third month of my husband's first deployment. It was March 20, the day before my birthday. To my horror, our nation was now at war in Iraq, and my husband's platoon was in the thick of it.

Jon was unusually upbeat when he called on St. Patrick's Day. He gave me the news that he was off the ship and in Kuwait. While I was nervous, his happy spirit and positive attitude calmed me down.

By the end of the call I was feeling very loved and peaceful. Natalie and Kat told me their husbands had also called that night. I found out later the guys had made those calls to us knowing they were headed into battle.

As the war raged on TV, I knew Jon was in the midst of it. Watching the helicopters land on Iraqi soil, and hearing about the terrible things happening there was terrifying for me. This was the beginning of both of our personal hells.

This man, who was so much a part of my life, was no longer around. And I wasn't even sure he was coming back. I had a life with him—a future, a present—but we were now in limbo. He was fighting, risking his life every minute of every day, and there was nothing I could do for the man I loved. I felt helpless knowing that I could lose the love of my life at any moment. We had barely started our life together.

As the "Shock and Awe" campaign against Saddam's regime continued, I went through stages of heightened emotion and sensitivity, followed by periods of numbness.

I think I watched TV for four days straight before I snapped out of it. I knew I had to stop behaving like this. Jon would not want me sitting around dwelling on the war.

While I could not help these emotions, I could stop "feeding" them. Slowly I weaned myself from TV and left the house. I knew it was time to live again. I thought if Jon knew my peppy upbeat personality was being held hostage by the news, he would have been upset. I sucked it up, and got back to life.

TAKING A BREAK

I remember one night, in particular, that was very intense. We had planned a Bunco evening at Autumn's house.

It was just a few days into the war. When we arrived, the TV news was reporting on the fighting. We were all trying our hardest to ignore the elephant in the room when they reported a helicopter with Marines out of Camp Pendleton had crashed.

Many of the wives freaked. Natalie's husband and Jon were in Golf Company, which traveled on CH 46 helicopters.

The reporting originated from the place that Jon had been when he called. Out of the twelve women in the room, eight of their husbands were fighting in that region.

Two of the older Captains' wives—Melanie and Trina— took control of the situation. They stood up and declared, "That's it! TV off! No more for the rest of the night. We are here to have fun. We are taking a break from the war."

I will always be thankful to them for doing that. We ended up enjoying the remainder of the evening. I remember laughing and carrying on with those girls as if it was just another normal night as a Marine officer's wife.

It was good to break away from the drama for a bit—even though the war was always in the back of our minds.

When I got home, there were four frantic messages from my husband's family. Each message conveyed how worried they were about their son, nephew, and brother. With each message, the tone became angrier. You could tell they were angry that I was not home to call them back.

I was hurt because I was equally afraid and worried, but I had made the choice not to live in constant fear.

Indeed, I knew nothing more than what the news had reported. And now they were trying to make me feel guilty because I wasn't at home watching the news. It didn't mean I didn't care about my husband's safety. I just knew that other than praying there was nothing I could do to change the situation. It was also important for me to take care of my stress levels so I could remain strong for Jon.

One wife, who had walked home with me, urged me not to return their calls. But I felt I had to.

When I called Jon's parents, his sister answered the phone. I told her I had been playing Bunco with my girlfriends. I had no idea if they understood why I was off playing a game when we both knew the fighting had gotten intense.

What could I say? Jon's family asked if I knew if Jon was OK. I guess they thought that I knew more than they did and they began to bombard me with facts and fears garnered from the news.

Then one of them said, "Well, we realize you are the next of kin now, so the Red Cross calls you first. But if Jon was dead, would you have called us?"

My heart broke.

Would I have called them?

I knew they were raw with fear. Still, I was shocked by that question.

I can't know what it is like for the extended families far away from the support and familiarity of the military base. Without a support network, I can only imagine what it must be like for them.

However, I had to wonder if they had the same empathy for me. You can not assume that everyone reacts like you do or that everyone grieves or worries like you do. There is simply no room for judgment at times like these.

I think what I went through that night is a perfect example of a misunderstanding that can develop between wives and their in-laws. If my story can serve no other purpose, it is that you have to put yourself in the other person's shoes before you react or pass judgment.

Most of all, when there is a conflict within the family, remember you're all there to love and support the serviceman. If you can keep that fact in mind instead of competing over who loves him more, who is worrying more, or who is grieving the correct way, you will be able to work together.

Neither one of us was in the wrong that night. We were just handling our fears in different ways.

SETTLING IN

I felt as though I was a widow. I didn't know what to do with myself. I could not move on with my life because Jon was still my life. And yet, nothing was happening to nurture that love or relationship.

The only way I could describe my marriage and feelings at that point was that I felt like the "un-married." Like zombies in a movie were the "un-dead," I was the "un-married." I was not a widow, not single, definitely married, and yet all alone.

After that first week, I pulled a Scarlet O'Hara and declared, "I will not think about that now. I will think about it later!"

I stopped thinking about whether Jon was going to come home or not. Whenever that thought came into my head, I replaced it with something we could do together when he came home.

VOLUNTEERING

The military has many different organizations that can keep you busy. I encourage military wives, especially during a deployment, to get involved with one.

The best way to cope with your grief and loneliness is to contribute to someone else's well-being.

I got involved with the Key Volunteer network during both of my husband's deployments. I went through special certification training and had different handbooks spelling out resources to help the wives in my group. We also planned events throughout the deployment, like care package packing parties and socials.

I found my strength was putting together timelines—"to do" lists for the Marines. These lists included what a Marine needed to do to take care of his family and himself before a deployment. I have always been organized and efficient at telling people what needs to be done!

My other duties included serving as a contact person if a wife needed anything. Wives could call me to ask what to do if they lost their ID, to get their husband's paycheck straightened out, or to find out what doctors accepted Tricare.

I was also responsible for keeping track of these women when they went out of town, as well as where they lived. It was my job to pass on any info from the command.

The absolute worst part of being a KV was delivering the "all clear message." That's a call a KV gets stating that a Marine has died in combat and the family has been notified, so "all is clear." It's our job to call the women in our "phone tree" and alert them that someone has died, but it's not your spouse. It's now "all clear" since the serviceman's family has been notified.

What makes it particularly hard is that we are not allowed to say who has died. The rationalization behind these calls is that the next of kin may have seen the news that someone died and would be freaking out until the notification is made.

In the Marine Corps, notification of a death is done in person. Whenever a black Lincoln Town car would pull into a neighborhood, everyone would hold their breath.

Three people deliver the notification: a Marine in dress blues, a clergyman, and a CACO officer (Casualty Assistance Calls Officer). No one is ever notified on the phone when a service member has been killed.

And yet, the fact that I had to call a bunch of women to relay these "all clear messages" was absolutely unnerving. I hate to say this, but it seemed like I got a call every Friday night.

When you get this call, your first reaction is "Oh, thank God, it is not my spouse." Then you feel horrible because you realize that someone has lost a loved one.

I hated these calls and thought they just got everyone upset. I had many a fight with Key Volunteer Coordinators over not making these calls. I preferred to email them.

At one point those calls became so frequent that Michelle and I really got freaked out. If I left my house to run to the commissary, I would leave a note on the door that said, "Back in 30 minutes. Gone to the commissary." Or I would go next door and tell Michelle where I was going. She did the same. We lived in fear of CACOs.

Both of my KVCs had an incredible amount of patience. Kristine and Karen put their hearts and souls into caring about and being responsible for so many women.

The KV network planned many events for us. We packed care packages and videos to send overseas. My husband joked that the KVN knew more about what was going on than the Marines!

It was true most of the time. KVs knew about the extensions. (All deployments get extended. In fact, I suggest adding at least two weeks to the "coming home date.") The KVs gets their info directly from the command.

I enjoyed serving as a KV because I didn't have to listen to gossip. I had the most up-to-date information throughout the entire deployment. It was a great network as well as a wonderful opportunity to serve.

The KVN no longer exists. Its functions are now handled by the Family Readiness Officer.

DEPLOYMENT PROMISE

There is one guarantee during a deployment: the second your husband leaves, something will break.

During Jon's first deployment, the microwave quit and the smoke detector batteries died—screaming at me at 3:00 a.m. That was soooo fun, trying to remember where a ladder was and then climbing up and dismantling the sucker. (Yes, I realize I could have used the claw Jon gave me to get them down.)

All four tires on the car wore out.

Then the fridge died.

Of course, everything was smooth sailing when Jon was home. These things simply waited until he left before going haywire.

If you live on base, get cozy with maintenance. You will be seeing a lot of them.

My fridge had been out for a week when I called maintenance threatening to alert the newspaper. I told them the public would enjoy hearing that a Marine's wife was eating dry cereal three times a day while her husband fought in the global war against terrorism.

The problem was that maintenance "couldn't find the time" to move an old fridge from an empty house down the block into mine.

One simple threat, and I had a new fridge that afternoon.

We should get Hazardous pay for the crap we deal with back home!

DYI

There are plenty of horror stories about home disasters. However, the worst one I ever heard happened to Erin while she was at Camp Lejeune.

I was in the midst of our second deployment, while she was on her first. We were doing our best to help each other along.

Erin was upset that her husband had not repaired a few cracks in the bathroom shower before he left.

It was her first deployment and she was feeling restless and bored on a Friday night. Wanting to feel useful, she decided she had seen enough episodes of Trading Spaces and was confident she could make the repairs herself. She headed off to Lowe's to purchase caulking supplies and tools.

Three hours later, she called me. Since it was late on the West Coast (Erin was in North Carolina, mind you), I knew it had to be an emergency.

When I answered the phone, Erin was crying. The Southern heat combined with the complicated task of resealing the tub was compounded by her loneliness.

Erin was upset. It was her husband who should have been making the repairs, not her! As she worked, the stress built up until she broke the sealant gun. She was sitting there alone, covered in caulk. She had caulk under her nails, in her hair, on the walls.

Learn from Erin's mistake. Don't mess with strange caulk when your husband is deployed. Being covered with strange caulk is not a crisis call the Red Cross wants to get.

Better yet, if a complicated task presents itself, hire someone to make the repairs.

JJ

After hearing about Erin and other wives' home maintenance mistakes, I got smart.

I've also always been a spoiled daddy's girl, so there were some things I refused to do. Pushing a lawn mower was one of them.

Oh yes, I heard brave tales of wives who mowed three acres on a 105-degree day with colicky babies strapped to their backs. Good for you, ladies! But I am not doing that. I work smart, not hard. That philosophy has gotten me quite far in life.

Before Jon's first deployment, my Marine Corps mother, Mary, invited me to her house many times. I got to know her family quite well, including her teenaged son JJ, who was full of energy.

Mary volunteered her son's help anytime I needed it when Jon was gone. I didn't hesitate to take her up on that offer.

That first week I had that child push-mowing both yards, taking out the trash, bringing in the water, and tending to the bushes. JJ willingly did all this for five bucks an hour.

One day JJ was tending the yard. It was very warm. I was inside enjoying a sweet tea.

One of my neighbors called to ask who the man was in my backyard! I felt so secure knowing I had neighbors watching over me. I explained it was the Colonel's son and he was doing some chores for me.

Ten minutes later the phone rang again. Another inquisitive neighbor, equally concerned for my safety. Once again I calmly explained what was going on.

By the fourth call, I began to get suspicious. Did Del Mar Housing have a Neighborhood Watch program that I did not know about? Why were all these women being so protective of me?

Then Michelle called. "Mollie, how much does JJ charge?"

That's when I realized something was up. I ran to the window and looked out.

Let me preface what happened next by telling you something about JJ's personality. This young man was known for playing pranks on base. One time he changed the "Officers Club Pool" sign to "Officers Club Poo."

Anyway, I spotted JJ in my yard completely bare-chested, his rippling muscles glistening with sweat as he push-mowed *my* yard. He was putting on a show for the deployed Marine's wives!

As he tossed another article of clothing off, another set of window blinds went up and my phone rang again. And again.

This military brat had learned a thing or two in his years of being a "dependent."

Something told me he was getting something more than $5.00 an hour.

The scandal spread through the neighborhood like wildfire. I became the Del Mar Housing Desperate Housewife.

Ironically, the other wives also wanted to pay JJ to do "chores" for them! COOCOO CACHOO!

The next time I called Mary to arrange a workday for JJ, she told me that ever since that first work day he had been working out daily to build his muscles so he could do a good job. Oh, I thought, he's working hard to build up muscles, alright, but it has nothing to do with the money I was paying him!

Any given weekend during a deployment I would have a house full of teenage boys rearranging furniture, pulling weeds, or washing the car. The only problem was that they ended up eating most of my food, farting all over my couches, and riding the go-cart all over the neighborhood!

I gave them hell and yelled at them for putting their tennis shoes on my coffee table. But the truth is, they were great company and fun.

JJ was a big help to me throughout the four years we lived on base. He even helped out when I was out of commission from the medication I had to take for back pain.

Who knew two years later the TV show "Desperate Housewives" would become so popular? Still, Wisteria Lane had nothing on Del Mar Housing's lust for young men mowing yards!

Please note, I am not suggesting that young wives hang out with high school boys while their husbands are deployed. Hanging with a teenage boy spells a recipe for disaster. We all knew that, and with JJ, it was all just good clean fun.

DEALING WITH CIVILIANS

People say the darndest things. They try so hard to be supportive and offer advice. I got to the point when I was in town that I tried not to let people know I was a military spouse.

Then I would show my ID at the register or they'd see the sticker on my car and the advice would start rolling in.

"Oh, sweetheart, you're married to a Marine? Is he deployed right now? I bet you're lonely . . . you should have a baby!"

Great advice lady, but I think my husband would get pretty upset if I started without him.

I reached the point that I avoided letting anyone know I was a military wife when I was off base. I hid my ID. The military discount was just not worth it.

It always went down the same way. Someone would find out I was the spouse of a deployed serviceman. "Well, you aren't married to a Marine, are you?" (Like that's a bad thing!?)

I would reply, "Yes, ma'am, I am."

She would gush, "Oh, well, he isn't over THERE is he?" (Meaning Iraq, I guess it's a bad word and we can't actually say it.)

"Yes ma'am, he is."

"Oh, Lord! Well, he isn't FIGHTING, is he?"

"Yes, ma'am, actually he is in the infantry."

"Oh, sweetheart, are you ok?!" (She's crying now—her arms reaching out into my personal space.)

And I'm thinking, "Lady, are YOU ok?"

What I also think and don't say is, "Gee, lady, I haven't been laid in three months and you need a hug?!"

One time Kat came to see Natalie and me. She was very upset about what had just happened to her while she was getting a facial and lip wax. She was relaxing in a chair when a Vietnamese woman complimented Kat on her wedding ring. Then she started asking about Kat's husband.

"What does your husband do?"

"He's a Marine currently serving overseas," explained Kat.

The shop erupted with Vietnamese chatter and laughter.

Kat was so confused. "What's so funny?" she asked.

The lady replied, "Your husband cheat on you! My mother sleeps with Marine! My sister will sleep with your husband!"

The laughter erupted again.

Kat couldn't get out of there fast enough.

Trips off base got fewer and fewer as the war progressed. Wives began to travel in packs so we wouldn't be cornered by well-meaning civilians.

It's hard when you are going through something that difficult to also have to do it publicly. You find yourself being strong for others, which in itself is draining.

Dealing with strangers, though, helped me become more sensitive to other people's times of trauma and tragedy.

Being a military wife in the public's eye taught me to respect other people's privacy. I don't ask people, "When are you getting married?" or "When are you guys going to have kids?"

These may seem like innocent questions, but they are none of anyone's business. Having everyone in mine for a few years taught me to back off and let others share what they want when they are ready.

I also loved how complete strangers would think since I was married to a deployed Marine, I would want to know their political opinions. Why would anyone think that based on my husband's career choice I'm interested in knowing his or her thoughts on what he's doing? Would you go up to a dentist's wife and start in on your personal opinions on gingivitis or America's tooth decay crisis?

I wanted to put a bumper sticker on my car saying, "Keep your opinions to yourself!"

No military wife ever wants her husband to go off to war, no matter what the cause. But that is a commitment the family makes. We answer to the Commander-in-Chief.

So express your opinion at the polls, not to my face. And please don't think you can say anything you want as long as you preface it with, "I support our troops, but . . ."

Stop right there.

Nobody wants to hear what you think.

LETTING GO

It was several months into Jon's second deployment and I had just given up. I was nasty—hairy legs, greasy hair. Let's not even talk about the bikini line. It had taken over like kudzu—thick and out of control!

Not only that, I was about as together emotionally as I was physically. I was at that point when I wouldn't answer the phone unless I knew it was another wife on base organizing a get-together.

That's when a girlfriend from back home tried to call me. I realized if I kept avoiding calls, the rest of the world might start to worry and send me a Red Cross message, so I picked up the phone.

She was crying because her husband was leaving on a business trip.

When she started whining that she wouldn't be able to sleep alone in the house, fire began to shoot from my eyes.

Then she said she was going to take their child and go to her mother's for the weekend because she just knew she couldn't take care of the child by herself.

Smoke curled out of my nose while I bit my tongue.

I thought of Michelle with two boys managing for seven months without the help of her husband or her mother.

Really, I felt like barfing. I couldn't understand why she thought I was the best person to call for sympathy. Sure, I understood, but I was the wrong person at the wrong time. This was hard to figure out?

It took everything I had to keep from screaming at her. I couldn't stop rolling my eyes as I sat and listened to her.

I'm sure other military wives have gotten similar calls from civilian women unable to cope. These are women who could never cut it as a member of the Silent Ranks. I'm just glad they married bankers and executives and have left the real men to the real women.

I also remember the judgment I endured when family and civilians would call and be surprised I was in a terrific mood. By their standards I should not have been. They thought I should be down in the dumps because of what they were seeing on the news.

But I would not and could not watch the news, particularly because the reporter embedded with my husband's battalion was always on when I turned on the TV. I had to put a limit on my TV time to keep my sanity.

SCREEN YOUR CALLS

To all wives experiencing a deployment, may I suggest screening your calls? Or better yet, set up your answering machine to screen out unwanted conversations with civilians and family.

Consider using this recording:

> You have reached the 'BLANK' residence. If you are my in-laws wanting to know why you have not received a letter from your son, press one. If you are a member of the extended family calling to ask about something you saw on the news wondering if your son, brother, grandson, or nephew is safe, press two. If you are a friend calling to complain because your spouse is out of town on business and you knew I would understand, press three. I will return your calls in seven months. All military personnel, stay on the line. I will be with you in a moment.

If you become uncomfortable talking with friends or family, avoid answering the phone. Instead, send weekly updates via e-mail. It was my mom's idea to stop answering the phone. She was right. There were times when I was not in the mood to talk. I didn't want to appear rude, so I would e-mail them later.

Nor are you obligated to share intimate details of your emails, letters, or phone calls from your spouse with anyone. However, you can share a bit of information with family members. Often the battalion or company will provide updates from the Company Commander. You can pass these along as well to your extended family.

Just remember the rule: "Loose lips sink ships."

What I appreciated the most during those months were the cards and messages that friends and family sent letting me know they were praying for Jon and I.

Those made my day.

DATE NIGHT

There is something to be said for the tight bond that develops between military wives, especially during a deployment. These friendships become something more than the typical relationship.

In fact, many times wives become surrogate "spouses" for one another. This comes from sharing and relying so much on one another in the absence of our real spouses.

I recall only feeling comfortable talking to a handful of people because I was tired of explaining my moods or giving updates on how I was doing. But other military wives got it. Instead of your spouse, your neighbors and on-base friends become the ones you begin to share those little details with.

We could take comfort from one another. We didn't have to explain why we were having a bad day—or even a good day. It was a comforting community.

I saw Michelle and the boys almost every day. It was normal for Christa to drop by with Silas. Often, I would see wives out at the playground and just stop by and shoot the bull.

Kat, Natalie, and I got together at least twice a week. Those times were really important. It was our time to update each other on what our spouses were doing. Sometimes, one husband would tell his wife something about the other guys, which she would pass along.

On those gatherings, we would have dinner together, go out, or just sit around watching movies.

We took care of each other by checking in daily and hanging out weekly. We never cried in front of one another, but kept up a brave front. If one of us was having a bad day, it was understood if we bowed out of a visit or activity.

It wasn't until our boys were back home that we finally let our feelings out and cried together. We never burdened each other with our fears during the deployments.

I owe these ladies the world. While our husbands were fighting the war together, we kept the home front together—standing side-by-side.

In keeping with being each other's "spouses," we often planned "date nights." At least once a week we would go to someone's house to share a meal and watch a favorite show or movie.

These evenings were a great chance to get out of the house and have a good home cooked dinner. Eating alone can be so depressing.

We'd joke that "my wife cooked for me" or "my wife did the dishes."

Autumn and I enjoyed a "date night" at least once a month. We usually went for sushi, but sometimes Autumn would find a two-for-one coupon for Black Angus Steakhouse. We would gorge ourselves, then count the days till the next coupon was valid and head out and do it again.

One date night we arrived at the restaurant a couple of minutes before opening. We were waiting out front with two other families who also had coupons.

When opening time came and went, I became impatient. We were famished! I pulled out my cell phone and called.

A voice answered with some mumbled greeting that was, let's just say, less than enthusiastic. This sent me over the edge.

"Yes, I'm standing outside your location here in Oceanside. It says you open at five and it is now ten after the hour. You have several people out here wanting to dine!"

No response.

By now I'm starting to yell.

"I just want to know, do you ever plan on opening your Black *Anus*?"

Hearing my mispronunciation, these other families turn and look at me. Did I mention that some of them were African American?

Autumn started laughing, but I was felt pretty small right about then.

On the other end of the phone I heard, "No, ma'am, this is the Black ANGUS. The manager should be out there shortly."

The mispronunciation did not influence our appetites that evening. It did, however, earn me quite a few dirty looks from the staff.

SPA DAY

I lived for spa days. They were the most calming, relaxing moments I could have. After long periods of time of not being touched, those spa days became a medicinal necessity.

Not far from the base, there was an amazing casino with a full-service spa in the town of Pala. Beenie, Autumn, and I frequented it at that point in deployment when we couldn't stand it any longer.

There are a couple of ground rules at the full service spa everyone should know. Beenie and I learned them the hard way during our first spa visit in Vegas.

We did a couple's massage, which just means we were in the same room for our treatments. The massages were bliss. One of us became so relaxed that a little something snuck out, if you know what I mean.

All I'm saying is we blamed it on the massage therapist's shoe squeaking on the floor. Still, there were lingering suspicions as well as the stench.

The massage is enhanced if the locker rooms are equipped with these amazing saunas and showers. Here's the thing. It's a community locker room, so people are walking around naked.

Beenie and I were freaking out. We dashed back and forth from hot tub to showers to saunas. Each time we'd modestly cover up with our robes. Then some wide-open woman would walk out in front of us and do something over the top like bend over.

That's when we decided we'd wear swimsuits at the spa.

On one of our first all-girl spa days, Beenie was seven months pregnant and feeling really self-conscious about it.

We were undressing in the locker room, but Beenie began fretting that she didn't want Autumn or me to see her naked. I had to break the ice. I dropped my robe and started doing topless jumping jacks. My boobs were spinning in opposite directions and then smacking together, spinning and twirling. I yelled out—in time with the jumps and slaps, "You're getting sleepy . . . Very . . . sleepy." The girls started laughing.

Then just as my bosoms were starting their next rotation, one of the spa attendants came around the corner! Now it was my turn to feel uncomfortable!

But Beenie was feeling more comfortable with her body, particularly after seeing mine at its most ridiculous.

Finally we were ushered off to our massages. We planned to meet up afterward to put on our bathing suits before going to the whirlpool sauna.

The other two girls were finished before me and already had their swimsuits on, so I suggested they go on ahead.

When I finished changing, I went barreling around the corner and found them lounging on chairs.

I stopped in my tracks. "What's up?" I asked. "Why aren't you two getting your feet wet?"

As I followed their stares, I saw a completely nude woman lounging on the steps of the spa. She looked like she was posing for a Hustler magazine centerfold—except she was no model.

She was obviously European with a full bush and armpit hair. She was leaning back on one arm and had the other on her forehead wiping sweat off her brow. Her foot dangled in the pool and her vagina was staring straight at me.

I tried not to make eye contact. I had learned in high school Latin that if you looked Medusa directly in the eyes, you would turn to stone.

I was not mature enough to handle it. After getting an eye full, I turned and marched right out of there.

Forget about making eye contact with my girlfriends. None of us had the self-control for that.

When that woman left the community sauna, I swear the water was at least a foot shallower. It had been soaked up by all that hair.

I couldn't bear the thought of getting in the sauna after her. What if something from one of her orifices was lingering in the water? I know chlorine kills germs, but still, there was a lot of hair on that woman. I had to ask myself, what was she trying to cover up?

I decided to use the showers that day instead.

THE DEPLOYMENT DIET PLAN

Something snaps after you've been making meals for two and then have to cook for one. You stop putting the effort into preparing meals or even eating right.

I think this is why a lot of widows and elderly people develop such poor eating habits. Whenever I see an old man eating alone at a restaurant, I end up crying in the bathroom. Nothing is sadder.

My nutrition suffered during Jon's deployment. I have never been a fan of TV dinners, so I would create these bizarre food combos that I would eat every day for two weeks straight before moving on to something else.

Here are a few scrumptious meals I would throw together. Watch out, Rachel Ray! Arguably these combinations are better than an MRE:

Week 1-2: Mac and cheese with sliced tomatoes;
Week 2-3: Tuna fish on an everything bagel;
Week 4-5: Grilled cheese, pickle, Campbell's beef barley soup;
Week 6-7: Cottage cheese and fettuccini noodles with sauce;
Week 8-9: Fried okra, fried egg rolls, and strawberries (in season);
Week 10-11: Flank steak, cooked by itself on the George Forman;
Week 12-13: Hot dogs cut up with ketchup and mac and cheese;
Week 14-15: Tuna fish and a side of green beans with Crazy Salt.

Acceptable snack foods were a peanut butter apple, chocolate Teddy Grahams, vanilla yogurt, Kettle Corn (sweetened popcorn) and, my personal favorite, raw cookie dough straight out of the tube.

Remember, you can also depend on the Schwann's man for ice cream, or any party appetizer cravings. You can even substitute the above items for a well-balanced Schwann's meal. Call for a catalog.

BODY TROUBLE

It's during this time in the deployment cycle that you start noticing changes in your body.

Most of us get fat or skinny depending on how we deal with stress. If that is your case, you know what to do about it: either eat more, or eat less.

My problem is I tend not to eat, which makes crazy things happen to my brain when it doesn't get enough nutrition. I actually blacked out once while driving on I-5. It was at that point I understood that I needed to eat more than once a day.

For those of you seeking comfort in food, think how much you are going to hate yourself when your man emails you with the reunion date and you're up ten or twenty pounds.

Be smart. Instead of eating the entire box of cookies, stop at three. You've got to maintain discipline. In addition to not eating well, I developed some unusual body issues that threw my girlfriends for a loop. I am sharing this in the hope that I am not alone.

The first odd thing that occurred was the appearance of a single dark hair on my boob. It made me feel like a werewolf. I asked my friends if this was happening to them, or if it was normal.

Where had this odd chest hair come from? Was it because I was becoming so independent? Was I starting to produce an overabundance of testosterone?

I even began to think it was because I was no longer sexually active and my body was rejecting its femininity. After all, my legs were getting hairier.

Finally a vote was taken two months later, and the girls told me to just pluck it.

I did and it never came back. But I did later miss it!

At the time of Jon's second deployment, the war had become a political football. I thought I would be funny and grow my bush out to support President Bush.

I really was not invested in this politically. I was just being lazy and a little crass. My bush developed a mind of its own, however. It became so huge I lost everything in it—keys, hairbrushes, flip-flops.

One day when Michelle could not find Jacob, I really had to think about the last time that I had seen him. I worried that he could have gotten tangled up in there. Everything else had.

At our June Bunco night, somehow the conversation came around to my massive bush. The girls started laughing. I don't think they believed me.

I showed Natalie.

She screamed.

She thought I had been exaggerating, as usual. She told me it was an absolute fire hazard as well as completely disgusting, and ordered me to shave and trim it back.

In fact, she suggested I celebrate my independence by letting it go on Independence Day.

I said goodbye to my bush during a private ceremony on July 4.

THE SWARM

The attack by a swarm of mosquitoes was one of the most bizarre incidents of that summer.

Natalie and I had spent the day at the beach. When I got home, I hung my bathing suit on a rack on the patio. I was wearing a nightgown—one of my handmade muumuus—when I went to check on my swimsuit. As I walked up to the rack, hundreds of mosquitoes suddenly surrounded me. I screamed, swatting here and there in an effort to disperse the buzzing angry cloud of biting insects before running inside.

You know how some people are always getting bitten or attacked by bugs while other people are not? Well, I'm the one who attracts the bugs.

Later that night, I woke up in pain. I looked in the bathroom mirror and saw bites all over my face and chest. Upon further inspection, I discovered I had bites all over my body.

I counted more than sixty bites on my stomach, five on my "pee pee," four in each armpit, and too many to count on my back. I felt like something out of a freak show.

I cried as I poured myself an oatmeal bath. I became nauseated, itchy, and in pain. (Just writing about it makes me start to itch all over.) I covered myself in calamine lotion and put on mittens to keep myself from scratching.

I ended up bombing the patio as well as every room in the house. I was sure those mosquitoes were plotting a return to finish me off.

Imagine pretending you don't have mosquito bites on your pee pee while you're shopping at the commissary. You just can't pull off that type of discrete scratch and get away with it.

SEXUALLY DEPRIVED FOR YOUR FREEDOM

Instead of a yellow ribbon, can I get some kind of sign to tie around my tree that proclaims "Sexually Deprived for Your Freedom"?

What about wives who silently suffer for months, or a year at a time, while missing the physical act of love?

My neighbor Michelle suggested "self-love."

Some wives couldn't talk about it as boldly, but many did have a novel with Fabio on the cover as their choice reading material during those long months.

There was one particular group of ladies who suffered more than the rest: the "preggers." They were so horny with hormones racing, and no man was around to quench their desires.

Something had to be done to help these courageous mothers.

THE DILDO FAIRY

I heard from close friends that there is a stage in pregnancy when a woman can't get enough of their man's sweet lovin'.

And after learning this, I was shocked to find out that many women actually timed their pregnancy around deployments. Many wives wanted to be pregnant the entire time their husbands were gone so when their husbands got home they would be there for the birth.

I thought this reasoning was nuts for a variety of reasons.

First of all, I would want my man around to bring me all my cravings at all hours of the night. And what about those aches and pains? Who is going to rub your feet when your man is deployed?

And don't even get me started on the hemorrhoids. Who wants to go through that alone?

But many brave members of the silent ranks do plan to be pregnant during their husband's deployment. When he comes home, they're about ready to burst. I wanted to ask them if, when they planned this out, whether they had taken into consideration that horny trimester?

That's also the time when good little wives place a pair of panties in the window hoping for a visit from the dildo fairy.

The dildo fairy knows your husband is gone and you need help. Rather than have you sit on a pickle, the dildo fairy comes by your home one night and leaves a dildo on your front door (usually wrapped and stashed in a decorative bag. How horrible would it be to have an unwrapped dildo on your porch if you lived next door to your CO?!)

I was the Del Mar Housing dildo fairy. I spent my evenings dropping off various dildos for preggers, ringing their doorbells, and then dashing off the porch to hide and see the look on their faces when they opened the wrapping to find their new special toy.

Ok, I admit I found such joy in shopping for dildos! It was very much like shopping for a car. I would ask the sales rep, "What kind of mileage does this one get? Can it go off-road? Is it harmful to the environment? What is your service plan?"

But I never used one. I didn't want anything that could short circuit or electrocute me near my pee pee. Still, playing the dildo fairy was a hoot.

Many a "pregos" sleep through the night thanks to the dildo fairy. Word quickly spread when young children found their mother's new toy. Explanations of the device pushed the boundaries of creativity. Who would have thought that a toothbrush holder or doorstop would be so elaborate, or have such an odd shape!

In addition to serving as the dildo fairy, I discovered I had many of the qualities of being a good old-fashioned homemaker, including the ability to sew.

One night while I was making pillows I thought about using Velcro or a zipper to add a pouch to the pillow. That's when the potential hit me. "How nice to have a little discreet pillow on the bed for KY, condoms, feathers, and dildos! What JOY!"

So I began making dildo pillows. Why I am not a millionaire right now after making so many dildo pillows, I don't know. I guess the bedroom drawer is hard to beat.

Or maybe it's all in the Internet marketing.

SHOWER HEADS

I had heard there were other ways that military wives quench their sexual frustration. From QVC, a girlfriend purchased a unique showerhead that took care of her frustration.

Every time I called she had just taken a shower—sometimes three a day! Other times she would cut our conversations short, telling me she just had to take a shower—now!

The poor girl was walking around looking like a prune all day. At least she was a relaxed one.

SEX TOY PARTIES

Then there's the inevitable sex toy party, thrown just before the boys come home. All the ladies get excited and wild with anticipation for this risqué party, especially when they know regular sex is just over the horizon.

A wild wife usually throws these parties, which is good. That means what you purchase is safe with her. She is hosting the party so she can get free merchandise or a discount on her own purchases.

My girlfriends and I went to one of these parties and found it to be as outrageous as we had imagined. While Beenie and I were expecting it to be kinky and sassy, we ended up sitting in the corner like two prudes.

What I did not expect was the nut job freak show salesperson. Why are the most disgusting people—the ones you never want to imagine having sex with anyone, anywhere—the ones selling these products? They make the evening even more uncomfortable because sex is all they want to talk about.

Inevitably, the saleswoman began passing around these dildos and describing her experiences with each one. I was trying to avoid throwing up. Then it took a turn for the worse. The scene was no longer cute or funny as images of this obese woman unraveled before us.

Obviously in need of dental work, poorly dressed, and more than a little skanky, she painted a vivid picture of sex with her lover using the very device you were . . . holding in your hand! I dropped a purple dildo as fast as my hand could open! I must have let out a small shriek.

She laughed. "Don't worry, I wash all my toys and samples in the dishwasher."

Oh, how comforting! "Remind me not to eat at her house," I mumbled to Beenie under my breath.

I sank deeper into the couch as the rest of the girls laughed while touching and fondling this woman's collection of fake genitals. Things started to get very raunchy very fast. I felt like I was participating in something dirty.

"Oh no. Is Jesus mad at me right now?" I wondered. "I'm married, but for some reason I feel so dirty, like I'm sinning!"

It was all too much—the penis pencils, sex oils, giant dildos, the edible panties. I couldn't bring myself to buy anything.

When the party finally ended, and while others continued talking and laughing about their new toys, I applied layer after layer of hand sanitizer in an effort to help wipe the ickiness away and feel clean again.

I just prayed to God that after seven months it would be like riding a bike and that I would just pick it back up again. After the sex party, I was afraid I wouldn't be able to do it again.

THE HUSTLER STORE

My neighbor Michelle and I had many things in common, particularly our taste for a certain type of fashion. Without planning it, we would purchase the same lingerie at Wal-Mart (yes, the California Wal-Mart sells lingerie) and have a good laugh over it.

Our quiet Catholic husbands had a tough time with this. They didn't like our discussions of such scandalous topics as lingerie while standing in our respective bedroom windows.

Toward the end of the second deployment, Michelle and I decided we needed to put a little enthusiasm back into our lives. That's when we decided to visit the San Diego Hustler store.

God forbid we shop for oils, candles, feathers, panties, and such around base. We had reputations to uphold.

Well, the truth was Michelle was bored with the selection at the tiny porn store by the base. We wanted to find out for ourselves what was so great about Mr. Flynt's store.

We left Michelle's kids with a neighbor, telling her we were going shopping for reunion outfits. We had to tell a white lie. Who would watch children for free for a pair of horny wives who were headed to a porn store in San Diego?

For those of you ladies who have never been to one of these stores, know that your modesty will remain intact (slightly) if you stay downstairs. The downstairs is harmless enough—lingerie, soap, candles, and lotions.

Upstairs is the danger zone. And, of course, that's where Michelle had to go to find the special lube lotion she just had to have.

I became more and more nervous with each step. I began to sweat. I refused to lift my eyes off the ground for fear I would see something that I didn't want to see. Of course, the first thing I saw was a six-foot black penis pillow. Why would anyone want to take a nap on that?!

When we got to the second floor, I was mortified. Ten years of private Christian education had not prepared me for this. I was surrounded by things I had never imagined.

Questions whirled in my mind. Why would someone need a rubber fist? Or a giant head with an open mouth?

I decided it would be safe to check out the jewelry. I saw lovely pearl necklaces. Well, I thought they were necklaces until I read their purpose. Let's put it this way, I have heard of a pearl shooting out of a clam, but not a bearded clam. My husband may have been seeing some bizarre things in Singapore, but this took the cake!

My obvious embarrassment made Michelle laugh and taunt me with a fake rubber anus.

For once in my life I could not even make a joke. My eyes were taking everything in. My mind was trying to process things it could not begin to comprehend.

It was then that I found myself in the gay porn section. Before me was a picture entitled "Leap Frog." Something was wrong. I squinted and looked more closely. It didn't depict the way I played the game as a child. The name described the position of the men engaged in the little game.

I was backing away in disgust when I heard Michelle gasp. I knew something was amiss because there wasn't much that could shock Michelle. And, yet, there it was. On the giant big screen TV, in high definition, was a huge gyrating anus! We knew it was time to go!

We dashed down the steps to the first floor. I looked around and realized there were no other customers in the store. But the employees were running around frantically talking into their headsets.

We ran to the front door and discovered it was LOCKED!

That's when an employee approached us. "Oh, I am sorry we didn't realize you were still in the store. You will have to wait back here. We are expecting Mr. Flynt any second."

Just outside the front windows we saw a mob of men standing behind ropes waiting to get in. Behind them were TV camera crews from every network imaginable.

Our hearts collectively jumped up into our throats. Our dirty little secret, our husband's careers—everything—would be exposed simply because we wanted a little lube and a feather tickler.

We were frantic to get out of there, but couldn't risk appearing on TV. We pleaded with the 19-year-old female clerk to let us out.

"Please, you don't understand. We need to leave, now!"

The clerk stared at us as if we were from Mars. "What? You could have your picture taken sitting on Mr. Flynt's lap!"

"He ain't Santa, lady!" I yelled back.

She finally agreed to unlock the door when Michelle started crying.

As we walked out, trying to hide our faces, Michelle turned to me and whispered, "Oh no! We have to go past the entire crowd to get to the car!"

Of course, the car with its Camp Pendleton officer sticker on the windshield and bumper sticker majestically proclaiming its passenger as a Marine wife was parked right in front of the store.

Michelle was weighed down with purchases packed in large bags proclaiming "Hustler" in bright red lettering.

"We'll never make it," I thought.

I turned to her and said, "Your hands are too full. Give me the keys."

When the door opened, I dashed out past the TV cameras and perverts. Flashes went off all around us as reporters desperate to catch the frenzy that had exploded out of the store did their best to capture us on film.

I heard Michelle muttering, "Please God, don't leave me. I'm a mother! My children can never know!"

I leaped behind the wheel, cranked the engine, and squealed out of the parking spot. Within seconds I pulled up next to Michelle, who was standing helplessly on the curb holding a Hustler bag over her head.

Just then a news crews surrounded her and began taking photos. I rolled down the passenger window and yelled, "I'm here! Get in!" She jumped into the car and we sped off in our effort to escape Sodom and Gomorrah. But we never looked back.

We watched the 11:00 p.m. news expecting a report on Larry Flynt's visit to San Diego. We were sure they would report that two Marine wives had tried to run the billionaire over. We could see our sketches being shown while the reporter announced, "Not much is known about these women, or why they wanted to harm Mr. Flynt. They are described as blonde Marine wives, who enjoy strawberry coconut sex lubes and tickle feathers."

Our prayers must have been successful: none of the stations reported a thing.

WHO ARE YOU SLEEPING WITH?

Trying to sleep when your husband is gone is a joke.

My looks started to fade because I was not eating well, getting laid, or getting enough sleep.

Night was the worst time for me. That's when I felt the most loneliness. I dreaded going to sleep. I hated being in that bed alone.

My thoughts would start racing. I tried reading. I tried writing. Nothing worked.

I would lie in bed for about two hours, get up, and start organizing the house. I would climb in all the cabinets, throw things away, trash the place, and make a ton of ruckus.

I became a mad woman.

Sometimes Michelle could hear me. When she did, she'd call to see if I was OK.

There I'd be at 2:00 a.m., going through closets, digging under the beds, organizing photos. Sometimes I would just walk over to Michelle's house— but I would always take my phone in case Jon called.

I got into a routine of renting movies and sewing at night. I made purses or pajamas. I wasn't very good, but it was a project I could easily finish. Plus, it exhausted me, which was exactly what I was looking for.

A lot of wives started scrap-booking or finding any type of busy work to distract them from their loneliness and stress.

Eventually, though, I would have to crawl into bed alone. There I'd be, staring at Jon's pillow that no longer smelled like him. I'd reach out, close my eyes, and say, "One day I will reach out again, and he will be there."

I think the hardest part of those months alone was waking up in the middle of the night, reaching over for Jon, and discovering all over again that he was not there.

One night I started watching Joel Osteen on late night TV. What a lifesaver!

His sermons gave me hope, and helped change my perspective on so many things. Every time he preached I found myself thinking, "This guy is talking to me!" I started to look forward to Sunday nights because I felt such peace after one of his sermons.

If you have a strong church community, go every week. You need that support. If not, worship with devotionals, praise music, or watch Joel

Osteen, Dr. Ed Young, Joyce Meyer, or whomever you feel speaks to your faith.

Some moms would let their kids sleep with them, but I don't think it's a good habit to start. Most of the moms who let their kids sleep with them found themselves facing a nightmare when Daddy came home. By that time, the kids were not willing to return to their own rooms, while Daddy is eager to get back his spot in the marital bed.

In fact, it is even more important for kids to have a routine when Dad is away. Let it be a special occasion for the kids to sleep in your bed, not a habit.

Since I was lonely and had no children to cuddle, I tried to get the cats in bed with me. Cats have their own agendas. They prefer to come and go as they please.

If I put the dogs in the bed with me, they were sure to get into trouble when Jon came home. Most of the time, I just slept alone. I tried to keep my routine as normal as possible so when Jon came home we would fall back into our normal lives as seamlessly as possible.

One night I heard a horrible noise coming from the office (the bedroom next to mine). It sounded like someone trying to open the window.

So much adrenaline started pumping through me that I thought I was having a heart attack.

I was trapped in my bedroom, which was at the far end of the house. I was afraid to go down the hall. I was sure whoever was breaking in was also planning to kill me.

If only the damn dogs were in bed with me! Even though they were tiny they should have heard the noise and started barking! Where were they? As I stood in my bedroom door, my vision blurred, and I began to cry. All this time I had worried about Jon being killed, when the reality was *I* was the one who was going to die.

By the time the noise stopped, I was shaking violently from head to toe. I prayed to God to give me strength. Was someone in the house?

I waited for ten full minutes before moving.

When I didn't hear any other noises, I tried to convince myself that the intruder had heard me and left.

I took a deep breath, walked softly down the hall, and entered the office. Nothing was out of place.

What I did notice was the wind blowing the blinds back and forth, making a lot of noise in the process. I watched the window for a few minutes and saw the blinds scrape the sill. They were the cause of the noise. It was simply the wind moving the blinds.

I had gotten myself all worked up over the wind. Still, I had never been so frightened in all my life.

I laugh now when I think of this, but it's also really sad. It shows the degree of exhaustion a military wife can feel when she is alone while her husband is deployed in a war zone.

Let's just say this: the dogs were in bed with me for the next week. Screw bad habits! I needed to sleep.

ON BASE PREDATORS

There is a type of sneaky predator lurking around the base who looks completely harmless.

And you can't put your trust in the MPs. They're the ones who allow this predator on base. He's one type they just wave right in.

He arrives early in the deployment. You've not showered in two days. Your roots have grown out three inches. You've permanently stopped shaving (even your chin), and you lost your toothbrush three weeks ago. You're at the point in the deployment when your hygiene routine is on hiatus. Since you have no one to look nice for, you've given up.

This predator knows when you've reached this point of deprivation. Your pockets are now bulging with combat and separation pay that is begging to be spent. Worst of all, no man has paid attention to you in a long time. You're totally defenseless.

It's late in the afternoon and you're still in your PJs and house robe.

That's when you hear someone pulling up in your driveway. You look through the keyhole and see him. Your knees go weak. You know you won't be able to resist.

He approaches the door, rings the bell, and says, "Ma'am, I know you're inside. It's just me, the MEAT MAN!"

So now there's a man in your driveway tempting you with his MEAT! Some company has sent out this hot guy in a truck with a cooler full of meat for sale. On a base. With women who have been alone for a long time.

He begins to tease you by saying things like, "Just step outside and I'll show you a sample. You look like the kind of woman who can handle a lean cut of meat."

It has been wayyyyy too long since you've heard seductive talk like that!

The next thing you know, you're out in the driveway looking at this stranger's meat! It's in your hands. He suggests ways to treat it and baste it.

You're sweating. You can't remember the last time you held meat in your hands.

Before you know it, the meat man is telling you it will only be $2.99 a pound.

That's when you finally regain your composure, stand tall, and counter, "No, sir! I will not pay more than $2.49 a pound!"

The Meat Man at Camp Pendleton caused untold problems for the wives. Before we knew it, our freezers were bursting with strip steaks, ground chuck, and flank steak.

The Meat Man company knew exactly what it was doing, too. It sent in a sexy Aussie to seduce us with his Australian accent. BLIMEY!

I have to admit I bought enough meat that I turned it into my diet plan. Beenie bought half a cow.

Ladies, keep up your guard. Your husbands will not be pleased to hear you paid a couple hundred dollars for meat while he was deployed. Stand tall and don't answer the door! The Red Cross does not want to get a call reporting that you have exceeded your budget by buying meat from a man on the side of the road.

TEMPTATION

"Mollie, with a sexy Aussie meat man at your front door and a body building teen tending your back yard, weren't you ever at least tempted?"

OK, ladies, it's time for me to get real honest.

There was one man I won't forget. It is well known I am a sucker for a man in uniform, and this one had all the right moves.

The fighting in Fallujah had gotten really bad, which had me stressed. We met when I went out shopping in an attempt to distract myself. I admit I'd gotten really lonely. I couldn't remember the last time I had a conversation with a man. I was lost, and he was pointing me in the right direction.

That's when the small talk started, which quickly turned into a conversation. I was so flattered!

He found out where my husband was and what he was doing and said he could relate really well because of his own dangerous job.

All I can say is don't underestimate mall security. They really take charge and can handle their weapons. I love the way they hassle loitering teens. It's so masculine.

I'll never forget Marv. Well, at least that was the name on his belt buckle.

I can close my eyes and see his beautiful strawberry blond hair in a comb over, his rich auburn "molest-ache" tickling his upper lip. I will always think of how for just one afternoon, Marv made me feel wanted again.

Honestly, there's not much you can do during a deployment to grow and nurture your marriage. Let's face it, there's not much opportunity to communicate.

I called deployments, "Riding on my vows"—like a plane on autopilot.

My husband tried to do what he could. He sent flowers on all the major holidays he was gone. He hid cards all over the house, then called or emailed me to go look in secret spots to find them. He emailed or called whenever he could. It was so romantic. But he was still not here.

I received numerous letters during his first deployment, but none during his second. He just couldn't write me; it was too difficult. His mind was on something else: staying alive and keeping others alive. He was not thinking of the different ways to romance me.

This is going to sound harsh, but our guys don't need to hear you whining about it. A few times I caught myself whining, but quickly stopped because I knew I was causing a distraction.

If your husband is worried about you, or thinking you are mad at him, how is he going to completely focus on being a Marine? He can't, because no man wants his lady mad at him. You just need to be smart. Think twice before pouting or sending a whiney email or letter.

Trust your marriage vows and rely on them. I know it gets lonely, but stay around the other wives who are going through the same thing and you'll be OK.

My best advice? Never, and I mean NEVER, talk about your marriage with another man. I mean it. Not a co-worker, not a neighbor, NO ONE!

You may need to let off steam, but it's best to go to the other wives, your chaplain, or your therapist.

Men LOVE to make it all better for lonely military wives. Even if you do not have feelings for that man, he will develop feelings for you. I saw it happen over and over.

Overloaded with all the women on base? Call your brother, your dad, or a male cousin. Get a male massage therapist on your next visit to the spa (but don't talk to him!).

Do not participate in school activities, charity activities, or neighborhood activities with a man—married or not—while your husband is deployed. You'll find yourself starting to rely on him for things. Without knowing it, you will start to look to him for comfort.

The Marv story is embarrassing enough. Don't get yourself into trouble.

GETTIN' BUSY

How can you stay busy during deployments without getting into trouble? You have to get creative.

Avoid embarrassing yourself. Don't go out drinking every night. It's fun every now and again to go out with the girls for dinner, but drunken behavior in public can attract trouble. I made a rule I would never drink off base or without one of the wives beside me.

Small rules like this provide comfort to your husband, too. If you establish promises like this before he deploys, you can avoid a lot of fights and insecurities.

Use this time during deployment to learn something new.

Christa had her own company teaching ladies how to scrapbook and make homemade cards. I was very impressed with her creativity as well as her business sense. This was also a great outlet for neighborhood ladies to get together and socialize.

Natalie took up softball and played once a week. She was competitive and was getting lots of physical activity. Since she did this off base, she got to socialize with another group of friends.

Over a period of two years, I watched Autumn learn how to surf and run marathons!

I returned to stand-up comedy. I met an amazing comedy producer, Bill Word, in Orange County, who let me come to his club. He professionally coached me on how to perfect my routine, and made sure I was never harassed or bothered by the male comedians or audience members.

I performed three or four times a week between Orange County and San Diego. It made it easier to get through the nights. I was writing again, and performing! And, it was a positive outlet: all laughs.

One of my lifelong dreams was to be a stand-up comedian—and now I was doing it! Not only was Jon proud of me, but I was also proud of myself! I took the time during Jon's deployment to achieve that dream.

So ask yourself, what do I want to learn while my husband is gone? Take a cooking or tap-dancing class. Maybe even go back to school. Keep busy so you don't get bored and get into trouble.

I noticed that the wives who did not have hobbies drank a lot and sank into various stages of depression.

Even if you have kids, you can still have a hobby. It's possible to find an activity, like bike-riding, that the kids can enjoy with you.

Deployments can be a time of personal growth. You know what they say about idle hands.

Keep busy.

GETTING LEI-ED DURING DEPLOYMENT

Out of desperation, we managed to find a way we could get lei-ed. We threw a luau to celebrate Lauren's and Natalie's birthdays.

We got everything Hawaiian, including Hawaiian dresses, decorations, food, and drinks!

We got a kick out of planning and shopping for the party. It kept our spirits up for two weeks straight!

Often we get caught up talking about how many holidays and celebrations our spouses miss every year. It sucks, sure, but who wants to spend another holiday pouting about it?

Find a way to make the holidays special instead of sitting around bitching because your man's not there to share it. Make the celebration into a girls'-only event.

Our Hawaiian birthday luau was fantastic. And the guys got a kick out of the pictures we sent of us "lei-ing" each other.

MADE UP

As the fighting increased in Iraq, we found it difficult to go into town and deal with civilians. We preferred the comfort of our surroundings, so we found things to keep us busy on base.

We played Bunco once a month, and hosted Mary Kay parties. Those were always a BLAST! Who doesn't like to be made to look beautiful? It felt so good to have someone do your make-up, especially since wearing make-up and looking good rarely happens when your husband is gone.

Since we would be covered in make-up with nowhere to go, we'd sit on my back patio and entertain one another. I remember when someone asked me to get out my astrology book, and we read aloud our astrological destinies. Someone would get pissed whenever we agreed with the book's description of someone's personality. We all laughed and carried on.

When it was my turn and all my horrible qualities were revealed, I exclaimed, "See ladies, I can't help it! My quirks and faults are written in the stars!"

Then we would get out the cameras and take glamour shots to send to the boys. Our husbands really appreciated getting pictures of us when we resembled females, and knowing and seeing that we were on base, safe, and making the best of a difficult time.

ALL SKATE

My birthday during Jon's first deployment sucked. I received calls from family members and friends trying to wish me a happy birthday, but the calls eventually turned to the latest news about the war.

What a great gift! I got about fifteen of those calls in one day.

On the other hand, the girls on base were great. Natalie and Autumn brought over a cake. A few hung out at my house. Still, we were a mess. The war was raging and as much as we tried we could not celebrate my birthday. We were young, newly married, and scared to death.

By the second deployment one year later, though, we knew that life and celebrations must go on.

Natalie conspired with Beenie and Autumn and the next thing I knew we were having a 1980s-themed roller skating birthday party! We were all wearing 80s-style clothes with side ponytails and wristbands. Imagine twenty women with their kids, all dressed in 1980s fashion. It was wild!

When the party started, I received the best gift ever. Michelle had each of her boys come over and give me a birthday kiss. She was taking pictures, but I was not really paying attention.

Suddenly, three-year-old David was Frenching me! I drew back in surprise and said, "Dave, you kissed me with your tongue!"

He started laughing and grabbed my boob.

Michelle is really going to have her hands full in about ten years. It was the only action I had gotten in three months, so I wasn't complaining.

All of us laced up and hit the rink. We did the Hokey Pokey, the Chicken Dance, and, of course, couples skate. Autumn and I became a "couple" that day.

We were having a wonderful time when I met the boy of my dreams.

Autumn was trying to teach me to skate backwards. She and Michelle had it down, but I couldn't do it at all.

And here comes Jacob, flying around the corner at 100 miles an hour. Remember this child is five years old and looked like an Olympic skater after three minutes on the floor. Jacob is yelling, "Look at me, Miss Mollie!" The wind off his body blasted me backwards and I fell on my butt.

That's when my dreamboat arrived—my pre-teen roller-skating lover. A whistle blew and I looked up to see his extended hand.

He was about six feet tall, weighed all of eight-seven pounds, and was one hundred percent bird-chested. He looked kind of like the rapper Eminem, complete with the bleached blond hair.

He was also about fifteen, with braces. The sleeves and sides of his shirt were cut out. With most of his shirt missing, his glistening pecs, complete with a nice patch of peach fuzz, were fully visible.

He lifted me up back to my feet. I thanked him, giggled, and skated off. That opened the door. Then he found out it was my birthday. One of my so-called girlfriends compounded the situation by telling him I was . . . fifteen.

When he heard this, he exclaimed, "I just turned fifteen, too!" Then it was on. He followed me around for the rest of the day. When I went to get a drink, he jumped over the counter and prepped it himself.

At one point he asked me to couples skate and I did—for about five seconds. Then I started giggling so hard I couldn't continue and skated off!

I looked up and saw my friends practically peeing in their pants as they laughed at me. How could I resist?

Finally, though, I decided I had to get out of there before he asked me to "go with him." I couldn't break his heart. "Gee, I'd love to," I could tell him, but "not only would I get arrested, but I'm married!"

He can be seen in the background of every one of the photos taken that day.

When the guys came home six months later they decided they wanted to give skating a whirl. I swear to you that when I walked in the door of the rink, the first person I spotted was my "boyfriend." Natalie cracked up laughing. My husband thought we made the whole thing up!

That's when we heard my "boyfriend" exclaim loudly to his friend, "She came back!" Natalie couldn't contain her laughter. It was at that point that Jon realized we had not been lying after all.

I had to break my young lover's heart that night by skating the whole night with Jon. My fifteen-year-old heartthrob stood on the sidelines wondering why I was skating with my "dad."

BIRTH PARTNER

Three months after Beenie found out she was pregnant with Grace, Lloyd found out he would be deploying to Iraq. She was nervous, so I volunteered to be the baby's official Fairy Godmother and Beenie's birth coach. I promised to be with her every step of the way.

We started a birthing class to prepare for the many stages of pregnancy, as well as the birth process and the days after the baby comes home.

Beenie lived about forty-five minutes away from the base in a non-military town. I drove up once a week to attend the class at the hospital where she would give birth.

On the first day of class we arrived feeling nervous and frazzled. We went to the bathroom before the class started. For some reason I ended up in the handicap stall with Beenie. I think she needed help fastening her outfit or something. We started hamming it up and giggling.

I yelled out, "Beenie, quit trying to show me your boobs. Not here! Wait till we get home."

I was being my typical self—saying something outrageous just to make her laugh.

When we came out of the stall, there was a line of pregnant women waiting to use the toilet. This was only a slightly uncomfortable moment for us. Once we got to the classroom and settled in, some of the ladies from the restroom waddled into the room.

I'll admit I was a touch embarrassed. As the class filled up, we realized we were the only girl-girl couple. There were plenty of stares and quick glances.

At this point I was at an in-between phase with my hair. It had been a cute-looking shag, but was now growing out. I didn't style it that day, which meant it looked like a fierce mullet.

Every set of eyes were evaluating Beenie and me. The women who had heard us in the restroom while we were goofing around were carrying on a whispering campaign.

What were they talking about? Why were they glancing at us?

I felt their eyes burning into us. All the mommies and daddies were sitting there holding hands. By this time Beenie and I were trying a little too hard to act like we were not a couple.

The teacher arrived and I start sweating. Beenie is thinking what I'm thinking: "They all think we're gay." The teacher greets us and does the introductions.

Beenie and I were starting to relax while the teacher broke down her syllabus and took a few questions from first-time parents in the room.

I figured I was being a freak: everyone was just as anxious as we were, right?

"Let's go around the room and the mommies can introduce themselves," said the teacher. She looked right at me and added "and their partners."

Oh my God. She didn't say "daddies." She said "partners."

She was attempting to be PC and sensitive to our particular circumstance. Everyone looked directly at us. We knew what they were thinking: "Look at the gays. Aren't they cute? Look, the little one's the man. That's odd."

I had to let them know what was really going on. When it came to our turn, Beenie went first. She stated her name, how far along she was, and then added, "And this is my partner, Mollie."

I interrupted like a frazzled teen busted for drinking on prom night. "I'm her partner! I'm NOT her 'life partner'! I mean, we aren't gay or anything. Not that there is anything wrong with being gay. I mean I majored in theater in school. I know a lot of gays. I am just saying that we have husbands."

The couples were staring at me. I continued: "They're both in the military right now. They're both deployed, so I'm helping her have this baby. I mean, she really has a man and he got her pregnant. I didn't get a turkey baster or anything. Not that there's anything wrong with that. It's just we . . . her and I . . . are not gay. AT ALL. We love our husbands. They're Marines. . . . They're at war right now."

Dead silence.

A cricket chirped. Jaws dropped. They kept staring at my dumb ass.

I don't think I was very convincing, but I had certainly been emphatic. Beenie burst out, laughing her ass off at my expense.

At that point I decided, "Who the hell cares?" Some people dislike the military just like some people dislike gays, so you can never win, especially in California.

Beenie's laughter broke the ice. After that, many of the couples started asking questions about our spouses and were really sweet. I think they felt bad for Beenie, who was having her first baby alone, and for me, for being a complete idiot.

The class met once a week. Beenie and I learned a lot about childbirth and our friendship. The experience brought us closer together.

One night the teacher encouraged us to sit on mats on the floor. Mommies were supposed to sit in between the legs of their men, who would hug them around the back.

I was really uncomfortable doing this, but not because I had to straddle my best friend. I am only five feet tall with a 27-inch in-seam. The physical act was hard for both of us.

But not because Beenie was not a big pregnant woman, but because she's at least eight inches taller than me. My legs barely made it around her waist.

We kept tipping backwards and ended up rolling around on the ground. If she tipped backwards, I got trapped beneath her. Besides that, she couldn't get up and I could not push her off me. Some of the daddies in the class had to help us. We did a lot of laughing in the class.

I did get good at massaging her hands, arms, and lower back, but I just couldn't hold her up.

The class was an intense time for Beenie and me as we prepared for Baby Grace's arrival. I knew I could not take the place of her daddy, but I wanted to do whatever I could to make the situation as comfortable as possible for Beenie. I wanted to help soothe her fears and help her get through the newness of it all.

It was frightening enough to sit at home while our husbands were fighting a war, but it was an extreme challenge to be pregnant with your first child during this time. I could only imagine the anxiety Beenie was experiencing.

Looking back, we joke that Grace was my first baby, too. I really do feel a special bond with this little girl.

CELEBRATING FERTILITY

Beenie was ready for a baby shower and I wanted to give her one she would never forget. I knew it was hard enough to have your first baby far away from family, but she was going through it without her husband.

I determined to make it a fun, all-girl event. We weren't going to have a typical baby shower. It was going to be a celebration of fertility! In fact, it turned into a bachelorette-style party. I bought a fake mustache and cowboy hat and played her husband for the day, which made Lloyd jealous. What a nut!

We didn't plan any of these boring typical shower games, like measure the baby bump. NO, my shower games were R-rated and much more fun!

The first game required that we each write down the myths we had heard on how not to get pregnant. Then I collected them up and read them out loud. Was it a surprise that the wife with the most kids thought doing jumping jacks after sex would prevent pregnancy?

Then we wrote down ways to get pregnant, or how to insure the sex of your child. These answers were even funnier. You would not believe the bizarre positions some wives got themselves into just to secure a "junior."

My favorite game was the one that required the wives to write down the wildest place they had made whoopee with their spouse.

One wife piped up and said, "Does it have to be with your husband? I have a real good one!"

After all the ladies had written down their escapades, I read them out loud and we had to guess who had done what and where. I had never heard such stories. I thought I was creative, but clearly I had a few things to learn. I won't reveal who did what, but here are some of the best answers:

— a park bench in Charleston

— a dressing room at the Bon Marché

— a tanning bed (while it was on! Imagine those tan lines . . .)

— a roof top during a party, in the winter!

You knew Marines were wild, but now you know it takes two to tango.

BABY GRACE

Grace is now and always has been my special girl. Since I had been screaming at her through Beenie's stomach from the time she was the size of a peanut, we had gotten to know each other pretty well. I credit her great sense of humor to all the laughing her mom and I did during the pregnancy.

I was there for the labor and delivery and had the great honor of being one of the first people to see this darling girl enter the world.

She was a blessing from the moment she arrived. I enjoyed holding her and changing her diapers, being with her and Beenie in the hospital those first days, and then seeing her at home.

I had my guestroom fixed up for Grace, and even bought a high chair and crib for her to use when she and Beenie came for weekend visits.

Everyone in the neighborhood had such a great time visiting with Baby Grace. I was especially happy to have the sweet little girl in my home.

Some mornings I would hear Grace waking up and I would go in and sit in the bed with Beenie while she fed Grace. Sometimes the three of us would fall asleep together. She helped us get through a tumultuous time.

UGLY BABY

There was a surge of births around the beginning of the war. In fact, I can think of at least five other births in addition to little Grace.

I had planned to make the long drive to visit Beenie and Grace, but when I arrived, there was another mother with her newborn girl visiting. I know I am biased, but Grace was a precious, beautiful baby. She had this head of dark hair—more than my pitiful mullet had at that time.

This other woman's baby wasn't so lucky. How do I say it?

She had an ugly baby.

Bald, cross-eyed, white pasty skin—a face you couldn't say was "cute as a button."

The problem started when we sat around enjoying lemonade. The moms started doing what mothers do. They were watching and commenting on the antics of their children. "Oh look at her. Isn't she so cute? Isn't she petite? She is so darling and feminine. She is so beautiful."

The two went back and forth like a ping pong match.

Lies, all lies! I was trying so hard to keep my mouth shut.

The comments kept coming, faster and faster. Then they stopped and looked at me like, "Why aren't you saying anything?"

I couldn't say a word. My mother taught me if you can't say anything nice you don't say anything at all. Although I had never listened to her, I felt that in the presence of this defenseless child I just had to follow mom's orders.

I panicked, stood up, and announced, "I have to go."

It was an uncomfortable moment. I had been there less than thirty minutes and had driven an hour to get there!

When Beenie walked me to the door, I told her, "I just can't take it. The baby is so ugly. I have nothing to say. I just can't be a part of that." And then I left.

Many of you may not be impressed with me right now. If only I could include a photo of this child, then you could understand. But I can't because my mother would be ashamed of me. Besides, I'd hurt that child's feelings as well as upset her mother.

I will report that I have seen recent photos of the child. She has overcome her initial awkwardness and appears quite normal.

As I look back, I realize that my reaction to this little girl was really about the ugliness in myself. In my defense I will say this: deployment does crazy things to your toleration level. Even the simplest things can send you over the edge.

That was one day when I just could not deal.

GET ME OUT OF HERE!

You can get a little cage crazy during a deployment, especially if you live on base. I strongly recommend taking at least one trip.

But it will be bittersweet. You'll be relieved to get away from the drama. Then you'll be on vacation, far from base, and find yourself thinking, "I miss my security blanket."

Trust me, ladies, this vacation is vital. Just go!

Make sure you plan where you are going and consider whether it will be comfortable for you. In fact, plan to visit with family or friends who will be sensitive to your situation and your moods.

You might even consider visiting another military wife at another base. Or better yet, take a road trip with another military wife to somewhere fun! At least you'll have someone with you who understands you. Best of all, you'll be in a different environment.

During Jon's first deployment, my stress level was on high alert. We had been married for one year and I was far away from my family.

The war had broken out. I was a birthing coach for my best friend who was about eight months "prego." My other best friend, Erin, was marrying her Marine and I was flying east to be in their wedding.

I was afraid to leave the base. What if something happened to Jon? What if a terrorist attacked the base while I was gone? (Remember WMDs were an issue then.) What if the baby (Grace) arrived early? So many worries plagued me.

But I knew I had to surrender my worries to God in order to stop the insanity.

In the end, it was one of the greatest and most amazing trips I had ever taken. This vacation was needed and well-deserved. Erin, her family, and in-laws made me feel so comfortable.

And yet, I still got scared. A few times I had to excuse myself so I could cry in private.

Still, we laughed, shopped, celebrated her wedding, and had so much fun together. It was the perfect distraction at a time when I needed it the most.

I am so glad that even with the war raging I had the guts to go. Jon took comfort in knowing I was with good people who loved me and were taking care of me during a stressful time.

After the wedding I went on to Columbia, South Carolina, to see my girlfriend Holly, who was in medical school, and her fiancé Geno. I had known them for more than six years. It was extremely hot in the South during my visit.

Someone got the bright idea to buy fireworks from one of those reputable stands on the side of the road. We thought it would be good entertainment when it cooled off that night. We bought tanks, snakes, cherry bombs, and bottle rockets.

We were just a bunch of regular Southern good ole boys planning a night of drinkin' and setting off fireworks in a parking lot.

Keep in mind that Holly's fiancé was in his late 30s, and that she was studying to become a doctor. And there I was, married to the Marine officer. You would think that collectively we had some sense, right? After all, there is not much to do at night in the South.

Around 9:30 p.m. we cut through some trees behind their apartment complex and headed for an abandoned lot where truckers park their rigs. We started by setting off a few sparklers and tiny ground fireworks.

A short time later a couple of big fireworks went off in the distance, followed by sirens a few minutes later. We figured someone had just gotten busted for setting off illegal fireworks. The police were out in full force that night, so we knew we had to be on high alert.

We set off a big one. It was a beauty! The rocket was huge and exploded with bright colors high in the night sky.

When we heard sirens again, we put our heads together to guess which direction the sirens were coming from, and whether we had time to set off one more. We decided to go for it.

Holly and I stood about fifty feet away from the clearing ready to make a break for it, if necessary. Poor Geno was alone out there with a lighter, a bottle, and the last rocket.

The rocket was just starting its ride into the sky when huge high beams of light flooded us, followed by sirens and flashing red lights on top of a squad car. Holly and I simultaneously screamed, "Cops!"

Then we did what any two college-educated, mature ladies would do. We hauled ass toward the woods.

The car came in so fast I swear the bumper grazed my ankles. We didn't stop to look back, but kept running.

A cop jumped out of the car and yelled "Stop!" on his bullhorn. It was so loud my ears hurt. Somehow our brains took over and we did as ordered.

"I don't know what you two are thinking running from the pole-lease (police)!" he exclaimed.

We looked at one another and shrugged. Geno was laughing at us while he stood in the dark parking lot.

That's when it dawned on me that it was the middle of the night and I was standing in an abandoned parking lot with no ID. I had been drinking and was setting off illegal fireworks. I was sure I was going to be arrested.

I remember thinking how I was going to explain to the Red Cross that I needed a wire transfer from Iraq for bail money to get out of jail. As I stood there contemplating my husband's reaction to my imminent arrest, the officer and Geno had a conversation and it was agreed that he would not press charges if we would pack up and head straight home. I thought my heart was going to stop as I exhaled a giant sigh of relief.

Thank goodness I didn't have another disastrous event to report to Jon. I was afraid he would think I couldn't be left unsupervised.

PROZAC NATION: DEL MAR HOUSING

I want to talk candidly about the reality of depression and anxiety that military wives can experience.

My goal is to make you laugh or at least smile, and that's why I'm focusing on the humor of the situation. Maybe if I tell you what I went through, you can avoid falling into the same pits I did.

It took me a while, but I finally talked to a doctor about my anxiety attacks.

I remembered becoming frustrated trying to talk to a twenty-eight-year-old naval doctor who sat there reading off a checklist. Was he checking to see if I was abusing alcohol or being destructive?

He put me on one bizarre mind-altering pill after another. Nothing worked. In fact, they all had intolerable side effects. Sometimes I felt things moving inside my head. My personality changed depending upon the medicine I was on.

I tried to do "talk therapy" with a naval psychologist. That was a blast. After an hour of convincing her my husband did not beat me, my parents did not beat me, no one had raped me, and I was not out drinking and having sex every night, I walked out.

I wished she could have focused on the condition at hand. After all, I was twenty-four, newly married, separated from my family, and my husband was in a war zone. I couldn't sleep or eat. You'd think that was the reason I was upset and feeling unbalanced.

If you have trouble finding help like I did, don't give up.

I stopped going to therapy because I thought no one was listening. I also stopped taking the pills.

Instead, I turned back to prayer, watched Joel Osteen, and listened to Dr. Laura.

I have since found an excellent talk therapist who has done wonders for my attitude and perspective. I'm disappointed that I didn't find one to help me at that point in time, although I now know I shouldn't have given up so quickly.

Do as I say, not as I did. If you are having problems, don't give up until you find what works.

Prayer is great and so is positive thinking, but you can't ignore your physical body and the effects of anxiety and depression. I was having racing, unrealistic thoughts. I worried about everything, constantly.

When my thoughts were under control, the physical problems—panic attacks and teeth grinding—started.

It was the dentist on base who first listened to me and made me feel comfortable. During a routine teeth cleaning I mentioned my jaw was killing me. He looked closer and saw I had been grinding my teeth down.

"I can fit you with a $600 mouth guard," he answered. "Or like all the military wives I have seen this deployment, I can give you a prescription for Xanax to help you calm down."

Finally, someone had gotten it. He didn't look at me like I was someone who wanted to abuse drugs. He didn't treat me like I was about to kill myself. He was older and had been a dentist for the Navy for more than 20 years. He recognized what was really going on.

We talked about panic attacks and the physical signs of anxiety.

I didn't have to take Xanax every day. It didn't permanently change my thought process or thinking. The medication simply dealt with the physical side effects.

Who knew a dentist would be the one to figure it out?

Ladies, you know your body better than anyone else. Do the research. Get to know your symptoms. Be honest with yourself, and don't give up.

If one doctor won't listen, go see another. If one drug doesn't help, ask your doctor to let you try another. And don't rule out talk therapy.

At some time in her "career," a member of the Silent Ranks needs to confide in a professional. It is a necessary catharsis.

I recommend combining talk therapy with exercise and eating right. All factor into your well-being.

Also, let it be said that not every person needs to be put "on something" just because she's going through a deployment. Don't let anyone—friend, family, or doctor—convince you to take meds if you really think you are OK.

It's not a requirement. Just be honest with yourself.

Don't be in a hurry to throw your pills away when your husband returns, either. Consult your doctor first. Many SSRI (Selective Serotonin Reuptake Inhibitor) drugs have to be "weaned" from your system.

It's a step in the right direction to know you are ready to get off the anti-depression or anti-anxiety drugs, but it is a process and you need to do it right.

Now that the lecture is over, I want to share some of my not-so-fine moments while I was getting used to being on Xanax. This drug is pretty powerful.

If you take it at the beginning of a panic attack, it will stop the dizziness, tightening of breath, blurred vision, and racing heartbeat.

If you take a Xanax and you do not have a panic attack starting, you will become very loopy. I had delayed reactions, slurred words, and didn't care about anything else in the world.

It also helps to have a full stomach when you take Xanax, especially when you first start taking it. I discovered this the hard way.

The first time I took a Xanax I didn't know you're not supposed to drive, and that you should take it with food.

I was starving, so I took one and headed for the commissary (which makes sense if you think about it). By the time it hit me, I was standing in the checkout line. I don't know what came over me, but I went nuts.

I am normally very independent, but when the young and very muscular bag boy offered to carry my groceries out for me, I accepted his offer. (Maybe he offered to carry my bags because I was swaying.) I babbled non-stop all the way to the car.

Then I started harassing him.

As the poor boy loaded the bags into my car, I started to compliment him on his large muscles and how chivalrous he was to be helping out a poor lonely wife who was in need of a man.

He eyed me now and again as he began sweating and loading the bags into the car as fast as he could. I swear when I tipped him, I tucked it into the front of his shirt. He actually ran from me.

I am probably now on the list of "women who offend teenage baggers." I'm glad they didn't have a union, or a grievance against me would have been filed.

On another day, I had been freaking out pretty bad and decided to take a Xanax and go to sleep. I don't know what happened next, but a few hours later I "woke up" and found myself driving my go-cart up and down the street, weaving in and out of my lane.

Michelle came home to find me with eyes glazed over and drool on my face. I didn't even hear her yelling at me.

I was driving so slowly that she was able to walk up beside me. "Mollie, did you take one of your pills? I think you need to park your go-cart and come inside."

Who knows how long I'd been out there. I could've gotten a ticket for driving under the influence!

I should have learned my lesson, but this the first of many Xanax-induced vehicular mishaps.

On another day, I was scheduled to have a cavity filled. I knew I was going to freak out, so I took a Xanax on a full stomach.

I was fine, no panic attack. I even thought I was fine on the drive home. I waved to my neighbor across the street before I pulled into the driveway. Then the craziest thing happened as I pulled up the driveway. Out of nowhere the house JUMPED out in front of the car and hit the bumper.

I felt my body whipped around the car just before I threw it into park. Damn that Xanax!

Then I realized my neighbor across the street had seen the entire thing. How could I play it off? Oh, I know. I'll just sit in the car for a few minutes and maybe she'll leave.

Yep, that's the amazing, crystal-clear thought process you have while on Xanax.

I sat in the car for ten minutes. I avoided looking toward her house because I didn't want to acknowledge that I had wrecked my car in my own driveway. Finally, I grabbed my purse and climbed out.

As I opened the car door I heard her call out, "Mollie, are you OK? I saw you hit your house with your car. You've been sitting there for ten minutes!"

Busted.

A word to the wise: unless you want to humiliate yourself in front of your neighbors, friends, and commissary employees, take your meds at home on a full stomach and stay there until you get used to them.

SHOPPING SPREE!

Besides going out for a manicure and a pedicure, one of my favorite things to do with the girls is to shop.

Natalie, Kat, and I would pile into the car and head to the mall. You don't have to go to the mall to get all the good deals. Michelle gave me a great tip about "shopping" on base. When people PCS, they tend to leave a lot of furniture behind, often right in the front yard. The rule on the base is simple: "finders-keepers!" And the higher the rank of the household, the better the treasures left behind!

On our evening walks we scoped out families preparing to move. We found computer desks, high chairs, strollers, playpens, grills, wicker chairs—the list goes on and on!

Michelle and I became known for our quick acquisition of property. Michele often called me on her cell phone while she was driving home from the bus stop. "Meet me at such-and-such for a pick up!"

But let me offer a word of caution: make sure someone is actually moving *before* you take something out of his or her yard. This mistake can be quite embarrassing, especially when you have a yard sale and one of your neighbors recognizes their missing family heirloom in the middle of your pile of stuff!

One day Michelle and I set out on our afternoon walk and stumbled upon an old wooden ammo crate. Since one man's trash is another man's treasure, I decided it would make a great coffee table for the back patio.

It was pretty heavy, so Michelle suggested that I go get my car. We could slide it in the back and unload it at the house after we finished our walk.

I was so excited about getting another great "Del Mar Street Bargain" that I cranked the car and backed out the driveway at full speed—right into my neighbor's car. Of course, this is the same neighbor who watched me crash into my own house one week earlier. (I promise I was not on Xanax this time.)

That ammo crate ended up costing me more than $500 in repairs to the neighbor's car. My husband was not too impressed with the news of that bargain. Still, I went after the ammo crate. I was going to get my $500 dollars worth of pleasure out of that thing come hell or high water!

And we did, using it throughout the years we were on base.

FAILURE TO COMMUNICATE

Communicating with your spouse during a deployment often presents some challenges. There is very little you can do to enrich your marriage at this time. It's really all about sustaining it.

At times, I was guilty of thinking, "What can Jon do for me while I am so lonely here at home without him?" You can't have that attitude. You are truly on your own.

Maybe I am not the best role model because the only deployments I experienced were during wartime, when nothing is guaranteed. Phone calls, letters, and emails were sporadic at best.

I lived for the mail. During Jon's first deployment I received frequent letters. I would be so excited I would run back in the house and read them while sitting in the bathroom crying. I never shared my letters with anyone. They were mine and they were private.

Phone calls were different. All of the wives were really good about sharing info from emails or calls because those were so rare.

At that time we were desperate for up-to-date news as well as the assurance that our husbands were safe.

If Natalie got a call from Carl, she would call me and I would know Jon was OK. If I got an email from Jon, he would let me know Carl was OK, and I would pass this on to Natalie. We were all really good about sharing news.

No matter what form the communication comes in, it is still not the same as the daily one-on-one communication in a marriage. You both need to prepare for that and know your limitations.

I can just about guarantee that there will be a fight, and it will be horrible because during one of the middle rounds the email will shut down or the phone will go dead. Don't beat yourself up over it. It is what it is.

We all have spats with our spouses; it's a part of marriage. You can try to do everything you can to minimize fights and avoid arguments, but there will be one. It's not the end of the world. Just accept it.

Just like in the civilian world, the most common argument is over money. I had a girlfriend who hit the roof when she learned her husband had purchased a very expensive camera while he was deployed because his had broken. They needed to talk about such a large purchase, but there was no opportunity to do so. They had a budget, but the inability to communicate over finances really hurt them.

This fight dragged on for days. Neither was right, and neither was wrong. Still, they couldn't talk about it without fighting.

Today they laugh about the episode, but it was a real issue at the time. As should be clear by now, deployments add crazy stress to everyone.

Jon and I had a nasty argument over money during his first deployment. Some crisis happened at home and I had to buy a bunch of things in a row—a microwave, new tires and, of course, my hair needed to be bleached.

I thought I had it all under control. I was working and was expecting a paycheck. I figured I would pay the credit card bill off when my paycheck arrived. Logical, right?

Jon had been in the field for more than a month. When he came in, he went online, checked our banking account—and freaked out! After weeks of not hearing from him, I woke up the next morning to find a scathing email outlining how irresponsible I had been with our finances.

The battle was on! I emailed him back that he had broken my heart. I was deeply hurt that he could not trust me. I told him I couldn't believe he was questioning me about money when I didn't even know if he was alive! He quickly saw the error of his ways and we settled it.

Remember, tone can be very difficult to interpret in emails. We didn't communicate well. We didn't handle that situation correctly. Remember when I had thoughtlessly sent the life insurance letter to Jon? He should have sent me a thoughtful email first—and then asked about the finances.

When you are not around each other every day, these "outbursts" can blindside you. Jon knew I was in charge of the money and the house. But it was hard for him not to be part of what was going on at home. He also forgot that his first communication with me needed to be more lighthearted and upbeat, like, "Hey, babe, I'm all in one piece!" Not, "What in God's name did you spend all the separation pay on?"

I think the hardest part of getting calls from overseas is that they come in at all hours. Worst of all, you never knew when you would get another one.

The pressure is always on to keep the conversation positive. The toughest time is when you have had a horrible day and you just want your best friend to be there to listen and comfort you. But you know, deep down, that if you dump on your husband he will get worried and it will pull his focus from doing what he needs to be doing. You just can't afford to bother him with anything while he is deployed.

Trust me, these men feel helpless because they can't fix our problems. They hate that feeling, so spare them from it and don't rub salt into their wounds.

So here you are, you have cried off and on all day. The dog threw up on your pants. Your friends are in their own little world. No one wants to talk to you. You got a flat tire, and now you're feeling sick. The phone rings. It's your man and he needs a little phone R & R.

It's time to remember that as bad as your day has been, it hasn't been as bad as his day. Your husband has literally been dodging bullets to stay alive.

Now, I'm not suggesting you fake it or hide things from him. I'm just saying you need to think before you speak. As much as you have to act, you need to remain positive and upbeat. He needs that deposit made into his heart.

Write everything out you want to say in an email, journal, or letter. Then sit on it and wait for the right time to send it. For me, letters were a way to get everything out clearly, intimately, without being interrupted. And I lived for Jon's letters in return.

When you are on the phone, you won't be able to take your words back. Besides that, the phone could cut out at any time—and it is usually at the worst time.

I always thought of phone calls as quick ways to touch base, and never really put a lot of expectations into our calls. We used them as a way to hear each other's voices, not as a venue to discuss our feelings.

Phone calls are an art. You've got to work on the rhythm and flow. First, you have to get past the awkwardness of not having spoken in a while. Add being hyper and wanting to talk at the same time. Then there's the classic delay that comes with using government phones.

So you have a phone call that sounds more like two sixth graders with a crush stumbling through a first phone conversation.

When my husband first deployed, Weapons of Mass Destruction (WMDs) were a huge fear. Chemical weapons were something the troops prepared to face and the wives feared.

The one place that chemical weapons attack first is where cells multiple the fastest: the testicles. All of us had heard about the horrible disaster following the 1991 Gulf War. Some of the troops developed a problem with their semen. It felt like fire when they ejaculated, making sex miserable.

The wives were freaked. Not to mention, none of us wanted one-eyed babies. So the first couple of times my husband would call from Iraq I would blurt out, "How are your balls?"

I begged him to snag some extra kevlar and make a kevlar cup.

Sometimes during deployments you get calls from your husband at odd times, including the middle of the night. The phone rings when you're half asleep and you have no idea what's going on.

Some of my more organized girlfriends suggest keeping a list next to the bedroom phone so you won't forget to talk about the important issues when he calls.

I was never upset when he called late at night, but it did take me a minute or two to get my thoughts together.

PHONE SEX OPERATOR

There was an opportunist who thought he could take advantage of lonely wives accustomed to late-night calls from their husbands.

I heard rumors about a prank caller phoning wives and asking for phone sex in the middle of the night. I was appalled. Of course, we were all afraid of being raped.

This master of "self-love" had learned the base phone prefix and spent his nights dialing away. Wives always answered in fear that they would miss a call from their real husband.

I, too, fell prey to this creep. It was about 2:00 a.m. one morning, and I had not heard from Jon in more than a week.

When the phone rang, I heard a quiet whispering voice on the other end. This was not unusual because Jon liked to keep his conversation private. He called me "Baby."

"Are you ok?" I asked sleepily. "Are you getting my letters? Darius is in bed with me." Darius is our cat.

Pause. "How are the kids doing?" asked the soft voice.

The kids? Wait a minute—time to wake up! I had to think fast. I didn't want to offend my husband if I was wrong. Was Jon referring to our pets as kids, as I often do? But Jon never did that.

This is more of a mess than you think. You're thinking, "Well Mollie, just hang up!" I couldn't! My husband didn't know about the prank caller because I hadn't told him. Why get him upset about that?

If I had called my husband a pervert and hung up on him, what would he think on his end? And what if he could not call me back?

Just when I was starting to dismiss my paranoid thoughts my "husband" asked me to have phone sex with him.

That did it. Jon's a Scorpio, but he's also Catholic. There was no way this whispering, muffled voice on the line belonged to my husband.

I hung up.

This guy called a lot of ladies on the base. Can you imagine how many wives thought it was their husband and actually had phone sex with this perve?

Maybe they actually were grateful for a little action and refused to accept the fact it was a prank call. We'll never know.

I know Michelle sat by the phone every night with a bottle of wine waiting for this guy to call. To this day I'm not sure if she was looking forward to cursing him out or going along for the ride!

IN PRINT

During Jon's first deployment, a reporter from CNN was embedded with his battalion. It was bittersweet and surreal to see this reporter on the news knowing he was with my husband's battalion.

During his second deployment, it seemed like at least once a month Jon's photo was on the front page of the local paper. I would get a call from Natalie or Christa screaming that Jon's face was plastered across the front of the newspaper. That's when we would jump into action and go out and buy as many copies as possible to mail them out to family members.

That's also how I found out he had shaved his head. I cried when I saw the image of my husband praying on the front page of the paper. I didn't recognize him at all, and it shocked me.

I knew this deployment was harder on him because he wasn't writing as often. The fighting had escalated, and there were numerous casualties.

This shot captured such an intimate moment in my husband's life. He was frozen in time, caught in a moment of intense prayer. The photo shook me to the core. I could see things about my husband in these photos that others would not notice. It was an odd way of communicating, but I could sense his emotions.

But I had no one to share these feelings with. The other wives had their own issues, and my civilian friends couldn't relate.

WHY YOU NEED TO SHAVE YOUR LEGS

They say when a bunch of women are around each other for a certain amount of time, they start cycling their periods together. This phenomenon happened to those of us who spent much of our time together. Did I tell you how close the ladies of Del Mar had become?

During tough deployments we shared meals, secrets, tears, fears, exercise, and even helped raise each other's kids.

But I was not ready to share everything. I had to draw the line somewhere, and Michelle tried to cross it.

It was a hot afternoon. Just another lazy day in Southern California. The kids were playing in the blow-up pool in the front yard. Jon and Kevin had both been deployed for about four months. Michelle and I were both dragging.

When Michelle got thirsty, she asked her son David (who was four at the time), to "bring mommy a coke." He came back with a Coors Lite.

I don't think the confusion came from the diet coke can being silver like the "Silver Bullet." I think Michelle had been busted. And it was priceless.

She drank it. After all, it was five o'clock somewhere. From then on, Michelle referred to her beloved Coors Lite as "Mommy Coke."

After everyone was done swimming, Michelle needed help emptying the pool. Besides the water, there was grass, plastic wrappers, a swim diaper, and urine from all the neighborhood boys who had been swimming in it.

There was no way Michelle and I could lift it. It was more than two feet deep and weighed a ton. So we stood on the sides of the pool and pushed it down, letting the water leak out. We kept losing our balance because the plastic sides were so slick, and began laughing hysterically. We hooked arms and stepped on the edge at the same time.

It probably looked like a scene from a "Mentos" commercial.

We held onto each other trying to keep our balance and that's when my leg brushed up against hers. We had become close friends, so I didn't have a personal space issue with Michelle. Touching her didn't bother me.

That was when I noticed she had stopped moving and was staring at me.

I looked at her. "What?"

"Miss Mollie, your leg is so muscular and hairy," she answered. "It's quite masculine. I think I just got aroused!"

"Yeah, yeah." I thought she was joking. Then I realized she wasn't.

This is the price you pay when you don't shave your legs for a while. Gals, one of your hard-up, horny neighbors may get aroused. Before she could kiss me, I jumped off the pool and ran into the house.

The Bible talks about "Love thy neighbor," but I don't think this was what He was talking about!

For days, every time I stepped outside, Michelle would be waiting for me in the driveway we shared. She would stand there waving and giggling. It was too much for me to take, and I was beyond embarrassed. In fact, I was a little afraid and refused to face her. So I stayed inside my house for a week. Michelle would call, but I wouldn't pick up.

I really freaked out when I heard her purring outside my bedroom window, "Miss Mollie . . . I know you're in your room . . . I can hear you in there breathing. Why aren't you coming outside? Is it because I was having lustful thoughts about your legs! I have never been 'lesbian' before, but there was just something about you the other day . . ."

Then she would break out laughing. She was getting such a kick out of messing with me!

A week later, when I finally ran out of food, I was forced to leave the house. I waited until I saw her drive off with the kids before I stepped outside.

We laugh about it now. She'll still call me once in a while and tease, "Mollie, do you remember when I turned gay on you by the baby pool? Your legs were just so masculine. I'd never had thoughts like that before in my life."

I made sure to keep my legs shaved after that.

WAIT A MINUTE, MR. POSTMAN!

Michelle and I were what you could call connoisseurs of lingerie. We bought most of our nighttime fashions at Wal-Mart because we were afraid of being seen at some scandalous store off base.

But Michelle had also found a catalog source that would anonymously mail her selections. She spent hours at night pouring over the catalogs and asking me which I thought she would look best in.

Like I said, we were very close and did share a common bedroom wall. We had few secrets. But our husbands avoided making eye contact for the four years we were neighbors.

One day Michelle came over in a panic.

"You have got to help me! I have a package coming and it's not here yet. I called the company and they said their driver dropped it off this morning! That means they delivered it to the wrong house!"

I didn't think it was such a big deal until she reminded me of the selection she had picked out of the Adam and Eve catalog. The company, she continued, "assumed I was a man" and had addressed the package to "Mitchell." It got worse. They told her this particular package included a "free gift—just for him."

Then she flipped open the catalog and showed me the free gift. "Oh, no," I moaned.

It was a fake rubber vagina.

Now I realized her reputation was really at stake. What if someone opened the package without looking to see to whom it was mailed and then doubled checked to find Michelle's address on it! Someone on our side of base housing—a Navy Captain, or Marine Colonel—was about to find a surprise on his doorstep.

We took off on foot, deciding we would cover more ground if we split up. It took a while, but we finally found Michelle's box of love and her free fake vagina. With her naughty treasure in hand, she breathed a giant sigh of relief.

And now our Bunco boner had a friend!

Although I saw a few cute things in the catalog, after Michelle's delivery crisis I decided to stick with my Wal-Mart knock-offs.

LET'S GET PHYSICAL

It's important to get exercise weekly, whether your husband is deployed or at home. I am not talking about doing your kegals, although your husband won't complain if you do.

You need to make a commitment to get your endorphins up during the deployment. I'm not one of those people who likes to sweat or even exert myself. My theory is that since I had done competitive gymnastics for more than twelve years as a child, I was pretty much done with exercise.

However, my weight had fluctuated since meeting Jon. I knew I needed exercise—at least for the endorphins if nothing else.

I had some great neighbors, including Cathy and Brad (who is a Navy Captain) living across the street. Cathy works from home. Like Jon and I, at that point in their lives they were "child free." They took me out for sushi every couple of weeks and invited me to attend yoga classes.

I realized pretty quickly that I was not a yoga kind of girl. First of all, I am so hyper that all the meditating made me nervous. Then they would start the moves. Some of the positions do not work on my body. Let's put it this way, yoga makes me fart—a lot.

When that happened Brad would start laughing, really hard. Did he hear me fart? Was he farting?

Then Cathy would start. Was she farting too?

Who else heard me fart? I was trying so hard not to!

I got little accomplished in yoga because I did all the moves wrong. If I did them right, I farted.

Anyway, I don't care what kind of exercise you do. Just try to find something that gets you out of the house. Go bicycle riding or swimming.

But don't get wrapped up thinking you are going to have some hot body when your man gets home. That should not be your goal.

Exercise every day because you need to get out of the house, socialize, and release those endorphins!

Michelle and I walked regularly, but sometimes she couldn't go because she was watching her kids' games. So I started walking with another wife from the battalion. She and I were the same age and lived in Del Mar. And her husband was serving with mine in Fallujah. She usually brought her big male mutt along on our walks. Those outings were some of the best times I enjoyed at Del Mar.

By that time I had returned to the career I had in South Carolina before I met Jon. The company hired me back to work its territory in California.

Since this other wife had a corporate job, we both felt the stress. I can't even begin to tell you how great it was to get out of the house just after sunset and really move fast. We could blow off steam from our work days and vent at the same time!

We were both career women with no kids and husbands at war. It was so comforting to talk to someone who understood the pressure of an intense job and a husband away on a deployment in a war zone. I lived for those late night walks. The dogs loved it, too. Everyone felt better after doing two miles around the neighborhood.

And then one day she stopped calling. I called and left messages, but she wouldn't return my calls. I was really hurt when I saw her out walking her dog really late at night. I felt like I had been dumped.

I decided I must have done something to upset her. When your friends turn into your spouse, breaking up can get really messy. I was torn up over this for months.

It was not until my husband came home months later that I found out the truth. Apparently, she and her husband had a fight during this time.

So, it wasn't my fault. She had been unable to handle the issues in her marriage and chose not to confide in me. Not everyone wants to share. Nor is everyone strong. We just cope differently.

It was very hard to lose that friendship. I had thought it meant so much to both of us. We go through our own crap during these deployments. Obviously, not everyone can reach out for help.

HOUSE GUEST

There is this old saying, "Fish and company stink after three days." The rot seems to set in faster during deployments. Be mindful of who you visit or who visits you while your husband is gone.

Don't invite anyone into your home who will make you uncomfortable. A lot of people will want to visit or will invite you to stay with them. You're not being rude if you turn them down. It's difficult to be as moody as you are feeling, while trying to be on your best behavior for your guest or when you are a guest in someone else's home.

Sometimes those visits can be therapeutic, however. Jon's sister and cousin came for a few days and we had a blast. We dyed hair, watched movies, and went shopping. This was a good visit. Unfortunately, some of my trips to see close friends and family did not turn out as well.

Just plan wisely. Only you know your limitations. You have to put your needs first.

I did welcome a yearly visit from my mother. Since she had been an Air Force brat growing up on bases all over the world, she was familiar with the military lifestyle. She also knew why I didn't want to cook or get dressed. She understood why I got upset and cried over the smallest things. She would just hold me while I cried and never asked uncomfortable questions.

I was so grateful for her company. She came in and took care of me in a way only a mother can.

We took the dogs on daily walks, went the beach, planted flowers for Jon's homecoming, and sewed different projects for the house. She got me through some of the toughest points in those long months.

Many of my girlfriends asked their moms to come and help with the kids.

If your mom is a positive presence in your life, ask her to come and stay with you. You might need that other person to step in and help with the housework and children.

Michelle's mom was a great help. With her mother in the house, Michelle finally got to relax in a way she could not when any of us were babysitting the boys.

However, if your mom will only upset your emotional balance, tell her to visit at a later date.

Your home is your sanctuary. Keep it that way.

THE SECRET BEACH

Michelle found this little beach just down from our home outside an Amtrak Unit. There was a loading dock and just enough sand to create a private beach.

I didn't want to ask how she stumbled upon this beach, but it was a gem. We called it "the Secret Beach."

It had a slip for putting your boat in the water (a launch site for Amphibious Assault Vehicles), steep rocks on each side, and sand for the dogs and kids to play on.

The secret to the spot was you could only go there when the Marines were not using it for training exercises. If you did, you were in for a treat. Otherwise, you're greeting a Hummer full of Marines while dressed in a bikini and flip-flops.

Since my husband wasn't around during the summer months of our stay at the base, my beach days became ladies-only activities.

Often Mary, my Marine Corps mom, her son JJ, and her husband the Colonel would join me and the dogs at the beach. Beenie, Natalie, Autumn, and Michelle would also hang out there as well. The whole gang, including dogs, babies, and kids, would gather for weekend picnics at the Secret Beach.

One weekend JJ brought his jet ski down to the beach and started offering free rides. I joined him for one and we saw boats, dolphins, and sea lions sunning themselves on the buoys. It was great fun.

Then I made Beenie go for a ride. She was nervous about leaving Grace, who was just three months old, but agreed after Mary, Michelle, and I assured her the baby would be safe.

Before JJ left, I warned him to be careful since he had a new mom riding with him. I watched Beenie as she got on the back of the jet ski with this buff sixteen-year-old.

JJ said they would only be gone for half an hour, so when they weren't back in forty minutes I began to get worried. After about an hour I was definitely on edge. Grace would wake up soon and she would be hungry. I was also worried about Beenie. What if something had happened?

Finally, the jet ski came speeding around a bend and pulled up on the beach. I ran to the water's edge. Beenie was soaking wet. Her lips were purple and she was shivering uncontrollably.

"What happened?" I asked.

I was ready to ring JJ's neck, but Beenie just looked at me and started to laugh.

JJ offered a blow-by-blow report of what led up to what we would later refer to as "The Jet Ski Incident."

At first JJ and Beenie had enjoyed a leisurely ride over the waves. When they approached the buoys where the sea lions were sunning themselves, they stopped to watch them frolic and play.

While they were watching the animals, a large motor boat sped past. The wave it left tipped the jet ski over. The engine had flooded, so JJ and Beenie spent several minutes trying to get it started. Their presence, however, began to upset the snoozing sea lions.

Unable to start the engine, JJ and Beenie started swimming away from the sea lions while dragging the jet ski. For those of you unfamiliar with the

Pacific Ocean, it's not the same warm bath water its sister, the Atlantic Ocean, boasts. The Pacific is usually a very chilly 62 degrees. That's why so many surfers wear wet suits.

Beenie, however, wasn't wearing a wet suit and she'd been in the chilly waters for nearly thirty minutes. Just as aroused sea lions were closing in, JJ got the jet ski running.

The next challenge was getting a soaking wet Beenie on the jet ski. If you haven't seen someone trying to mount a jet ski after spending time in cold water, it's quite a sight. It can take several tries to get up on the seat. Beenie and JJ slipped, turned, and twisted in an effort to get back on, usually tipping the machine over again. And it's not any easier when you have ten sea lions hot on your trail!

After several failed attempts, JJ and Beenie finally made it back on at the same time and headed toward the beach.

Beenie later confessed that JJ had to help her on by pushing her ass up in the air as she slung her leg over the jet ski.

How humiliating for poor ole Beenie!

BIRD!

The Secret Beach became an exciting outing for the dogs.

During the week, Michelle and I would fill the cars up with kids and dogs and head down to the sand and salt water.

Maggie, Molly, CoCo, and Monsieur loved to dig in the sand, bite at waves, and chase birds.

My little poodle Monsieur would get so excited about his feathered friends that he would go crazy chasing them. Imagine this seven-pound body converting into a bird dog. He would actually "point" at his hoped-for prey! He particularly liked chasing seagulls. He would give a good chase, but it ended whenever they headed out to sea.

On one particular day, I let him run off leash since there was no one else on the beach. He set his sights on a particular seagull and went after it full force. When the seagull veered out to sea, Monsieur didn't stop, but instead dove in it and started swimming.

I panicked. I had never seen my dog swim, so I assumed he didn't know how. Boy was I wrong. Here was this tiny dog fiercely paddling out after a bird into the Pacific Ocean.

"Monsieur! Monsieur!" I yelled as loud as I could.

Suddenly, he turned his head to look in my direction. At the sound of my voice he seemed to realize, "Hey, I don't know how to swim!"

He started to sink.

We all started to scream.

A Marine who was in the building behind the beach heard us screaming and ran up to see what was wrong. When he realized what was going on, he pulled off his boots so he could perform a "Poodle Rescue."

Without thinking twice he dove into the ocean and swam out to my drowning pooch. He took a look around where the bird-dog wannabe had disappeared and ducked under water. When he resurfaced, he had my tiny "Monsieur" in his hands. Boy did we cheer for our hero!

Safely back on shore, Monsieur continued to bark and growl at the seagull, which had returned to taunt him. After that incident I kept both poodles on a lead anchored in the ground to prevent them from chasing any more birds.

Who knew that the gulls would start chasing after my dogs!? I guess word had spread through the bird community that my dogs were grounded.

I let a young boy walk Monsieur along the water's edge. I was reading a novel Michelle had given me when I heard screams and looked up. The boy was on one side of the beach, and Monsieur was on the other. A pelican was beginning his dive bomb attack, and Monsieur was the target!

By the time I stood up, adjusted my bikini, and started to run to the water's edge, the pelican had swooped down and was trying to get a firm hold on Monsieur with his beak.

I started screaming and chasing the pelican, throwing my book and flip flops at it in an effort to get him to drop my dog. Thank God he finally did. After that, I seriously contemplated putting little weights on my dog's feet.

GIVE ME YOUR DIGITS

One day Natalie and I headed down to Del Mar beach because the Secret Beach was covered with AV's and Hummers.

It was the weekend, and we were not looking forward to sharing it with a crowd. Since the lifeguards at the beach are Marines, helicopters often fly low over the beach to check out the girls in their bikinis.

Whenever I went with Beenie I would sometimes pull a boob out of my bikini top and wait to see how long it took for the helicopters to start buzzing overhead.

This particular day, however, I did not feel like playing peek-a-boo with my "girls." Natalie and I were determined to get a suntan on our shoulders before the big reunion at the end of the week.

Deployment was finally coming to an end and the ship was leaving Hawaii and heading home! Naturally, we wanted to look "sunkissed" for our men.

All we wanted was a few quiet, relaxing hours at the beach to clear our minds. So we went to a secluded part at least 500 feet from the crowd.

We got settled and were reading when some rowdy eighteen-year-old Marines decided to set up about ten feet directly in front of us.

We knew we were in for trouble because all they had with them was a cooler full of beer. They immediately started cursing loudly and bragging about their Mitsubishi Eclipse. A few of them started talking about the hot Oceanside ladies that were expecting a call from the boys tonight.

Natalie and I started to laugh. The youngsters misinterpreted our giggles as flirting. One, who claimed he was down to his last payment on his "rent-to-own-rims," decided to respond to our "mating cry."

He walked over, definitely determined to find love. Natalie and I were lying on our stomachs on chairs so we could see his feet shuffling up. I think in his drunkenness he even kicked sand in Natalie's face.

"Want a beer?"

"No thanks," we both replied, turning our attention back to our books.

He reconsidered his game plan and tried a different plan of attack.

"Are you all here with anybody?" was followed by a huge hiccup, which almost knocked him back in the sand.

This Marine was checking out our availability. Young women on base are only allowed to be unattended if they are: (A) in the service or (B) a dependent wife or daughter.

If he had been paying attention, he would have seen our wedding rings, but he kept on talking. In fact, I think this Marine had a future in recruiting because he refused to give up.

I didn't want to humiliate him in front of his friends, so I dropped a well-placed hint. "We live over in Del Mar Housing. We just came over here to read our books."

If this Marine had any sense, he would have realized we lived in housing for company-grade officers. Clearly, we were spouses.

However, he was too drunk to understand, so he continued to talk to us while blocking out the sun.

He pulled out his cell phone. "Can I get your digits?"

We tried to tune him out and kept our eyes down.

I noticed he kept digging his feet into the sand and heard him rambling on about his toes. That's when I took a closer look at his feet. Most of his toes were buried, but something didn't look right. That's when I realized he had six toes on each foot.

Talk about "digits!" This guy had plenty; he didn't need ours. I looked over at Natalie, who was also staring at his feet. Then I focused in on what he was saying.

"Yeah, I see you girls are trying to skunk me 'cuz I have extra toes, but the Marine Corps doesn't care. They are still goin' to send me to Iraq. I can still train. My fit reps are good. I think my extra toes make me run faster."

I was done being polite. I had gone through seven months without my husband. I had bit my tongue a hundred times in public when strangers said outrageous things about my husband or the war. But I could no longer remain silent as this drunk kid tried to hit on us. I burst out laughing; so did Nat. He found out the hard way that we weren't interested. He finally walked away.

You know, those extra toes really did help him move quickly.

REVEALED

"War does not build character; it reveals it." Jon had read that quote while overseas.

No other statement summed up the journey of my character over those four years and two wartime deployments. I look back now and see how much I learned after that first deployment, and how much I matured. The Silent Ranks experience the effects of war as well. We just do it on the home front.

During that time in my life, I was at my best when I had to be and at my worst when I was at my lowest. I can honestly say I never failed my friends, my husband, or myself. "I never turned to booze, drugs, gossip, adultery, or any behavior I would be truly ashamed of. Sure, I was a little sassy at times, and I had to grieve alone at home and miss a few get-togethers, but I never took anyone down with me."

I remember one tantrum I had while Jon was gone on his second deployment. I can't tell you what set me off, but I was screaming, pounding my fist into the ground, yelling, cursing Jon out, and kicking my legs as I was face down on the floor. Sobs rang out of me.

I emitted guttural sounds—like a child unable to calm down. I carried on for at least twenty minutes.

Finally, Michelle tried to call, but I wouldn't answer. I continued to carry on finally crying out to God to hold and comfort me. When I calmed down, I went into the bathroom and splashed water on my face.

When I checked the message from Michelle, I heard the panic in her voice. That's when I realized I was a 25-year-old baby throwing a fit. I had held all my anger inside for months, but it had finally exploded.

Most of the time, I chose to cry privately in my home.

I was not the only one.

Members of the Silent Ranks keep brave faces around each other or in public. It was critical because we needed each other's strength.

There were a few wives who could not handle the stresses of military life or deployment at all. One called me to report she had been hiding under her bed since her husband told her he was being shipped out. I wondered how she got to the phone.

That was a little too much drama, even for me.

I hated to do it, but I distanced myself from the weak during those months. I didn't need anyone bringing me down farther than I already was.

Natalie and Kat became my constant companions throughout both deployments. Michelle and her family were right next door. We didn't pull each one down. If one of us was upset, we stayed away from each other.

If we noticed one of us had been pulling away for too long, we would go to her house and draw her out.

True friendship means being patient and understanding with each other, but being careful about not dragging others down with you.

STAGES

You go through the stages of grief when your husband leaves. I have talked about this a bit before, but not quite like this. Recognize these stages.

First, there is denial that he will actually leave. You try to convince yourself that he may not deploy. Once he leaves, you feel the shock that he will be gone for a length of time.

Then you get really angry. It floods over you.

You think: "Why do you have to do everything alone? Why does this have to break right after he leaves?"

Until you accept the reality that you are alone and stop fighting it, you will find yourself in turmoil.

Acceptance is the key for all military wives. You have to accept and be satisfied that this is your life. This is your sacrifice and your cross to bear. If you want a life with the man you love, then recognize you are being called to serve alongside him.

About the time you accept being alone, is the time for a "halfway celebration." These celebrations would really piss me off, because you are halfway—and still have so much more time to go.

YOU'RE A SURVIVOR

The last stage is when you discover you have found your groove. You're finally comfortable. You've developed a routine and then the news arrives that they're coming home. That's when the panic starts. You alternate between nesting and freaking out.

Just when you've gotten used to being alone and are able to sleep through the night, your routine is about to change again. Be proud that you survived. Now you get to cuddle again.

Everyone may be celebrating that they are coming home, but you're afraid something could still happen and he won't. In fact, you're afraid to get your hopes up.

I realized I had to let that attitude go. I had to allow myself to reconnect with Jon. It was time to celebrate his homecoming and allow myself to get excited.

By the second deployment, the stages of grief were all mixed up for me. I skipped a few steps and revisited a few others.

When Jon returned the first time, I told him, "I am just so glad that I have you home for a while."

Jon's response was, "I'm going back in less than six months."

I can't really put into words what that statement did to me emotionally. I was in mental limbo and shock. I tried to fit in every life experience I thought we needed to have in that short time.

We took dancing lessons, ate at every restaurant. I went crazy trying to fit so much in. I just could not shake the fact that I would have to face losing him again—and so soon—after he had safely returned home.

I really did live every minute like it was our last, but I failed to relax and enjoy the quiet moments. I felt like I had to make a million memories.

I did a lot of the "disconnecting" behavior during the six months between deployments. And I felt no shock at all at the beginning of the second deployment. I already knew it was going to suck.

I look back on those four years and realize that was a lot for a newly married couple to stomach.

But I think it really is best that newlyweds move away and start fresh. When you go through this experience together, you establish a strong foundation.

Jon and I made a new home and found new friends together in a new place. We did this on our own without family or friends.

We went through more in our first year together than most couples go through in a lifetime. We learned from our own mistakes and forgave each other our imperfections.

I know there may be more obstacles ahead, but we have the strength to endure. No matter what this world serves us, nothing else can pull us apart.

KEEP YOUR HEAD ABOVE WATER

I have had civilian friends ask me to explain the dynamics of friendships between spouses of deployed service members. They want to understand the dynamics of our support network. I put it this way:

The wives are up to their chins in a large body of water. We must link our outstretched arms so the currents won't carry us away. We need to stay connected by holding tight to one another.

Each wife must remain still—not creating waves for the others. If she does, the water rises above the others' heads. The wife making the waves could cause the rest of us to drown.

If one wife begins to sink, she can pull the others down. If one wife tries to push the sinking one up, she could cause the water to go over her own head. It's impossible for her to save another by herself.

To remain strong, the wives must hold tight and be responsible to and for one another. Hold fast to the links in your chain because you are a proud member of the Silent Ranks.

SIMPLE THINGS

Many military wives e-mail me, writing that they are having a really bad day. They ask for jokes to lift their spirits.

Here are some of the things that can help you stay positive and in good spirits (and they can serve as your life jackets when you are feeling blue):

*   Watch a funny movie. In fact, keep a ton of them around.

*   Play some dance music and dance to it. I am serious. Get some R&B, praise, or my personal favorite, oldies from the 50s and 60s, and turn it up! You can't be sad while listening to "Itsy Bitsy Teeny Weenie Yellow Polka Dot Bikini."
*   Make a mix CD for your car and another for the house.
*   Get out of the house. Walk or bike ride. Do something physical.
*   Do something constructive with your hands, like crafts, sewing, knitting, making beaded necklaces. Do anything that results in a finished product so you feel you have accomplished something.
*   What has always been your dream? Something you have always wanted to try, or learn or accomplish?

Pursue it. Make it come true!

Chapter Seven

REUNION

They extended the deployment twice. And then finally, word comes down from the command that you have a reunion date! You've made it through your husband's deployment and now he is coming home. You feel so excited—like it's your honeymoon all over again.

Then your excitement turns to . . . bitterness. You have finally learned how to work the weed whacker, unclog the toilet, and sleep through the night without him. Now you have to make room for him in your life.

Don't feel guilty about this. These feelings are normal, but it's important you find a positive direction for these emotions. Be proud that you were able to do these things on your own. He will be proud of you as well!

Channel your energy and emotions and be thankful he is coming home. You can incorporate the amazing changes you've both been through as you start the next chapter of your life together.

Surprisingly, some ladies remain bitter. It's hard to have good sex when you are bitter, ladies. So . . . let it go.

When you start thinking about having your man back in your home, panic may set in. What do you talk about? Where do you start? He has missed so much of what happened to you during his absence. How do you go back to sharing your day-to-day lives together?

Much of this chapter falls under the "do as I say, not as I did" rule because I learned quite a bit from my own experiences as well as those shared by other wives.

I have to be honest with you: The reunion is the hardest part of the entire deployment cycle. When someone warned me the reunion would be tough, my first reaction was, "That's crap." I honestly wish I had listened more carefully and prepared better.

While I can give you some tips to ease you through the transition, be ready for some serious screwin' and some serious scrappin'. Emotions are raw as you readjust to being together again.

Keep in mind that you are different people than you were before the deployment. Hopefully, you're both better and stronger. It's important, though, to be patient as you adjust to the changes in both of your personalities.

NESTING

As the reunion date got closer, I went into super speed mode preparing the house and myself for Jon.

I cleaned the house from top to bottom and brought home all his favorite foods. I wanted to be able to stay home for days with plenty of his meals. I had a feeling he wouldn't like any of the selections from my deployment diet plan.

I also went shopping for a dress. I wanted to look perfect for the first time we would see each other. I wanted a dress for my first reunion, something really special.

For Jon's second homecoming I made a skirt. I worked on it for weeks. Sewing became my way to stay busy and focused. I really needed an activity to keep my mind busy, and sewing and shopping fit the bill.

I discovered it's good to have distractions during that last week because you can and will go nuts if you don't. Getting out of the house to shop for a dress and all Jon's favorite foods kept me in a positive and fun frame of mind.

BUNNY TAIL

In the week before Jon's homecoming, I went to the tanning bed, the nail salon, and the hairdresser. It was like I was getting ready for my wedding all over again.

Bottom line: I needed professional intervention for the lack of attention my body had undergone. I needed help to look attractive once more. And I needed something really extreme to pull me back from my drab existence.

I had read a lot about the Brazilian wax in magazines. It was all the rage and supposedly really sexy. The Brazilian was a step up from just a normal bikini wax. In fact, it was the extreme procedure I was looking for.

So, I decided to give it a try. Since I wanted the job done well, I went to a reputable place in Oceanside called Magic Nails.

There I met Helen, a Vietnamese woman who kept yelling, "Cash only!"

"Ok," I kept replying. "Cash only."

"Cash only!"

"Yes! Cash Only!"

Satisfied (I guess), she took me into the back to a private room. "Take off clothes below waist," she ordered. "Up on table." She nodded toward a folding table.

For a second I got really nervous because she didn't understand English very well. Not only that, the room looked like the backroom abortion clinics I had read about.

I tried to relax when she came in the room with a tub of wax. There I was, laying on a crappy table with my privates exposed. I kept thinking, "If God wanted everyone to see your privates, he would have named them 'publics.'"

With second thoughts racing through my mind, I decided to get up just when she approached me holding a wooden stick dripping with wax.

Helen was smiling, and suddenly appeared very friendly. I began to relax. She said the most encouraging things to me as she proceeded to rip large chunks of hair off from around my labia.

She looked at my privates and said, "You beauty down there!" I was flattered. My privates had been in hiding for so long. I did flinch once or twice as she continued her waxing job.

Each time I did she exclaimed, "You want beauty?" When I nodded in reply, she would exclaim, "Then you get pain," ripping off another patch of hair. I think she enjoyed doing that.

Halfway through my treatment, a woman outside the door spoke to Helen in Vietnamese. Helen turned to me. "Be back." She left me there—lopsided and quite sticky.

Within a short time I could hear loud music coming from the lobby and Helen's voice singing Celine Dion's version of "Beauty and the Beast." At an instrumental break in the song, the door bursts open.

I'm spread-eagled on the table as Helen walks in with a microphone in her hand.

"Mollie, you want sing Karaoke? I put you on list. You're next!"

And then she slams the door!

Three minutes later she returned to the task of grooming privates.

"God I hope you washed your hands," I prayed. She was not even wearing gloves.

At this point, I could hear the next Karoke contestant singing "Vogue" by Madonna.

Helen chatted on while she tediously labored away. "Your husband will kiss more now . . . down there!" Even I didn't know how to reply to that.

"Lift leg," instructed Helen. As I did, I felt something warm in a place that usually felt kind of dirty. What was she doing?

"Ah, what are you doing down there?" I asked

"It look like a bunny tail back there!" she answered as she stuck a paper strip right next to my anus and jerked it off.

I screamed.

She showed me seven black coarse hairs on the strip of paper. Who knew? It's so dark back there. How long had those been there?

You hear news reports about a scientist who discovers a new species of fish that had been in the bottom of the ocean for centuries. Since it's so dark in those regions, no one had ever explored it. Now I understand the mystery.

Helen finished up with a few more pulls and rips. After it was all done she handed me a mirror. "Look!"

"That's ok," I replied. "I trust you." I really didn't need to see for myself.

Before I could move she pushed the back of my head forward between my legs. "See, I make you beauty down there!"

"OK!" I answered, summoning up the courage to look.

I'm from the generation that was taught not to look at your own genitals or even touch them. I think my mom put a "Mr. Yuck" sticker on the front of my underpants. She made it clear bad things could happen if you go near your genitals.

I took a deep breath, let go of my past, and looked. I paused for an instant waiting to be struck by lightning. Nothing happened.

Helen did a great job. My pee pee looked a little strange. Frankly, she looked a little "naked," but she definitely looked better. My hope now was that Jon would recognize her!

Oh, and the bunny tail? She let me keep it. I use it as a good luck key chain.

BANNERS

After the house and I had been groomed, I started on the "Welcome Home" banner. Many families go all out on this one. They get their kids to do hand prints in paint. They do huge collages and add cute sayings. The banner is an excellent way to get kids of all ages involved in the homecoming plans.

Since Jon is really low key and an introvert, he requested something small. I purchased a simple welcome home sign and American flag pinwheels. In the yard I planted flowers and dressed my pink flamingo in an Uncle Sam costume.

It was all simple, but really warm and cute. It was a perfect welcome home for Jon.

FIRST KISS

My husband and I had visited his family before he deployed. We talked about how great it would be when he finally came home. His sister kept asking how the reunion works. Then Jon's mother piped in and exclaimed, "I'm going to be the first one to run up and give him a huge hug and kiss when he gets back."

That was it. Unable to hold back my anger, I spun around and retorted, "No, you won't because I will be the first one to see him. After that, we will be up in the bed for at least a week before any of you can come to visit!"

That wasn't particularly tactful, I admit, but I really needed to make the point. My day-to-day life had been the one most impacted by his absence, and, damn it, I was going to be the first to kiss my man and didn't want anyone else there for the reunion.

I believe it should have been my husband who addressed this issue with his family instead of making me look like the bad guy. Many families arrange their reunions the same way they do their "goodbyes."

Since every family is different, you need to be honest and prepare in the same way. Some families with kids want the extended family on hand so they can help with the kids. They plan for mom, dad, grandma, and cousins to be present when their serviceman returns.

In the end, you need to talk about what works best for your family. Jon and I simply didn't want to be overwhelmed by our extended family.

I recommend sending out an email to friends and family explaining when your husband is coming home. Politely inform them that your husband will be jet-lagged or at least adjusting to being on land again, and will need lots of time to rest during those first few days.

Let them know that he won't be accepting phone calls, either. The last thing you need to be doing when he first returns home is to exchange small talk with fifty people. You'll catch some grief for this, but do it anyway. Encourage them to send a "Welcome Home" e-mail, which he can respond to when he is rested.

I was pleasantly surprised by how many friends and family sent heartfelt messages. Jon really appreciated them.

Of course, he will call mom and dad to let them know he is on American soil. It's up to them to call their friends and family.

If he wants to call more people at his leisure, that's his decision. He doesn't need the pressure of having to call a bunch of people under the false pretense that he needs to be "polite." He's going to need down time, and so will you.

E-mails are the ideal solution.

Your husband will be given leave when he returns and I encourage you to take a family vacation.

When I say "family," I mean just you, your husband, and the kids. If you have kids, I believe it's important you and your husband find alone time away from the base and the kids. It may only be an overnight stay while someone watches the children. Regardless, you need time for just the two of you.

Many of you will have family that will want to visit or have you travel to their home. Make sure you decide what is best for your family and make the decision based on the leave as well as your budget.

We took a week to be home alone. Then we took off for a week to get away from the base. Only after that did we invite family in. Your job when he comes home is to serve as the gatekeeper.

Our priority was each other. Since Jon and I did not have kids, it was hard for his family to understand why we needed time alone.

I got a pretty bad rap for being overprotective of Jon. But I knew the most important thing when he returned was to get our relationship back on track.

Wives are traditionally the ones in families who plan for his return. Your husband has no idea what's going on. He is just relieved to be home. Politely set boundaries, but do it in a loving, patient manner.

If your husband serves in the Navy or Marine Corps and is deployed by ship, he has the option of inviting someone to join him on a Tiger cruise back to the mainland. A Tiger cruise is when the ship stops at its last port before heading to mainland America.

There is a lot of hype over these Tiger cruises, but I heard they are really boring. Frankly, I think it's like being in prison. You play a lot of video games, lift weights, and smoke cigarettes. It's not a Carnival Fun ship.

If you cruise from Hawaii to San Diego, the ocean can be really rough so get ready to puke.

Many times families will actually meet in Hawaii and do a reunion there. Many men take their leave then and honeymoon with their wives at this last port. This is great for families with kids. The wife flies to Hawaii. She and her hubby get alone time, then when they get back to the states the kids get to see their dad.

Jon's dad wanted to meet him in Hawaii and do the Tiger cruise. Unfortunately, he had some medical issues and decided he couldn't manage the trip.

Instead, Jon's parents flew to Hawaii and visited with him there. Jon and I had mixed feelings about their trip. We had been considering flying me out to Hawaii for a little honeymoon. Since his dad couldn't do the cruise, we thought if they saw him in Hawaii that we would have our own time back in the states.

In one way, it was the best thing to do. But I was sad and jealous when they called from Hawaii to tell me they were about to see Jon. In a way, his mom did get her "first kiss."

Jon called me that night to say that he felt weird because all the guys were honeymooning with their wives and he was with his mom and dad. It was a no-win situation for us.

No matter how you think your "first kiss back" will go down—who will be there or what you will wear—relax. Avoid high expectations.

Life in the military always has some drama attached. It's like when women put all their emotions and thoughts on the wedding and not the marriage. Keep that in mind and make sure your priorities are in order.

Our friend Kat received really disappointing news right before the homecoming. Her husband's ship had been redirected to help with the rescue of a capsized fishing boat crew. That meant the reunion wouldn't happen for another three days.

Can you imagine finding out two days before your husband is scheduled to arrive, "Sorry ladies, it will be three more days."

I felt so bad for her.

Be sure to take your camera to the reunion. I was blessed to have photos documenting both reunions.

Natalie snapped the most amazing photos of our first kiss afer his first deployment.

On his second deployment, Jon went with an early party so he came back before everyone else. He was the only Marine at the reunion.

My girlfriend Karen followed me on the 20-mile drive to pick up Jon so I could have photos of our reunion kiss. I will never forget her thoughtfulness.

THE DRIVE HOME

When Jon returned, I was surprised to discover it was like he had never left. I didn't feel like a huge weight had been lifted; I just felt at peace.

I will say this. I hadn't felt as though my husband was really safe until I saw him in America with my own eyes.

Calls from the airport in Iraq didn't calm me, nor did calls from Germany. Nothing helped until I saw him myself. At that point I thought, "He survived this war. I can breathe now."

He drove us home. During the long drive we chatted like old friends. It wasn't awkward or strained. All my worries about how we would get along were silly. My best friend was back and we were a couple again. It was as if seven months of hardship had never happened. All the time we had been apart didn't matter.

We had a lifetime ahead of us.

YOU ARE NOT ALONE ANY MORE

When people ask if we had trouble adjusting after Jon returned from Iraq, I explain that I learned very quickly not to come out of the shower with a towel wrapped around my head.

Ladies, since you've spent seven months or more alone in the house, you might want to curb your recent unattractive bachelorette behavior.

After all, you're now sharing your home with a man who is sexually attracted to you.

One wife told me she had to stop cutting farts while watching TV. She had never done this in front of her man before he deployed, but during his absence she had gotten comfortable letting herself and her crude behavior go.

So ladies, avoid burping, farting, and using the bathroom with the door open. You're not alone anymore.

I had to work through some adjustments. I wanted to show Jon I could relate to what he had been through. I tried to show him that I could live like he had in the desert. I knew he had gone without a lot of amenities in that sandbox over there. So I started to do the same around the house. After about a week he pulled me aside and said, "Sweetheart, I appreciate it, but you have to stop using the litter box. It's not right to blame the cat."

SEX

To be honest, sex was a bit awkward when Jon came home. The first time I was so scared I screamed and ran. I had forgotten how to do it.

After being everyone else's dildo fairy, I didn't practice what I preached. Let's just say I wasn't properly "prepared" for my husband's return.

In hindsight, I wish I had at least sat on a pickle or something. Many wives reported having to put ice on their pee pee after their first encounter. Frankly, I think you really do revert to virginity after six months of inactivity.

I heard from one of my girlfriends that her husband popped a hernia from their lovemaking escapades. Look ladies, you don't have to make up for seven months all at once. Surgery is no fun for anyone.

Jon started wanting sex at the weirdest times. We would be driving down the road in bad traffic and it would set him off. He would look at me and say, "If I had a Hummer right now, this would be a lot easier."

I was really shocked. My husband was not one to ask for sexual favors while driving.

I told him to get in the carpool lane if he was looking for that. He got into the lane and immediately relaxed. "You're right, honey, this is easier. I forgot about the carpool lane."

What? I was confused. When I tried to oblige his request he looked at me like I was crazy.

We did have some communication problems when he first returned, which took us a little while to work out.

SLEEPING TOGETHER

Sharing a bed with your spouse after a deployment is a totally different subject. I had acquired some bizarre sleeping rituals in order to get some rest during the months of separation.

At one point in the deployment my bedtime had moved from 11:00 p.m. to about 2:00 a.m.

Instead of sleeping on the left side of the bed I now slept in the middle of the bed surrounded by all the pillows. I made a nest of pillows. I had also bought this tiny squishy pillow that I put on my stomach to make up for the fact that Jon was not there. By the time Jon got back, I was used to this ritual.

Jon took an instant dislike to the pillow on my stomach. In fact, the new pillow became his arch rival.

Jon would toss it across the room when I wasn't looking. I would go insane when I couldn't have it. I felt like Linus without his blanket.

Whenever Jon complained about sleeping with one leg hanging off the side of the bed because there was no room, I would tell him to be glad I no longer kept the Taser under my pillow.

I also had a cat on the pillow above my head, another at my feet, and sometimes the dogs in the bed. With the bed jam-packed, Jon had to fight for his share of space. Often when I fell asleep I would spread out into an "x" shape and Jon would wake up squished into a corner of the bed.

As payback for my sleep routine, he would tell me in the morning that my breath "smelled like Iraq." One morning I rolled over to find him wearing a gas mask.

I had learned how to sew while Jon was gone—hand stitching ten different muumu-type nightgowns. I was quite proud of my handmade designs. These gowns were a cross between the dresses worn by Mama in "Mama's Family" (complete with ruffles, a high neckline, and lots of lace) and a dress worn on "Little House on the Prairie." I completed my ensemble with a thick pair of socks.

For Jon, these outfits were a huge turn-off. I thought of them as really soft and comfortable.

When I emerged from the bathroom in one of my handmade gowns, Jon would hiss under his breath, "MOO MOO!" Somehow this sounded like a threat.

I would try to initiate sex, but he wouldn't respond. I told him, "Let's play fantasy! It's the Civil War. You've been injured on my father's land and I hid you in the barn . . . go with it."

My role playing fantasy, however, didn't spark anything. I couldn't understand why he cared what I wore to bed. We had a healthy sex life. What was the big deal?

Deep down I knew I was being selfish and was putting my comfort before my man's needs of seeing his wife looking attractive.

Thanks to Dr. Laura, I eventually saw the error of my ways and put all my muumus in storage.

After I bought cuter, hipper looking jammies at Target, I enjoyed the new attention I got from my man. Now I looked cute and sexy instead of resembling a grandma.

My sex life and sleeping habits improved as well. All was back to normal. My man was happy.

I did ask for one compromise, though. Since I was wearing cuter nightgowns, Jon allowed me to keep the socks on.

The pillow, however, is still an issue. I'm working on it.

HIVES

In our battalion's reunion brief, we were told to keep everything positive for at least three days while our men became acclimated. We were told that no matter what, we were not to argue or bring up anything that would upset them.

That's certainly easier said than done.

I had kept some serious family issues from Jon while he was on his first deployment and still had to hold them back after he returned. I had had some problems communicating with his family while he was gone. It was a problem that had been building since we eloped. We didn't know each other well back then, so we didn't know how to communicate. This led to misunderstandings.

It was to the point that I needed Jon to address his family directly. He needed to take care of the problem so it didn't repeat itself during the next deployment.

But I had to find the right time to raise this issue with him. I kept to the three-day rule and said nothing. Even when he asked me how things were going with his family, I bit my tongue. Still, Jon could sense there was a problem.

We went down to the USS *Tarawa* to pick up the belongings he had left on ship. While there, I sat on the wool blanket on his bunk. I was wearing shorts. Wool and I have never gotten along, so by the time we got home I was itching all over.

I had these welts up and down the back of my legs. It got worse over the next few days. My legs were beginning to swell and the bumps went all the way up to my bottom. This is not so sexy, particularly when you have not seen your man in seven months and you have a lot of lovemaking to catch up on.

Jon took me to the doctor, who diagnosed hives. He thought I caught it sitting on Jon's wool blanket on the ship, and gave me antihistamines and calamine lotion.

There I was, covered with pink cream all over my legs. I looked like a kid at camp who had gotten into the poison ivy.

To make matters worse, Jon and I were leaving for Las Vegas. He only had a week of leave and his family had planned a big welcome home party in his hometown.

We had to split his leave between his family and our alone time. I was simmering emotionally. I had all these pent up emotions that I still had not shared with him.

I was miserable in Vegas. The heat aggravated the hives. My legs looked disgusting—even more so when Jon lathered me up with lotion every night. Who needs kinky foreplay when you can use calamine lotion?

I wanted to keep this trip positive, so I continued to bite my tongue and avoided talking about what had happened. But the longer I held it all in, the worse I got physically.

Beenie and Lloyd were with us for a few days in Vegas. Beenie freaked when she saw my legs. Really, I looked like a monster. She knew what I was upset about and was hoping I had finally talked about it with Jon. "No," I replied. "I just want this vacation to be fun and positive."

I had the burden hanging over my head and all over my legs the whole trip.

Partying with Beenie and Lloyd helped loosen me up. I was glad to have my best friend with me.

Jon and Lloyd had all this Iraqi money and used it to tip all the valets and waiters. It was hysterical. The money was worth nothing, but a rumor was flying all over Vegas that two Marines had found Saddam's money and were handing it out. We got free drinks everywhere we went. Those definitely helped calm me down.

After we got home, Jon asked me if there was something wrong. That's when the floodgates opened. I told him everything in a surprisingly calm manner. I told him about the issues I had had with his family, and how upset I had been. We talked about everything rationally and calmly.

He could understand the communication problems I had had and he understood my feelings. As we talked, I realized that I had been having a panic attack almost from the start of the reunion.

He immediately got on the phone with his family to discuss the problem. I took a Xanax and went to bed. When I awoke, my legs had nearly cleared up. Every night for a week I took a small Xanax before bed and each morning the hives were smaller and smaller.

I had stressed myself out and made myself physically ill. After talking with Jon and straightening things out with his family, I was able to calm down and begin to heal. Many newlyweds go through adjustment periods with their new families. Unfortunately for us, there was a war thrown into the middle of our growing pains. Great communication and a lot of love got us right again.

It's important to find that balance when your husband returns. If there's something pressing that you need to address, don't put it off.

I'm an advocate for the "three-day-nothing-negative" rule, but I took it way beyond that to three weeks. I wanted to pretend everything was perfect, but that was the wrong choice.

I had endured a lot during Jon's deployment. Once he was home and settled, though, it was time to take care of me.

Might I suggest that you write all your concerns down in letters, but don't send them? When he gets home you can decide if those letters are something he needs to read.

A lot of wives get into this martyr routine of, "I suffered more than you." They want their husbands to believe they gave just as much.

It's like their emotional needs are a bag that needs to be filled up. And yet, there's a hole in the bottom of it. No matter how much their husbands try to fill them up, it leaks out of the hole leaving them feeling empty. Eventually they will stop trying to fill the bag. The marriage is never the same.

Find acceptance and address legitimate concerns that can be changed. Don't bitch just to bitch. It becomes an endless cycle.

Nor is this a competition. I have had civilian friends ask Jon, "Who had it worse? Your freaked-out wife back home? Or you at war?"

Jon and I have the same answer. We both believe the other had it worse.

Jon says that he knew when he was in danger and when he was safe. He knew when to worry. He knew he was alive and breathing. But, he always felt bad for me because I never knew from one minute to the next whether he was dead or alive.

I say he definitely had it worse. I could get distracted, go to the movies or out with friends, drink a soda or a beer, eat out at a restaurant—all without someone trying to kill me. He was on alert 24/7 and in constant danger.

The point is we both recognize it was hard for each of us in different ways. And we love and honor each other for the strength and character we exuded in those times.

SHARING

I didn't push Jon to talk about what he had gone through or experienced over there. He shared what he wanted to share. I didn't have to prove that I could understand. He knew I did. He only told me what he knew I could handle, which was not much.

I believe wives don't need to know everything.

We pulled out photo albums so I could show him pictures from all the parties and celebrations the other wives and I threw.

It warmed his heart to know I was not home crying and sulking during his entire deployment. It brought Jon peace and joy to know that I had been taking care of myself and hadn't been crying and depressed every day. That made me proud of myself.

To this day there are photos of his time in Iraq that I have not seen, and I will probably never see them. While he was gone, I never told Jon when I was afraid, when I had had a bad day, or when there was a family crisis. Jon's ongoing gift to me is to never share the gory details of the missions and dangerous events he experienced.

We kept our concerns and fears in our own hearts. We didn't need to burden the other. That is love.

Over time we began to share some of what had happened in our separate lives during those months.

FALSE PREGNANCY

After Jon's second deployment we took a cruise to Mexico. It was our official "honeymoon," although it took place three years after our wedding.

Carl and Natalie were also going on a cruise, so Natalie and I went wild shopping for "cruise wear." I wanted to get some tops that would be comfortable as well as cool since it gets hot in Mexico

I purchased a ton of these smocked baby doll tops. They are gathered with elastic at the top then flare out in a baby doll fashion at the torso. The tops made my boobs look bigger than usual, which was annoying. My chest looked like one big boob in the middle.

Despite this, I liked the fact that the design flared out so much you could not see my stomach. Cruise ships are notorious for encouraging gluttony. I knew that I could eat as much as I wanted and would not have to worry about hiding a huge bloated belly. Covering my bloated gassy belly was more important than having deformed-looking boobs.

When we reached our first port on the cruise, I was feeling comfortable in my smocked top and shorts. We met another couple from the ship near the cab station and decided to share a ride. We were chatting about the cruise, what excursions we would being doing, and general chatty stuff you would expect.

The other couple said they were going to swim with dolphins. I was thrilled for them. I started my typical whining, asking Jon if we could also swim with dolphins.

The lady started to giggle. She patted my knee and said, "Well, you certainly can't do that now in your condition, but maybe next time." She looked at her husband. They smiled at each other and then looked back at me.

After we reached their destination and they got out, I found myself wondering if there were size restrictions for dolphin riding.

Later that day, as Jon and I were shopping, the locals kept trying to sell us goods. One by one they approached me with different items. They were calling back to each other and then pointing at me and calling me "Momma." I was flattered. I thought they were telling each other I was a "hot momma."

When one of them brought me a baby onesie that said, "Mexico" on it, it dawned on me what they meant: the locals calling me Momma, the baby onesie, the lady in the cab.

I turned to look at myself in a full-length mirror in the shop and saw my luxury "cruise wear" top made me look six months pregnant! So that's why people had been letting me go to the bathroom first if there was a line. I vowed to toss all the tops as soon as we got home.

By that night I had forgotten all about my "baby" and was tearing it up at the Karaoke bar on the ship.

Since we were on vacation and didn't have to drive, Jon and I were throwing down the vodka.

I was on stage with my drink in my hand singing and slurring Tina Turner's "Private Dancer" when the couple from the cab walked in. They stared at me with their mouths hanging open, their eyes moving from me, to my drink, at Jon, and then back at me. Finally, they shook their heads and walked out. When mommy boozes, baby loses.

PEEPING TOM

The cruise was the best vacation Jon and I had ever had. We finally relaxed. No more deployments faced us. We felt like newlyweds and were acting like them, too.

After a fun afternoon at the pool, we would go up to our room to shower and change. We had this amazing room with a balcony and would fall asleep with the window open listening to the sounds of the ocean. I kept the curtains open so I could see the open sea.

After rinsing off one afternoon I ran out of the shower buck naked and started running around the room like a wild woman. I started doing jumping jacks and various exercises to make Jon laugh.

He peeked his head out of the bathroom to watch me, and his eyes went wide. The next thing I knew, he jumped out of the bathroom and plowed right over me. For a split second I thought it was some sort of weird sexual advance, but he kept going, shouting like a mad man.

As I watched from ground level, Jon grabbed the curtains and pulled them shut. He turned around with a horrified look on his face and said, "Someone was out there on the balcony WATCHING YOU!"

He turned back to look through a tiny section of the curtain. He was totally freaked out.

Jon is so modest he would prefer to jump overboard rather than face the fact someone had been peeping in on us.

I got up to look and spotted someone out on the balcony, but he didn't have a pair of binoculars or a camera. He was washing windows, dancing to the music coming from his headphones.

Scrubbing away at his railing, this guy obviously had no idea I was in my room doing nude Jazzercise. Excuse me, the *ship's* railing (just in case you interpreted that as a metaphor for something perverted).

Jon watched him until he moved on a full five minutes later.

For the rest of the cruise, Jon gave all the janitors and crew on the ship the stink eye. He was convinced they were all looking at me as if I was not wearing any clothes.

The ocean view just wasn't the same for the remainder of the cruise. But I did get a great idea for a new type of exercise video.

GET THE FACTS:

Find out the true symptoms of PTSD. Don't fall for these tricks like I did.

* The smell from taking out the trash does not lead to flashbacks;

* Playing Wii an entire weekend is not a positive coping mechanism;

* Despite what he tells you, the FDA does not guarantee giving him oral sex before bed will cure nightmares.

BACK TO NORMAL?

Ok, so it's been a few weeks. You've been on vacation and have had your family reunion. The kids are sleeping in their own beds. Your husand is back at work. The excitement has worn off.

Now you think as you look at him, "Who is this stranger in my house?"

Basically, you're done being nice. You've done everything for at least the past seven months—paid the bills, taken out the trash, done the dishes, shopping, yard work, everything. Even during the first few weeks after his return, you continue doing all these tasks.

Your husband feels a bit worthless as he watches you buzz around the house like a queen bee. You need to realize men need to feel important. You need to put this man back to work as a member of the household. But do it the right way.

You must slowly get him used to sharing responsibilities again. You're the matriarch. This is your home. You know how it runs.

Although your man may not be facing another deployment, he is still in the military and has many responsibilities. You need to make the major chores your responsibilities.

Here is the key. Give him simple tasks that you know he can complete without screwing up. Have your man do things like take the trash out or carry a basket of dirty laundry down the steps for you.

Don't even think about allowing him to do the laundry. You know that will be a disaster. He'll mess it up even though he is trying to help. And you will be a nasty bitch complaining because he didn't do it the way you do it.

This is the stage in the reunion adjustment period where you both start to get nasty.

This is where I have a beef with the DIs (Drill Instructors) out there. I have noticed Marines do not listen to a word their wives say unless we scream at them. You can't gently and calmly request your Marine to do something around the house. He won't respond.

I would go so far as to say they don't even hear you unless you go into DI mode. The DIs have trained these men to respond to certain tones and inflections. They block out everything else.

If you want them to do something you have to get in their face screaming, "3, 2, 1! ON YOUR FEET!"

"Get up right now and take out the trash."

"NO!"

"Do it right! Get it back."

"GET IT BACK!"

"ZERO!"

It is bizarre, I admit. I still feel really weird when I have to do it.

Your main argument with your man once you're back to normal becomes, "You're not doing enough around here to help!"

And when you give him something to do, you find yourself yelling, "You don't do it right, so I will just do it myself!"

Ladies, if these men are constantly being told they can't do it right, they will stop offering to help. Ask yourself this: when he stops wanting to help, where will you be?

Pick your battles wisely. Be patient. Give your husband chores that will make him feel like he is needed and part of the family without overwhelming both of you or the balance of the home.

Ladies, in military life you hold the power in your home. You call the shots. Most importantly, you are responsible for maintaining the balance there.

I remember Jon wanted to do some things, so he offered to unload the dishwasher. I thought I would have a heart attack as I stood their watching him handling my dishes. He was putting cups away next to the soup bowls, and forks next to the cups.

I wanted to scream, "What is your damn problem? Did you ever live here? Quit fucking up my kitchen! Do you even know where anything goes? The colander doesn't go next to the baking sheets! You are a moron! How is it you can search all over Iraq for weapon caches, but you can't take a second to find out where the damn soup bowls go?"

I simmered as I watched him, curse words ready to fly. And then I remembered: he knows about as much about a kitchen as I know about Iraq.

I'm not going to say we didn't get into it at various times because we did. I simply learned to pick my battles.

A lot of wives complained about how their husbands interacted with their babies and small kids. Children can go through a lot of changes in six months and dads miss a lot. Routines and responsibilities change. Take the time to incorporate dad into the new structure at home.

A common complaint I heard from my girlfriends was, "He wiped the baby wrong, bathed the baby wrong, burped the baby wrong." These wives were fired up.

A week later I would hear, "He never wants to help with the baby."

You think?

Adjusting to having Jon at home was frustrating and exhausting. Sometimes I felt like there was a child in my home but, Lord knows I was thankful that he was there.

Many of us put too much emphasis on our homes because it was the only thing we could control and make stable and safe during the deployment. It was an effort to let go of that control, but Jon also needed a sense of belonging.

Take deep breaths before blowing your cool over how he does something. Just be thankful he's home.

SEPARATION ANXIETY

After Jon's second deployment we were both experiencing the effects of wartime deployments. I went through a phase where I could not go anywhere without Jon. He could go to work and I could go the commissary and I'd be fine.

But after work or on the weekends I wanted him to be with me. I could not go to the bank, Wal-Mart, or even to the mall. If it was off base, I wanted him with me. If we were on base we were "safe."

I even had to go with him if he needed to take a trip to Lowe's.

It was all very subtle; no Xanax needed. I wasn't having panic attacks or irrational fears. I just wanted to stay physically close to Jon. I know it was because we had been separated for so long and I was afraid to lose him again. And I wanted every minute back that we had lost.

I didn't even realize the extent I was doing this until months later when I actually went to the mall or bank alone.

It took me months to overcome the panic of two consecutive deployments. It took time to trust that we could be in separate places at the same time and that no one was in danger.

It also took me months to be secure enough to go someplace without him. I remembered one day driving to the store alone and thinking, "I am OK with this. I actually left Jon at the house and am going by myself to the store."

I remember smiling and thinking a new leaf had been turned over.

Jon went through personality adjustments as well. He became extremely forgetful and seemed to have no short-term memory. You can call it what you want— PTSD, combat stress, whatever. Jon and I were different people after those two years.

It took a while to redefine ourselves, but we did it together. And our love for each other is stronger because we survived those changes.

WHEN YOUR SPOUSE MEETS YOUR WIFE

The wives had been very supportive of one another—until the guys came back. Then we started to get a little catty.

I don't know if it was because we were all getting laid regularly, but I suspect it may have been the competition over the gifts our husbands brought home.

One wife at a barbecue would start, "My husband brought me back gold from Bahrain," which was countered by, "My husband brought me back opals from Australia!" That was topped by, "My husband brought me black pearls from Hawaii!"

But there was always that one lady who ruined it for everyone when she piped up, "My husband brought me Chlamydia from Singapore."

It gets awkward when you're together again and your husband meets your "wives." You have shared so much, but now that your husband is back the communication between you and your "wives" has stopped, and you miss them. When your friends have become your surrogate spouse or "new wife," you can have some serious misunderstandings. Sometimes wives can expect a little too much from each other, or jealousy over intimacy arises when the guys come back. It's not even in a co-dependent way, but more like siblings fighting.

It's hard for some spouses to let go when the true spouse returns and the friendship is not what it used to be. Maybe a wife stops calling or wanting to hang out. Or another wife comes to you complaining about her husband, which makes you feel weird because you can't relate.

Some men have trouble slipping back into their role of being a husband. Many are content to act as if they are a guest in their own home, letting the wife run the house and raise the kids while her friends play the role of spouse.

Remember, ladies, you are only treated the way you allow yourself to be treated.

These are military guys. They are used to taking orders, not deciphering clues. Say exactly what you want and expect from them. Jon and I had way too many arguments over his inability to read my mind.

I remember when Beenie was pregnant for the second time. Lloyd was a little freaked out because he had missed the birth of their first daughter. Pregnancy and giving birth were old hat to Beenie, but Lloyd was unsure what to do or what role to play.

When Beenie went into labor, Lloyd called me from the Naval Hospital. He was whispering, "Mollie, I think you should come up here. I think Beenie hates me. I think she'd rather have you here."

I scolded him and told him, "Lloyd, it's your turn! Get back in there and rub her back and arms and give her some encouragement, damn it!" I ordered him to go be a husband and a daddy!

I hung up on him. I had to issue a little tough love.

Lloyd ended up doing just fine. And they were glad to share the experience.

The biggest transition for me was that once Jon was home our marriage was just us again. While he was gone, I had had all these women involved in my life. We had shared everything.

But when it was just Jon and me, my girlfriends were no longer a part of my marriage and day-to-day life. They were just my friends again.

I have to admit that my girlfriends knew more about me and my feelings than my husband had learned in our first four years of my marriage. They provided advice for decisions and comfort when I was struggling.

It was very difficult to give that up and transfer those roles back to my husband. If fact, it took years.

GET OUT

Although I had separation anxiety when John left the base without me to run errands, I was conflicted about wanting my own space around the house. I had had enough of our time together. After two weeks of spending every minute together, I asked if he had some place to go. He was a little shocked.

I felt bad, but what I really wanted to yell, "I love you, but GET OUT! I need Bunco and girl time!"

I couldn't remember the last walk I had had with Michelle, the last date with Autumn, a phone call with Beenie, or my last conversation with Natalie and Kat.

Although I remembered being sad and miserable while he was gone, there is this weird point after the reunion when you start to miss that alone time.

I wanted that time when I could just do nothing, with no one to clean up after or cook for. I wanted the time when I could watch my shows or movies whenever I decided.

Take my advice: do not tell your husband you miss being alone. You're adjusting to having his company again. The only people who will understand are the other wives who have gone through the same thing. Everyone else will think you are a complete asshole. You're not.

So, it was time for a Bunco night. I needed some girl time after weeks of testosterone. I called Autumn and suggested a reunion Bunco.

The husbands moaned and whined: "But what will we do all night while you're gone?"

"HA! Try it for seven months. You'll figure it out!"

(We weren't that cruel, though.)

Lloyd stepped up and offered to host a poker night for the guys at his house.

Our reunion Bunco was a blast. All of us carried on and on—giggling about the sex we had been having and how our husbands could not remember where anything in the house went. We talked about the cruises and trips we had gone on. It was like old times, but so much happier because the stress was mostly gone.

After a few rounds of Bunco and a couple of drinks, we started wondering what the guys were doing at their poker night. "I wonder if they carry on like we do," someone said, "talking about us and sex?"

Everyone got quiet. Then I had one crippling thought—"Moo Moo." I had to stop this poker party! I piped up, "Let's spy on them! Let's crash the party!"

Off we went—all twelve of us—down the dark streets of Del Mar trying to be inconspicuous. Karen lost a shoe. Someone else stopped to pee in the bushes.

As we approached the house, we could see the men inside drinking beers and playing cards. "It's a trick!" I whispered. "There is no way they are this boring! They must know we're out here!"

We decided to send in a few recon snipers to get a better look. Amazingly, I was chosen to approach the house. We got right under the windows and listened in. They were actually playing cards and betting. No one was talking about boobs, sex, or nagging wives. We sat there for ten minutes. I think Lloyd was even petting the poodle sitting on his lap.

That was it?!

I popped my head up so they could see me and yelled, "You guys are so lame! What are you doing?"

They all looked at me in shock. Jon answered: "We're doing what you told us to do. We're playing poker."

At that point, the ladies decided to go get wine coolers, cigarettes, and rap music so we could crash the boy's card game. Their party was just too pathetic.

If only those men had known what went on at a Del Mar Bunco Party. Either they would have been proud of their wild wives, or they would have had the entire game shut down.

COOK OFFS

After that night, we decided it was time we started having normal neighborhood parties again.

Lloyd and Beenie's home became the designated place for a barbecue or a neighborhood picnic.

Lloyd is very competitive. The cook-offs started after I made chicken enchiladas for Beenie one night during deployment. Lloyd, as usual, got jealous when Beenie said they were the best she ever had. He challenged me to a cook-off when he returned from Iraq.

At the scheduled cook-off, we had three different types of chicken enchiladas. Many threats and fighting words were exchanged. And yet, I don't remember who won the challenge that day. I do know Beenie still insisted mine were better than Lloyd's. That drove him nuts.

He wants all of Beenie's affection, approval, and attention. He's like a kid yelling at his mom, "Watch me! Aren't I the best?"

It was cute, and it was a sign that we were getting back to normal.

PAMPER YOURSELF

I learned the hard way that there are some things you can do with your wives that you can't do with your husband.

I booked a spa day for Jon and me at a San Diego casino. I thought we both deserved a little relaxation and pampering, but it didn't turn out as well as I had hoped.

It all started when Jon found out a man would be giving him a massage. He said he didn't want to have a man touching him "like that." I didn't want him to be tense the entire time, so I requested a female masseuse for him.

Then he got upset about the female "touching him like that." He said I was the only one who could touch him.

I thought about asking him about his theory on massage therapists touching everyone "inappropriately," but figured I'd better leave it alone. Wherever he had gotten the negative impression of massages, I didn't want to know.

Instead, I assured him it would be OK since we'd be in the room together.

The couple's massage session included a private whirlpool tub spa and six-jet shower afterward. Jon was freaking out the entire time that someone might see his penis. I was surprised, since this is a man who had taken showers out in the open in front of about 2,000 Marines and Iraqis during the war.

I later realized his irrational fear stemmed from an incident when we were first married.

Before we left South Carolina, Jon and I had a gathering to say goodbye to our friends. My parents came in from Virginia and Jon's dad flew in from Idaho to celebrate with us.

We had a great party. I got a little ripped. My dad kept telling me all night to "cool it and eat more meat."

My parents stayed at my apartment that night. They were sleeping on the fold-out couch in the living room while Jon and I were in the bedroom.

Later that night after we had had sex, Jon got up to use the bathroom. When he came back to bed, he said my dad had walked in on him while he was peeing.

Yikes! Why would my dad barge in on him? Jon explained that he had not turned the light on, so when my dad opened the door and turned on the light, he got an eyeful of his very nude son-in-law!

I wanted to die of embarrassment. My parents knew Jon and I were sexually active (we were newlyweds, after all), but my dad seeing my Jon naked was so over the top.

Jon was setting a pattern that would follow him through the next few years. I assured him that the massage therapist would not see his pee pee, and that he would always be covered.

The massages went off without a hitch. Neither of us got so relaxed that we tooted. Nor were our genitals exposed.

When the massage was done, the therapist told us the room was ours for the next hour and to enjoy the complimentary champagne and strawberries.

Jon and I headed to the next room to enjoy the whirlpool. We laughed about how silly Jon had been with his fears about being exposed in front of a stranger. He even admitted that his massage therapist had acted very professionally.

We stripped down and settled into the huge tub. Jon offered to go into the next room to get the strawberries.

He returned white as a ghost.

"What happened," I asked.

Jon explained. While he was collecting the strawberries and champagne, the door opened and the female therapist walked in.

"Oh, I'm sorry. I knocked, but you must not have heard me. I just left something in here."

With the strawberries and champagne in his hands, all Jon could do was stand there unable to cover his pee pee.

I told Jon he got his wish. He had used the negative law of attraction and been granted his wish of being seen naked. He was upset and no longer able to relax.

In the end, I decided Spa Days are just for girls.

Then again, what if she had walked in him while he was doing naked jumping jacks?

Chapter Eight

ON THE L.A.M.
(LIFE AFTER THE MILITARY)

After four years of service to our country, it was time to make some major decisions. Jon had the option to augment and stay in for two more years, or get out of the service.

Ultimately, we made the tough decision to leave the military.

My husband told me I had supported him in his lifelong dream to be a Marine and to serve his country. Now it was my turn to pursue my dreams, and he was willing to support me.

It was a true sacrifice for Jon, and one that was very tough for me to accept. Leaving life in the military behind us was like leaving our family.

In truth, everyone was being reassigned. Although Camp Pendleton would no longer be the same, it would always be my home.

But Jon knew what was best for us. I had been doing stand-up comedy off and on, but had not been taking classes, writing, or regularly performing. He knew that in order for me to be happy we needed a home base so I could pursue my dreams more easily and more diligently.

We were still young and unsure what we wanted to be when we grew up. It was time to explore other options. We moved up to Los Angeles to what I would call a "transitional neighborhood," meaning it was ten minutes from the sunny California coast and ten seconds from the ghetto. It was what we could afford.

I tried to settle into my new house and neighborhood, but I was afraid of no longer living on base. I remembered how worried I had first been when we first moved on base, surrounded by tanks, helicopters, men with guns, and a big fence. Now I felt naked and insecure without them.

I have to admit that living in Los Angeles was a lot like living on base—lots of random gunfire, sirens, and men carrying weapons. While those sounds once made me feel safe, now I was truly scared. I was even afraid to walk my dogs at night. I asked my husband to teach me some self-defense moves. I wanted to know what to do if someone tried to rape me while I was out with Monsieur and CoCo.

He told me to just start nagging. In no time at all, he continued, my attacker would get frustrated and leave me alone. I guess the sound of a woman nagging is a universal sexual turn-off.

I quickly learned that our neighborhood had an appreciation for the arts. Our local neighborhood "Crips" representative welcomed us by letting us know we were part of his territory. He left his spray-painted message on the side of our house.

One night as my husband and I were driving home through our neighborhood, we saw the cutest little fur ball scurrying across the street. Was it abandoned? Injured? Hungry? There was no oncoming traffic so I begged my husband to stop the car so I could run out and get it.

Jon knows my love for animals, so he slowed down. I jumped out of the car and started running after my new pet. My heart quickened with anticipation of an animal rescue! That is just what I needed to get my mind off how miserable I was feeling in this new city. I was sure if I put my energy and effort into an animal, my depression would quickly fade.

I bent down to touch my tiny rescue and flinched as it lay lifeless on the road. I picked it up (it was so light!) and held it close to my chest to give it warmth. I was so frightened—it was not moving! And it felt, well, empty. When I looked more carefully I realized I was holding somebody's weave.

After that I decided I needed a new strategy and attitude. A new neighborhood, like a new base, is what you make of it. I was focusing on the negative.

My husband and I set out to look for local attractions and restaurants to visit. We picked two a week and started looking forward to getting to know our surroundings. We also developed a passion for riding bikes along the beach and going to the theater. Before long we had more things to do than we had time for.

By the way, I kept my pet weave. I just couldn't bear the thought of her living the rest of her life on the streets. She is really an ideal pet. She doesn't eat much and only needs a good brushing once a week. We have not named her yet, but if you have any suggestions email me. She hasn't answered to any names we have tried so far.

She sleeps in the bed with us at nights. However, she's put outside when it comes to private time between my husband and I. My husband doesn't like the look she gives us when we are being "intimate."

Making real friends, however, was another matter. Our Los Angeles neighbors were not like our friends on base at Pendleton. They weren't interested in poker nights or cook-offs. And none of them had ever heard of Bunco.

I tried inviting my massage therapist to go with me for a pedicure, or to take a trip to Target. She stared at me like I was a mass murderer.

I made a few friends in my acting classes. For the most part, though, Los Angeles folks stick to themselves. If anyone lived more than five miles away you had to make an appointment to get together. Appointments to see friends? Unbelievable! I clearly was not on base anymore!

Not only that, we quickly learned that traveling five miles in Los Angeles takes at least forty minutes. It seemed that no matter where we wanted to go, we had to set aside an hour to get there.

In other parts of the country, if you want to do something rain is the determining factor. In L.A., it's traffic and gas. No one wants to drive anywhere since the traffic is always horrible.

I tried to think positive. I was finally living in a place where it is acceptable to have fake hair, a fake tan, and fake nails, but I couldn't afford the gas to travel to get any of it done!

And everyone in Los Angeles has these weird food hang-ups. They're either on the dog beach diet or the south beach club diet or something. They would have freaked if they knew what I had been eating the past few years—Kettle Corn, cans of tuna fish, and raw cookie dough.

We decided to try a dinner party with a few friends we had met, but it turned out to be a disaster. They responded with little notes saying, "We no longer eat carbs." Or, "Just so you know, we do not eat meat anymore. Hope that won't be a problem."

My favorite was, "We are gluten free now. It keeps our autism levels low." (Yes, I am serious!)

I had no idea what to serve any of these people, so I bought some cabbage and bean soup.

It's funny, but they were all freaked out about eating dinner at our home. "Why?" asked Jon.

"Well," one of them admitted, "You're a Marine family, and we thought you might serve something . . . barbaric."

Jon was speechless. I wasn't sure what that meant. So I asked. "What do you mean?"

"We thought you might serve Iraqi meat."

Did she mean meat from Iraq, or dead Iraqis? Either way, I was pissed. "Don't worry," I told her. "We save the good shit for family."

We never saw them again.

We eventually connected with friends we met through work and classes, but I really missed the community we had while living on base. In the Corps we had shared a common bond. And yet, with all the diversity in L.A. there is no common bond.

Thank goodness that Jon and I are each other's best friend.

FRIENDS AROUND THE WORLD

I stayed in touch with my military girlfriends, who are now spread all over the world.

Erin was on the East coast and we continued to talk regularly. When she and her husband got stationed in my parent's hometown, I was delighted to be able to fly home and visit them quite frequently.

Erin and Mike had their first "B-billet baby" after his two deployments.

*   *   *

Beenie and Lloyd chose to be stationed in Okinawa, Japan. Beenie was cautioned by a seasoned wife who had lived there to watch out for the "Okinawa Surprise."

Beenie replied, "Eeeeeww. Is that like fried octopus or something?"

The wife laughed and replied, "No, it's the baby your husband will give you when you get stationed over there."

Indeed, Beenie did have her third baby in Okinawa, but she was no surprise. She was very much wanted. Okinawa, however, was tough on Beenie.

The time change was not like coast-to-coast in the States. Catching each other on the phone was difficult. Add to the equation the fact she was taking care of three kids now.

She called me just after her third daughter was born and said, "I'm done having all these babies, and I'm going back to drinking and smoking!"

She called a week later to report she had drunk all the Amaretto on base and they were placing a special order just for her! In fact, the PX on Okinawa had a permanent waiting list for pregnancy tests and Amaretto.

Life without Beenie is boring.

*   *   *

Michelle stayed on Pendleton for a while, so we were able to have them over for Thanksgiving dinner in our new home in Los Angeles. Jon fried the turkey, which turned out great. We were surrounded by family and our favorite neighbors.

By the first of the year, Michelle and her husband had PCSed to the East coast. I missed their boys so much.

Michelle once told me she had dreamed about Jon and me before she moved onto Pendleton. She said she actually saw our faces. So when she first met us, she felt like she knew us already.

I told her I had prayed and prayed for the Lord to bless us with good neighbors. And He did.

I will always be so thankful for sharing so much with Michelle and her family. I consider it an honor to have watched those boys grow up.

*   *   *

Natalie and Kat followed in Grunt wife tradition. Natalie had a "B-billet" baby in her new duty station. I greatly missed seeing those girls every week, especially sharing a smoke with them on the back porch.

I have since given up my social cigarettes at parties. (I never wanted to be thirty and smoking. I like my skin and lungs too much.)

Unfortunately, I now have "smoker's lips"—deep groves on the skin around my lips from the smoke. When I put on lipstick it bleeds through the lines and I look like I have catfish whiskers.

I miss both my conversations with Natalie and Kat and the female companionship. Shopping at Target is no fun without them.

* * *

Autumn and I remain in touch. Her marriage ended after her husband's third deployment to Iraq.

I used to cast judgment on military families getting divorced, but what happened to Autumn opened my eyes.

Her husband returned a very different man. They tried going to counseling and talking things out, but finding a compromise proved elusive.

Autumn found out in a message from her in-laws what their next duty station was. Her husband had not bothered to tell her they were moving.

By this time Autumn had returned to school to get her teacher's credential so she could work wherever they were stationed. She had accepted volunteer positions and found hobbies to keep her busy during his deployments. Wisely, she had bettered herself and her health prepping for a life as a military wife.

Then her husband came home one day and said, "You have lost too much weight with all this exercising you're doing, I liked you better when you had big boobs and a big butt."

I hit the roof when I heard this. Jon had been thrilled to hear Michelle and I were walking everyday. He would have been overjoyed if I had taken up a more aggressive hobby like surfing or running, as Autumn had done.

The final straw for Autumn, though, came after one counseling session when her husband said to her, "I just can't see myself having a family anymore." He didn't mean children; he meant her as his wife. The marriage was indeed over.

Earlier in the book, I wrote that in order to make a military marriage work you have to make your man your number one priority and accept that you are number two. But I meant you are number two behind the military, not behind his wants. The biggest part of being married is to live for someone else, and to strive to make them happy.

Autumn was the one wife who accepted the military lifestyle and role as a housewife better than the rest of us. She became my role model. Because of her example I embraced being a housewife and took pride in being a good one. I was shocked to see her marriage fall apart. I knew she had done her best to contribute to the union, but he had changed beyond what could be repaired.

Autumn is very happy now. We still have the most fun together and can be around each other for hours without getting on one another's nerves. She has moved on and is thriving in her new life.

OUR SORORITY

Since our time on Camp Pendleton and surviving the war together, all of us report we just can't find that same magical chemistry in the new places we live. Whether it's a new base housing community or a civilian neighborhood, my "sorority sisters" across the world now have the same complaint: "It's just not like Camp Pendleton!"

Indeed, that time together was like being in a sorority. I had worked my way through college and never experienced being in a sorority, but I imagine it was similar to our neighborhood on base.

I was chatting with Michelle's husband, Kevin, on a visit to the East coast and he confided that Michelle was just not as happy on their new base.

"Mollie, I think she thought all bases would be like it was on Camp Pendleton, but they aren't. I've never seen anything like that and I don't think we ever will again. You all were just so bonded. You can't repeat that."

He was right. We had all shared so much at such a unique time. It left us forever bonded.

After that conversation I stopped searching for that type of friendship. I no longer needed to. I already had it.

In the end, if war had brought us all together, then distance could not keep us apart. I love each of those women and their children with all my heart. I always will, no matter where we are in the world.

NEW MARRIAGE

Jon started growing his hair out, which I found totally disgusting.

He started off slow by wearing a "Med Reg" when he returned from his second deployment. Then it moved into a "Low Reg." I was getting suspicious. It was not sexually appealing at all.

There was no smooth shaved feeling on the back of his head. Now there was HAIR! It was really freaking me out.

I thought of all the tantrums I had thrown over the massages given by the Vietnamese ladies when he was getting his "High and Tight" cuts. Now I was begging him to shave it off.

He told me that he would look "too militant" wearing a Jarhead haircut working in a civilian job. He was right. I finally accepted that he was growing his hair out.

But growing hair was not the only change occurring in our marriage. I figured that since we had spent so much time apart in the military that the time for separation was over. I was wrong.

His new job sent him out of town for weeks at a time, which forced me to PCS to Los Angeles alone. Jon's new gig also meant working holidays and weekends. It was worse than the Corps because there was no pride behind it. To be honest, that first year out of the Corps was tougher on our marriage than our years in the military. Who would have thought *that* was possible?

We had purchased a home and moved to a new city, but had no friends. We both had new jobs, but we were working opposite schedules. Jon was working nights and weekends. I worked days and had weekends off.

In addition to adjusting to this new lifestyle, we were both coming down from military life and the effects of war. In the military we had spent so much time away from each other that it was like being on a perpetual honeymoon. There had been loving calls home, love letters, emails, flowers. In our new life, there was no romance.

I thought we had had our fill of hardship when we left the military behind. I soon realized that all marriages require hard work, and that life is even harder. You just have to constantly work on it.

We now had to overcome new misunderstandings with everyone around us. We were no longer military, and yet that was a huge part of who we were. Jon and I both went through a time when we felt we didn't belong anywhere.

The military had been such a huge part of our lives, but many folks in Los Angeles aren't that receptive to military families. Jon had difficulty with the lack of pride and respect exhibited by his co-workers.

I, on the other hand, had problems socially. Making new friends was hard for me for the first time in my life.

Once again, we only had each other. And yet, we weren't around one another very much. I found myself lonely and depressed—again.

Jon started to withdraw. I could tell he needed time to be alone. I sensed he felt more comfortable doing activities by himself.

Still, I was becoming increasingly needy and miserable.

It was a very long, rough year. Our communication sucked. We were once again "riding our vows."

God blessed us by finding a new job for Jon one year later. We were relieved and thankful. We had not had a day off together for a year. Now we could spend holidays with family again. We were able to sleep together and Jon was sleeping better because he was working days.

We accepted that we were very different people from the couple that had met at a fish fry years earlier. We also knew our marriage had changed.

We accepted the changes in each other and we thanked God for each other, our love, and our marriage. We dealt everyday with the changes. It was so much a part of our lives that I barely noticed the changes in each of us.

We were both working full time and I was pursuing my stand-up comedy and writing. But I was overwhelmed. At times I felt like I had three jobs—homemaker, sales rep, and entertainer.

I had done everything for Jon for four years. I covered all the bases, from paying the bills, to cleaning every dish, to buying the groceries.

This made me mad when I came home exhausted from a day at work and had to cook dinner and then write or study for a couple of hours before bedtime. How could he walk by a pile of dirty dishes and not do them? Resentment started to build inside me.

I was finally living my dream (stand-up), but I was tired all the time. I was not as happy as I had been when life was simpler. That's when I decided to go back to talk therapy. I needed a neutral ear to help me navigate back from all the deployments and separations from Jon. This time Jon joined me. We had a lot of new adjustments to work through.

In therapy, I finally got it through my head that Jon is not a mind reader. He didn't know I wanted him to do the dishes. I had never asked! We were still living as though we were in the military and I was in charge of the house.

Jon and I had to talk through how to run our new home as well as figure out how to share the housework. We addressed issues from our childhoods as well as the war. It was an amazing release for both of us, and we found out so much about each other's feelings.

I have to admit I miss our old way of life. It took me a while to understand that just because I could do it all it does not mean I have to.

Jon started to pitch in around the house and we started having lovely dinners together as well as date nights. Our home was once again a place we both wanted to be.

Our marriage began to improve. I can honestly say that our marriage is better now than it has ever been. I owe that to therapy and the commitment we have to each other.

CAMO COMEDY

As I began to incorporate more military wife jokes into my stand-up act, my identity changed to "The Military Wife." Audiences laughed at the idea of military people trying to fit into the Los Angeles lifestyle.

One day on stage I asked myself, "Why am I doing these jokes for these drunks in a Hollywood club? Why not do them for the wives on base who are trying to survive a deployment and need cheering up?"

That's when I began performing Military Wife Comedy just for the military. I placed edited sets on Youtube and my website so military wives could watch at their leisure, no matter where they were stationed.

And then I geared up for a tour. I was determined to give back to a group of women I loved so much.

I have found as much peace following my dream as I did supporting a group of ladies who are the strongest women I know. I am proud to be a member of the Silent Ranks.

THE CALL YOU DON'T WANT

In November of Jon's first year out of the military, I received a call that his Commanding Officer had been killed in Iraq. It shook me to the core.

I immediately drove to his wife's home. I thought about how lucky we had been during those two deployments not to lose anyone so close to us. We got so many "all clear" calls from the Key Volunteer Network every week. What a blessing that we didn't suffer the death of a close family friend.

Those calls would shake me up, but I would thank the Lord that it was not my husband who had been killed. At the same time I had to pray for the families that were dealing with the devastating news.

Now my friend was dealing with the loss of the love of her life. Jon and I were there for Karen and her kids. We went to the funeral, visited often, and sent a lot of emails.

We continue to stay in contact with her. Her husband's death was the first loss of someone who was close to both of us.

Karen had been my KVC, my friend, and had come to numerous Bunco parties, birthday celebrations, and hang-out sessions in the backyard with kids bouncing and screaming on the trampoline.

I was used to her comforting me; now it was my turn to comfort her. Jon and I keep a photo of Karen's husband in our living room as a daily reminder of him and his family, and of how precious life really is.

I pray for the widows of war every night. I pray for their courage, and blessed memories of the love they had, as well as for new companionship in whatever form it comes.

WHAT THE MILITARY CAN DO FOR YOU

The Marine Corps offered us an instant group of friends and a ready-made family. As I've said, the people we met in the Corps will be our friends for life, no matter where they live.

I know that it's not the Marine Corps that provides these great people and experiences. The Corps is a business. Like a machine, it functions automatically. It's the people working within it who make it great. And it's those people you must put your faith in.

Too many men will chase after a rank or a goal in the military while leaving their families in second place. After twenty-five years of service, they expect that the military is going to do something for them, remember them, honor them, or thank them. Instead they retire and someone else takes their place. All they have after a quarter-century of dedicated service and sacrifice is a plaque and a hat. They mistakenly believe there would and should be more for them.

Servicemen need to recognize the military doesn't hold their hand when they're ill, or have grandchildren come over for visits. The Corps will not be sitting by your side when you are old and feeble, but your family will be.

You have to use the military like it uses you. The military has many wonderful opportunities, but it will not be there for you at all times; nor does it see you as an individual.

Find pride in what you did for the military and your country (and for what it did for you), but realize that other things matter greatly. Families and servicemen with the right priorities and perspective will find a fulfilling life outside the service. Those who put too much into the structure will lose more than just their identities.

HONESTY?

One lazy day, months after Jon was out of the Corps, I heard this rumbling sound coming from Jon. I was blown away! My husband had just farted in front of me.

In more than five years of marriage Jon had never done that. He is from one of those families where no one farts or poops. I, on the other hand, come from a family where my dad waits for us in the car with the windows rolled up. When we open the car doors, we're blasted with toxic ass gas. My dad has turned farting into a sport. My two brothers and I used farts as a weapon.

The only time I ever saw my mother cry was when dad farted in public. She laughed so hard that tears ran down her cheeks.

I respected that Jon came from a family that had different values when it came to bodily functions. I had always given him his privacy, but here was my husband of five years tooting in front of me.

Of course, he instantly denied making the noise and made the same sound again by moving his foot along the couch. I was disappointed. He really hadn't tooted in my presence.

Not willing to let the subject go, I playfully teased Jon by telling him that he sometimes farts in his sleep. This was much too much. I had hit a nerve. He countered that I also farted in my sleep. The battle was on.

I demanded to know when I had supposedly passed gas in my sleep. I had made every effort to hold back my frequent gas attacks for at least five years. In fact, I had purchased so much GAS-X during our marriage I should have also bought stock in the company.

It was at that point that Jon revealed the most humiliating story I had ever heard in my life. He recalled the romantic story of the first time we had made love. After a very passionate night, Jon had awakened to find me still sleeping soundly. He stood up and gazed at the woman he loved. My golden hair was spread across the pillow and the morning sun was dancing over it.

He described me as his tiny angel. As he stood at the end of the bed staring down at me, filled with happiness that we would share every morning of the rest of our lives together, I farted.

The story made me scream and immediately burst into tears. My husband is no storyteller, nor does he know how to lie. I knew he was telling the truth and I was humiliated. Frankly, I believe that honesty is not always the best policy, especially in a marriage.

To this day we do not fart in front of each other. That's our new family rule. However, I can't say the same for my dad. Jon is on his own there.

CONCLUSION

Jon and I are enjoying our new roles as civilians in service to the military. We hold the motto "Once a Marine, Always a Marine" close to our hearts.

We enjoy meeting new families in the military and get such a thrill when we find ourselves sitting next to another veteran at a wedding reception or event. Finding another Marine in Los Angeles is like finding a diamond in the rough. We treasure each meeting and experience.

Recently Jon bought tickets to go see the opera "Miss Saigon." It's the story of a Marine who has an affair with a prostitute in Vietnam. As the story goes, the Marine discovers some years later that he has a child in Vietnam.

After the show, I turned to Jon: "That was lovely, but are you trying to tell me something? The doorbell is not going to ring this weekend, is it?"

GLOSSARY

ALPHAS: or service alphas: a semi formal uniform worn when reporting to a new duty station.

BAH: Basic allowance for housing.

BCGs: Birth control goggles.

BOQ: basic officer's quarters; temporary housing for officers.

BUNCO: Dice game popular with military wives.

CACO: Casualty assistance calls officer who helps the family in the event of a service member's death.

CAX: Combined arms exercise.

CO: Commanding officer, the boss.

COMMISSARY: Grocery store for military on base.

COVER: A hat.

DEPENDENT: A legal term given to those receiving financial support from the service member.

DEVIL DOG: Nickname and term of endearment for Marines.

DI: Drill Instructor.

DITY MOVE: Do it yourself move. The military reimburses you to move yourself from one duty station to the next.

DRESS BLUES: Formal uniform worn to the ball, or any formal event.

DUTY: Standing guard, or having guard detail.

DUTY STATION: Location of your service member's job.

EAS: End of Active Service.

GRUNT: Infantry, artillery, armor, men of combat arms.

HAZARDOUS DUTY PAY: Increase in pay given any time a service member is stationed in an area deemed hazardous.

ICE: Interactive customer evaluation. Online comment card for MWR and MCCS.

IOC: Infantry Officers Course.

JAG: Judge Advocate General, a military lawyer.

KV/KVC/KVN: Key volunteer is the person who relays information from the battalion to the dependents back home, a deployment support network. A KVC is the coordinator of the volunteers. The KVN is the network of volunteers. The Corps has since replaced this system with the Family Readiness Officer.

LAV: Light Armored Vehicle; looks like a small tank with six wheels.

LINKS: Lifestyle Insights Networking Knowledge and Skills class.

MEU: Marine Expeditionary Unit. About 2,000 Marines, of different MOS's deployed overseas. A MEU usually is attached to a Naval ship.

MOS: Military occupation/specialty; a Marine's job.

MP: Military police officer.

MRE: Meal ready to eat.

MWR/MCCS: Moral welfare and recreation, an organization on each base that plans functions for families and military personal living there.

OOD: Officer of the Day, who stands watch for 24 hours. Considered "on duty."

PCS: Permanent change of station. Moving from one location to another.

POGUE OR POG: Person other than a Grunt; non-combat arms Marine.

PT: Physical training, exercise.

PX: Public exchange or shopping mall on base. You must show a military ID in order to purchase anything here.

SEPARATION PAY: Issued after 30 days of separation from one's dependent while on deployment.

SGLI: Service member's group life insurance. Automatic life insurance issued by the military. Given to the dependent at the time of the service member's death.

TAD: Temporary additional duty. When a service member must go for training or to complete a service away from the permanent duty station.

TMO: Traffic Management Office. Responsible for arranging moving your belongings with a PCS.

TRICARE: Military health insurance.

UTILITIES: Standard camouflage uniform.

The 2015 Update

50 SHADES OF CAMMO

The sun was high in the sky, but the heat she was feeling wasn't from the weather, it was from the view. She had been watching him labor for over an hour. Most men would be tired after stacking their 100th sandbag, but this Marine was just getting started. His biceps looked as if they might explode from under his utilities; although his sleeves were rolled up, it was still too constrictive. He slowly unbuttoned his digital desert cami top and it fell to the ground in a heap. He pulled his green undershirt over his head and when he did it she gasped . . . what she had imagined was not nearly as good as what was in front of her. Pure hotness. The years of daily PT had obviously paid off. His dog tags were lost in a mountain of muscles. Sweat glistened off his awesome pecs, his shoulders were massive. Atlas would be shamed. She imagined him throwing her over those shoulders, carrying her off, her body underneath his massive chest. Suddenly he turned around, brushing away beads of perspiration, their eyes locked and she knew what would happen next, the fastest thirty seconds of her life . . .

Did I have you there for a second? Did you think, "Wow, I know the book is called *Confessions of a Military Wife*, and I knew there was some scandal, but GEEZE, she really took it to a whole new level!"

I'm sorry to disappoint you. I am not writing military wife erotica now. I'm just trying to sell a paperback. And sex does sell, but if you are a military wife, married to a grunt, you know that if someone wrote a steamy sex novel about being married to a ground pounder, it would take all of three minutes to read . . . about as long as the foreplay. My husband is way fine to look at, but when we first got married our foreplay consisted of three French kisses, a nipple grab, and a five-minute round of, "Hey Mollie, quit hitting yourself." I am happy to report things have improved (somewhat) in ten-plus years of marriage. I mean, we did eventually have a baby.

But, what is hot right now is erotica and vampires. But come on, how would vampire Marines kill anyone in the Middle East when it's so goddamned sunny all day? Plus it's the werewolves who are all buff, not vampires. Maybe I've missed the boat here. I mean, there is probably a HUGE market for military wife erotica with all these deployments that never seem to end. The back of the book could have a secret place to hide a sex tool. I could make millions, and women would be satisfied and not so bitchy when their spouses deployed!

But I couldn't write that kind of book—not because it would mortify my mother, but because I wouldn't know what I was talking about. Once you've been married to the military for a few years, different things turn you on. After my husband's second deployment, if he took the trash out without being asked or just did the dishes because "they were piling up," that was all it took for me to get really aroused. Or at least get me to shave my legs. I don't see a story like that hitting the silver screen.

Jon asked me the other day what the recent phenomena of erotica for women was all about. I explained that, for women, foreplay was 50% in the mind, and that it can sometimes take all day for women to get "in the mood," and how we gals really need to "think about it" and work it up in our minds. Women, I continued, weren't like men, who can just bump into their wives in the kitchen and get a raging boner. We have to mentally "get" there. And that, I continued, is why these erotic books were so popular: they speak to a woman's imagination. Jon went silent and I could see the wheels turning. I was impressed that he was taking this into consideration.

Then he turned to me, excited and serious, and replied, "Great babe, so the next time you want to do it, why don't you go into our room, cut off the lights and imagine all the foreplay you want and then yell for me when you're ready. I'll come in and we can just get straight to business. It's a win/win for both of us!"

I doubt there will be another child.

I do hope, however, that you enjoy these additions to the paperback and find them funny and informative. If not, there is always *50 shades of Camo*. I'm sure someone has written it—or will soon.

Mollie on stage. *Mollie Gross*

You may be wondering, "Why did Mollie feel the need to update her book with the paperback release?" The answer is easy: because of you.

I wrote *Confesssions* when I was in my late twenties. So much has transpired since then. In the book, I was reflecting back on my life during that time as a young military wife, supporting my husband during his two wartime deployments to Iraq. My twenty-something was so hyper that if my thirty-something met her, after five minutes the thirty-something would have a headache and need a nap.

However, I still admire that young bride. I love that girl. She was courageous and self-sacrificing and strong. She was always responsible, and occasionally mature. She loved to laugh. She enjoyed helping others. As a young bride I may have made mistakes, but I have learned a lot since then.

Since writing my own story I have also met thousands of young brides who have told me their stories—and discovered there are so many similarities. Regardless of the husband's rank, branch of service, or where stationed, the experience of being a young military wife during wartime has many parallels. I wanted to bring to new readers some of the exciting ways other wives used *Confessions* as a tool not only to laugh and learn, but also as a catalyst for book clubs, social gatherings, and keepsakes.

I also wanted to update my fans on how my life has evolved and assure you all that I am still laughing. There are many aspects to my "platform": a major part of which is to offer you more laughter, more confessions, more support for your journey as a military wife, mother, veteran's wife—and beyond.

In the years since *Confessions* first appeared, while on tour or via social media, I have had the pleasure of meeting so many of you and I am still humbled by your response to my book. I had no idea it would have this kind of impact. I wanted not only to thank you, but also include in this paperback some of the amazing feedback I received from my fans, and present a few of the tools that they shared with me.

There are some fun things in store for you in these new back pages. (Everyone knows all the craziest stuff went down in the back of the bus.) So I hope I can offer you so many more reasons to love this book. I've included book club questions/ideas, a yearbook section, and a scavenger hunt game, as well as up-to-date information on where you can find more of me on social media, through my writing, my podcasts, and even personal appearances.

I hope the paperback—unlike the false lead above—doesn't disappoint!

Semper Fiesty

Mollie

*   *   *

Ok, then what happened???

No one tells you when you write a book that people are going to read it. I mean, I KNEW some people would read it, like my mom and grandma, and maybe a few friends, but I never really thought *real people* would read it. In fact, I don't recall having any specific expectations for *Confessions*. Being a military wife taught me that it's best to "lower your expectations!" So I didn't have any. I just knew I had to get it out there. There were instructional books when I was a young military wife, but what I ran across read like a textbook. They were informative, but out of date and dry.

I was facing my husband going to war! What was that like? Separation from a deployment is difficult, but what about the added stress of danger? There was nothing available for reference. Many personal memoirs were negative and depressing, or frankly had nothing to do with a husband being involved in combat or a war zone. I wanted to do something different.

Never before had a military wife written a FUNNY, POSITIVE, RAW, REVEALING, "say it like it is" book about being the military wife of a real combat Marine.

One of the lines of people waiting to see me perform. It is such an honor to do so for those who take the time and trouble to see me. I feed off their energy and want to give them the best show I can. It is always my prayer before I perform that I take the gifts and talents God gave me and let them be of service to these amazing families. It warms my heart to see every smile and hear every laugh. If you want me to perform at your base or post, please go to www.molliegross.com to see how! *Mollie Gross*

Frankly, the fact that I was the wife of a combat veteran really complicated things. I mean, war isn't funny. Having a husband deployed and going through combat is disconcerting, and I wanted to talk about how I used humor to survive. About how much we managed to laugh back home.

So, I never thought I could get published. Then there was an added factor that I was a comedienne, and although I had been writing comedy and sketch for years, a book is a completely different undertaking. If you remove the content that had never been done before, you have to look at the fact that I can barely type, can't spell, and have no idea how to keep tense or be grammatically correct. And yet, threw—I mean through—perseverance, I found a great publisher and we were off to the races!

And then the strangest thing happened. People read the book, and recommended it to their friends . . . and they read it and reread it and the next thing I knew, it had this Rocky Horror–like cult following. After standup shows, when I would sell and sign books, wives were asking me to sign their Kindles, or they bought a hardback copy in addition to the digital copy, so I could sign it. It was taking two or three volunteers to wrangle up my fans and keep them organized. People were waiting an hour to get their selfie with me! (Seriously, I was dumbfounded.) Wives were sending me photos of their cats reading the book; they showed me how they used it as a yearbook when they PCSed off a base, for their friends to write a memory in . . . and so on and so on. Somehow, trying to do what had never been done before, worked.

Years after its release, I'm thrilled for the opportunity to update a few things, and add to the book to make it a better, funnier tool for military wives. My readers tell me I've given them so much with the book, including laughs and wisdom; it goes both ways. You've given *me* even more in return.

I never set out to be a writer; I just wanted to write down what happened to me on the home front during the war. I thought maybe I could make people laugh when they really needed it, and maybe, just maybe, help a few young brides not take life so seriously, or be too hard on themselves. Maybe a few would read my words and not make the same mistakes I did when I was a newlywed in the military community. Maybe they could laugh at me and then learn to laugh at themselves.

I remember soon after the book came out I was performing standup comedy for military wives in the Marine Corps community. I had a few videos on YouTube. Word got out that there was a *funny* military wife out there. The war was still raging, and military wives *needed* a laugh, and I was happy to provide it. Momentum built and, the next thing I knew, I had a global fan base on social media and was being asked to write for magazines and various publications. Radio shows were interviewing me for my insight on the military community; TV producers were seeking out my professional opinion. I was performing standup all over the U.S. and was reaching hundreds of thousands on social media. My lifelong dream of being a comedienne had come true.

To date, I have been to so many different states to perform that it's all a blur. I have performed for as few as five people at a private event to more than 5,000 at USAA on their live broadcast feed. It has been a whirlwind. I get so pumped up for each show. When I did my third show in Yuma, the line was out the door and wrapped around the parking lot! I was moved to tears. It was such an honor. In addition to the comedy and speaking, many more doors were being opened—ones I did not know would bring me such fulfillment. I launched "Ask Mollie" on my website, where women could anonymously ask me direct questions and receive my advice. I have always been bossy and like to tell people what to do. Luckily, I give some pretty good advice (or so I have been told).

In each situation, I "handled it with humor," solving problems and still making them laugh. The questions kept pouring in. Women started to reach

I am honored and humbled that *Confessions* has been selected again and again to be on the First Lady of the Marine Corps Recommended Reading List! Even with six-inch heels, the giant promotional cutout of my book towered above me. I was freaked for the entire book signing event that it would fall and crush me. And . . . I was pregnant here and did not even know it! *Mollie Gross*

out to me for more help than the book. I found that by using humor to convey my advice and feelings, I also gained their trust. By "handling it with humor" I showed women that we can laugh through just about everything. When you make someone laugh, borders fall away, and defenses melt. There is something visceral—something raw—about laughter. Laughter is about who we really are. To laugh is often to be vulnerable.

Because of all the women reaching out to me directly for advice, I decided I needed a venue to convey an inspirational message. I started training with Jack Barnard in Los Angeles to be a motivational speaker. Jack is still my speech coach. In addition to being a comedienne, author, and advice columnist, I was now speaking to military wives all over the U.S. We were laughing together, crying together, and with humor, I was encouraging—and inspiring—them to take control of their lives.

Four years after *Confessions of a Military Wife* first appeared, sales and interest were still going strong. The First Lady of the Marine Corps, Mrs. Bonnie Amos, created a recommended reading list for military spouses, and, to my surprise and delight, my book was chosen! In addition to touring with Spouse Buzz Live, Military.com, and my own "Military Wife" comedy, I was now speaking with the First Lady of the Marine Corps.

All this started from doing stand-up for military wives. Everything else —my comedy, my message—grew from that point. While I love all of these various ventures, they are also hard work that included extensive training and coaching. It's been as fulfilling and life-changing for me as it has been for my fans. I have met wives from every branch, married to every rank, and there is definitely a common thread: with the lifestyle we've chosen, we all know that if you don't find moments to laugh, you won't make it.

I have learned so much from these amazing women, and I hope to take that wisdom and share it with my audiences in a variety of ways. I've grown and learned so much from my fans. And for that I am eternally grateful.

If you have a question for me you can submit it at www.molliegross .com/askmollie. If you have a more extensive issue you wish to speak to me about, I offer Life "Laugh Coaching" in a private one-on-one environment. Whether it's mentoring your next dream project or you need advice on handling day-to-day stress, you will be sure to get hard hitting advice with a comic twist. Send your request to: laughcoach@molliegross.com.

I had a blast hosting a friendship event for military wives in San Diego. Whether I am asked to speak, host, or do comedy, I always try to use each event as an opportunity to teach the crowd to "Handle it with Humor." *Mollie Gross*

Proud Veteran's Wife

Active-duty military families will always hold a special place in my heart. I get my greatest high performing standup for them. It fulfills me like nothing else to make these wonderful people laugh, to let them, for just one

(Left, and below right): It isn't easy being my assistant. It's more like being a babysitter or wild animal trainer. Judith, ("Judy") is amazing. Each day she impresses me with her quest to learn, explore, and better her life. Oh, and she gets me on stage on time and makes sure I spell your name right, too! *Mollie Gross*

(Below) "Military Wife Comedy" in Yuma! The women there are so wild my husband no longer assists me when I perform. Yes, I'm wearing silkies, and no, I won't tell you which Marine I got them from. All I can say is it is a good thing Jon wasn't there! *Mollie Gross*

evening, see the funny side of this intense lifestyle. Many things have changed since I wrote my book, and many years have come and gone. I no longer identify myself as a military wife, but as the proud wife of a USMC Iraq War veteran. My husband has partnered with me to provide awareness for our nation's veterans, helping them and their families transition to the civilian world and adjust to life after wartime deployments. I hope and pray that just like *Confessions of a Military Wife*, I can help military families make the transition with humor through my comedy, speaking, and writing.

Motherhood has also provided a lot of new material, so every day I am writing about that as well and putting many of these thoughts into my podcast. That's right, I have launched a comedy podcast to share laughs, insights, and updates with my fans! Marriage, parenting, women's jibber-jabber, bullshit; this podcast is raw, informative, and funny. Advice you can listen to, so subscribe! In every aspect of what I do, my focus remains, "handle it with humor." Visit my website or Facebook to check it out.

Why don't you ever come to my base to do a show?

Unfortunately, because military bases are, well . . . military bases . . . I can't just set up a comedy show on a base. I have to have a government contract to come onto the installation. It takes a wife to contact her Family Readiness Officer (FRO) or Marine Corps Community Service (MCCS) or *Morale, Welfare, and Recreations* (MWR) and request a show. MCCS and MWR have budgets and are always looking for ways to bring in something new. The more wives who send in requests to the FRO, the more likely MWR/MCCS will contact me to book a show. They provide a government contract, I can get on base, and then we all laugh for hours till we pee our panties.

If this interests you, just go to my website or Facebook and see how to book me for a show, and my management team and I take it from there. I do comedy, speaking, and workshops, and best of all, I meet you after the event. We get to dish, and I get to hear from you! So *start nagging*, and I will see you soon.

Thank you!

What I am happiest about with this paperback is the opportunity to speak directly to my fans and to thank them.

Fans: Thank you for every YouTube hit and "like" on Facebook, for the books you bought, for the books you shared, for the articles you commented on, and the time you spent waiting in line to see me perform, and then waiting in line to meet me after a performance.

Thank you for each time you interacted when I gave a speech, for every kind word you wrote on Amazon as a review, for each time you defended me on a dumb-ass "dependa" hate sight, for sharing me on social media, for sending me a personal message about how my work helped you, and for trusting me to give you advice. Thank you for nagging your FRO, MCCS, or MWR to book me on your base/post, so I could come perform for you.

And most of all, thank you for your service on the home front. Thank you. Thank you one million times. I love meeting you; I love hearing from you; I have pictures of you all over my office (I really do!). I'm sincere when I say you mean so much to me because each one of you have helped to make my dreams come true and because of you, I am able to help more people.

It is one thing to tell a fart joke and make people laugh, but it is an entirely different thing to reach people through humor and change their perspective on daily life. It has been an honor to take a gift that God gave me and use it to serve others. The more each of you talk me up to other military wives, the more people hear about me, the more women are laughing and embracing their life choices and thriving in the military lifestyle. So thank you, because you are helping others as well. Thank you for helping me spread the message of handling life's challenges with humor.

Kristine Schellhaas: Double LL, Double AA. Cue the music from *The Phantom of the Opera*. I am obsessed with Kristine Schellhaas and Christine from Phantom. There was a period of about four months when Jon came home from work and I was playing the sound track to Phantom. Every day, for four months. I cried over the lyrics; I tried to sing along. I wanted to discuss the theme of the opera over dinner. "The phantom was misunderstood: he loved Christine!" I played the movie on a loop and the soundtrack in the car, and blared it on the Bose in our kitchen. I ordered the novel, read it before bed, and asked Jon to cover half his face with a white mask when we made love. I guess that was the tipping point, because then my CD went missing—only to resurface six years later in the bottom of Jon's tool box: SUSPICIOUS! When HBO stopped airing the movie, I started listening to talk radio. The last season of *Smallville* was about to air. And slowly, my love for Phantom diminished.

Until, that is, I reunited with Kristine Schellhaas, my longtime personal friend. Our husbands were both in 2/1, and she's the founder of USMC LIFE. I don't have a problem spelling her name because I sing it: "Kristine, Kristine!" And I am as obsessed with this Kristine as I was with the Christine in Phantom. And my real Kristine is sexier, smarter, and more talented and gets shit done. Kristine, thank you, my love, for letting me eat all the bread at Claim Jumper, for watching my iPad at Panera Bread during our business meetings when I had to go to the bathroom fifteen times when I was pregnant. And most of all, thank you for your support, not only promoting *Confessions* on your radio show, website, social media, and speaking events, but for your guidance and help with social media, my branding, and this paperback. You are the strongest woman I know, and you inspire me each day. I love you. I will stay up all night braiding your hair next time Ross deploys, or maybe just kidnap you through a mirror and take you to my underground lair and sing to you all night, while wearing a white half-mask. Read about Kristine's own motivational story at www.kristinespeaks.com.

Jack Barnard: Do I love you because you are the most talented person who can write upside down? Or because you have the highest tolerance for my ADD rambling? Or because you eat the rest of my food on my plate when I order way too much and spend our meetings running my mouth instead of stuffing it? Yes, all these things contribute to my love for you. But really I love you most of all because you are brilliant, hysterical, and kind. You are never surprised and never flinch when a far-fetched idea or horrible statement flies out of my mouth. You believe in me more than I believe in me. Your guidance and wisdom has meant so much to me over these years. Thank you for the focus, the patience, the guidance, the encouragement, and for telling me what I needed to hear, even if I caught on so slowly that Helen Keller would have thought me a lost cause. I would not have come up with half of my ideas if it was not for you collaborating with me, pushing me to answer questions and seeing in me what I never saw in myself. You are so important to me. Not just as a manager, a coach, but as a friend. Thank you.

Sarah Keeney: For coordinating, communicating, and constantly wrangling all that goes on behind the scenes when getting a book published and promoted, thank you! You are beyond patient and kind. You are so good to my fans and charities who want info and promotions. Without you I would have no idea how to get half my crazy ideas to fruition. You are the best!

Terri Barnes, Holly Scherer, and Kathy Hightower: If you have not yet read one of the numerous books by any of these ladies, do so right now. These women are the leaders in all things military family. Whether speaking, writing, encouraging, educating, or inspiring the new generation of military wives, all they do, they do for the home front. And here is the thing: they help other women who aspire to also lead. A lot of speakers and writers out there are not into paying it forward. Not these terrific women. These women have helped me so much. Because of them I have grown and been able to reach so many more military spouses. Ladies, thank you.

MJ Boice, Bonnie Amos, Ashley Houchins, Cherie Cain, Randy Plunkett, Andie Hurley, Vince Patton, USAA, Monster.com,

Military.com, and the many, many other FRO, FRG, MCCS, MWR, and event coordinators globally who booked me to speak or do stand-up, and who supported this book. Thank you for getting that I am not just a big joke, and that there is a message to embrace life under all the silliness and hijinks. Thank you for understanding the use of laughter as a healing tool. For knowing how important it is to laugh, and how powerful humor is as a tool to communicate a message of gratefulness. Thank you for supporting young wives and for knowing they are the future, and they are strong, and they are to be celebrated and encouraged. Thank you for allowing me to reach them.

Jon: Thank you for supporting me to write, for allowing me to reveal the most intimate and often embarrassing details of our marriage in words, on paper, in jokes, and on stage. Thank you for marrying me young and growing up with me. Thank you for watching our son while I update this paperback from the table in the camper in the driveway. Thank you for telling me daily I'm beautiful, and that I am your best friend. Thank you for laughing at so many of my old jokes, but also allowing me not to be funny.

Who says book clubs are for nerds? Here I am having WAY too much fun with the amazing ladies in Beaufort, South Carolina, led by the lovely MJ Boice. After two amazing shows, I sat down with this book club for a few questions and a lot of laughs. I was five months prego here . . . for once it's not gas! *Mollie Gross*

Book Club Questions

After performing two back-to-back shows in Beaufort, South Carolina (one standup, one speech), I was asked to speak with the local military spouse book club known as "Read Your Way Through Deployment," led by Marine spouse MJ Boice. These were some dynamic women, and this was much more than just another book club. These fantastic ladies in South Carolina did not just discuss the books they read; they used the military books on their list as a catalyst for discussing ideas, life choices, and dreams. In addition, they formed bonds with each other, encouraging, motivating, and becoming confidants. It was an honor that my book was one of many they discussed. I had a blast meeting all these amazing women, learning from them, laughing with them, and eating all the delicious food they made for our meet and greet. MJ and the group were kind to me, and encouraged me to add book club questions to the back of the paperback.

I hope you take their lead, call some gals to come over, start your own club—and make some life-long friends.

Book Club Questions

1. Soiled silkies on the kitchen table, combat boots on the counter, garage taken over with gear. Mollie asks herself, "Why didn't I marry a banker?" but instantly realizes she loves the man she chose and the lifestyle that came with that choice. What aspect of military marriage do you find is both a blessing and a curse? Bitter and sweet?

2. Mollie and her husband eloped in a town best known for discount fireworks and cheap cartons of cigarettes. Shockingly, not everyone supported them. What were the circumstances of your own wedding? Were you supported?

3. Unpacking the diaper genie, still full two months later or hauling all your old high school yearbooks, unopened wedding gifts and the scary stuff you were trying to ignore stored under your bed in a U-Haul across seven states. Did you have the military move you or did you Dity? Which is better?

4. Beenie Weenie and Mollie were BFFs even after she moved to Okinawa. And Mollie and Erin never shared a duty station. How do you foster friendships after you PCS?

5. Crying over every news report, freaking everyone out at bunco with a doom and gloom attitude. Mollie said she had to distance herself from negative wives she suspected would bring her down during the deployment. Have you ever had to distance yourself from a "friend"? If so, how did you do it without making it worse?

6. Mother-in-law insisted you share every email, text, sext, and letter with her? Wanted to stay at your house in a sleeping bag in your room when her baby boy got back from deployment? What boundaries have you set with extended family when it comes to communication, visits, deployments, reunions, and holidays?

7. Sewing a muumuu didn't do much for her sex life when her husband returned, but Mollie thinks the best way to deal with your loneliness and grief during a deployment is to focus on things beyond yourself by volunteering and staying active with a hobby. What do you do to help cope?

8. Binge-watching a TLC show about a 600-pound "little person" with hoarding tendencies and nineteen kids, while passing judgment eating cookie dough and drinking wine to zone out—Not good! What's a more positive way to treat yourself or improve your mood during a deployment?

9. 2:00 a.m., stepping in dog crap barefooted, tripping over the baby bouncy seat . . . all while trying to remember where the G-damn ladder is . . . because the smoke detector batteries are dying and you must change them before everyone in the house wakes up. The second they leave something is going to break. Do you have a funny deployment disaster story?

10. Waxing off your deployment mustache, actually putting on deodorant, and buying *real* food for the house. How did you prep yourself and your home for your spouse's homecoming?

11. Everyone talks about the men adjusting when they return, but how did *you* adjust? Were you "different"? . . . and if so, what did you do to create harmony and balance in your marriage again?

Scavenger Hunt

I ran into a wife after an event who said she had been stationed at Pendleton, and at that time she and a few of the wives in her neighborhood were all reading *Confessions of a Military Wife*. They decided as a bonding exercise to go to some of the places I mentioned in the book. She told me they had a blast.

I want to take her idea to the next level. I think it is very cool if you can get some wives together and go to some of these places and have fun, but if you want to be "Semper Fiesty," I DARE you to not only go to these places, but do some of the things mentioned in the book! Good luck, and have fun!

1. Hit on a toothless bagger at the Commissary.

2. Find the secret beach and get an on-duty Marine to rescue your drowning dog.

3. Go to the holiday harbor parade and puke up hot buttered rum.

4. Visit the barbershop in Oceanside with the ninety-year-old barber and get a high and tight SANS widow's peak.

5. Get married again at the Ranch House Chapel.

6. Yell "black anus" outside a Black Angus restaurant.

7. Do nude jumping jacks at the spa at Pala Casino and Resort.

8. Couples skate with a fifteen-year-old boy at the roller rink in Escondido.

9. Get a hot doctor at the Naval Hospital to tell you have "no anal spillage."

10. Have diarrhea at the McDonald's on Vandergrift.

11. Go to the Hustler Store, avoid the third floor, get lost trying to dodge Larry Flynt, end up on the third floor, see something hideous, feel shame, and then go to confession.

If you do all this, you can sign MY book and write my next one, because you are a BOSS.

Use Your Copy of Confessions as a Yearbook!

Have you ever had a friend you thought you were really tight with, with whom you could share anything? You spend so much time together and disclose so many secrets that she becomes your surrogate spouse? Then one night when your spouses are deployed, you call her, and after two hours of talking on the phone, you move to the bathroom to pee, and she's like, "Umm, what are you doing?" UNCOMFORTABLE MOMENT! You then realize, "Whoops, I guess we aren't that close."

Being intimate enough to not be timid about your bodily functions can indicate you and a friend are pretty tight. That's when the friendship has moved into "we are so close we are family." A lot of my military friends are family. Whether we communicate daily, weekly, or just twice a year, the closeness is still there. It's safe.

Unfortunately, this is not always the case. So many military friendships come and go. The military lifestyle is very transient, and you must work to keep the connections with those you love, long after they PCS.

I met Rachel in Hawaii after a speaking event. She brought her copy of my book, and she told me when she left Twentynine Palms it was devastating parting with her close group of friends. This is what Rachel told me:

> "My husband's first duty station, and my first experience with military life, was in Twentynine Palms, California. During our time there, my husband deployed to Afghanistan for several months. Instead of moving back home to be near family, I chose to stay in California to continue to work and pursue my college degree. I became very involved in the unit Family Readiness Program, and I met many wonderful ladies whose husbands were also deployed. We had pot kicks, book clubs, craft nights, etc. They were a great support system with my husband being away, and I can never express my gratitude for them in words. When my husband returned and it was time for us to move to Hawaii, my friends had a going-away party for me. During the party, they presented me with a copy of *Confessions of a Military Wife*. They all knew I loved this book, but what was special is that they had all signed it with loving and supportive messages. I will always cherish the book and the memories of the friends that became my sisters."

There may be friends along the way you make a point to reach out to every few months. Maybe there is a wife you won't see until three duty stations from now, and it's like no time has passed. If you're diligent, and work at it, you may have a friend you text daily, use social media with weekly, and call when the kids are asleep. Time zones don't matter, nor does the separation of continents. In truth, some of your friends you never see again, but you will always have precious memories of your time with them.

I hope this special page allows you to capture some of the friendships you had at the time in your life when you read this book. Thanks again, Rachel and the dynamic ladies of Twentynine Palms!

The best part of my live events is meeting, learning, and laughing with the fans afterward. I met Rachel Brand in Hawaii after a motivational speaking event. I was there to inspire, but it was Rachel who inspired me! She showed me her copy of *Confessions* that was signed by all of her girlfriends as a keepsake from 29 Palms! I was 10 weeks prego here and attempting to cover my bump because we had not yet told anyone. *Mollie Gross*

This is us with Kevin, Michelle, David, and Jacob—ALL GROWN UP! Not a day goes by that I don't wish I could walk out my door and see these boys playing in the driveway. And now Jacob is DRIVING! When we lived on base, we shared more than a backyard and master bedroom wall. We shared hopes, fears, prayers, joy, and love. That created a bond that will last a lifetime. I more than LOVE this family. Words cannot describe how much they all mean to me. My goal in life is to live next to them again, even if it's just Michelle and I at the old folks home! David—it's your turn to change MY DIAPERS!
Mollie Gross

My baby shower. Autumn is STILL on fire and still inspiring me to DO, LEARN, LIVE! She filled me in on her new hobbies of Salsa dancing and jumping out of airplanes. (Michelle is seated at the table.) *Mollie Gross*

Erin and I have never shared a duty station or time zone . . . and are still BFFS! Vows for my Surrogate Spouse: I will understand when you don't call me when you husband is about to deploy. I won't judge you when you eat raw cookie dough for breakfast the first week he is gone. And I promise to fly to Hawaii and help you get dressed when your children have fried your brain and worn you out. I am just thrilled you got dressed today. *Mollie Gross*

Military friendships last a lifetime when you work at them. Even after multiple duty stations, different time zones, different continents, pregnancies, babies, and deployments, Beenie and Lloyd are still a huge part of our lives. We make time for each other. We call, text, and visit each other whenever we can. I have not lived next door to Beenie in more than ten years, and she is still my BFF! *Mollie Gross*